The Filthy Thirteen

To Richard Reynolds

Jack Agnew
FILTHY 13

Jack Womer
506

Thanks
Jake McNiece
Sgt Filthy 13

THE FILTHY THIRTEEN

FROM THE DUSTBOWL TO HITLER'S EAGLE'S NEST: THE 101ST AIRBORNE'S MOST LEGENDARY SQUAD OF COMBAT PARATROOPERS

Richard Killblane
Jake McNiece

CASEMATE
Philadelphia & Newbury

Published by
CASEMATE
1016 Warrior Road, Drexel Hill, PA 19026
United States of America
and
17 Cheap Street, Newbury, Berkshire, RG14 5DD
United Kingdom

Reprinted May 2009

Typeset and design by K&P Publishing.

Hardcover Edition: ISBN 978-1-932033-12-0

Paperback Edition: ISBN 978-1-932033-46-5

Cataloging-in-Publication data is available from the Library of Congress

PRINTED AND BOUND IN THE UNITED STATES OF AMERICA.

Contents

PREFACE

I had known of Jake McNiece for a number of years before I considered writing his story. He and a friend, Truman Smith, were favorite guest speakers at local schools and social organizations, and both were always willing to speak at any veterans' event I coordinated. Both of them truly gifted speakers, Truman finally put his own words into print with *The Wrong Stuff: The Adventures and Mis-Adventures of an 8th Air Force Aviator*. It was subsequently at the urging of Jake's friend and fishing buddy, Richard Sherrod, that I agreed to personally record Jake's own version of the war.

Sherrod, probably the biggest fan of World War II veterans, originally had a notion that every soldier's story should be recorded, though without realizing exactly how much work oral history entailed. Yet it was thanks to his encouragement that with Jake I finally took the first monumental step. The hours of effort required far exceeded my initial expectation, but I was overwhelmed with what I discovered. I had heard Jake speak to audiences before, but in one-on-one sessions I encountered the full uncensored version. With me as his sole audience, I was at the mercy of his unique talent for storytelling. Jake has a way of leaning back with his laugh; that grin just spreads across his face. He looks at you with that gleam in his eye and knows when and how long to pause before hitting you with his punch line. At times, he fed on my laughter. Sherrod, who had also heard all the stories fit for print, again became instrumental when I sat down to chronicle the accounts to see if I had missed anything. With his help I recorded them all.

Jake is one of the most gifted storytellers I have known. This is not to imply that any of his descriptions are untrue, but only to say that he is a skillful practitioner of the American art of first-person narrative that extends back to the days of Davy Crockett. This tradition continued with Samuel Watkins after the Civil War and Samuel Clemens (later Mark Twain), and in that same eighteenth century the famed frontier trapper and army scout, Jim Bridger, who attracted people from as far away as Europe to hear him spin his yarns of adventure. Storytelling is a talent which takes life's experiences and relates them in an interesting manner. Like a fairy tale they often have a moral at the end, or like a joke they end with a punch line. There is no way I could ever tell the story of the Filthy 13 better than the man who inspired and led it. Even when Jake's words are captured in black and white they do not quite convey his gifted original style.

After innumerable interviews to record Jake's personal recollections, the second part of my task was to ground his accounts in the context of the broader campaign in World War II Europe, and to crosscheck them with the stories of other survivors of the Filthy 13, or men who fought alongside them. On occasion I have placed the stories of other veterans within Jake's narrative in order to flesh out events. More commonly, the additional context and analyses are in footnotes for each chapter.

There are places where Jake's memory of an incident differs in varying degrees from other veterans' or what has been described by official histories. For anyone searching for the truth, no matter how fresh the memory or how recent the event, versions are going to differ depending on the perspective of the individual and what he felt was important. For example, Virgil Smith and Jake McNiece, who both live in Ponca City, Oklahoma, tell nearly identical versions of the same stories, though with different emphases. When Jake ate in the officers' mess in England, Jake concludes with how Virgil introduced him as a major. That was funny enough for Jake. Since Virgil's neck was on the line if Jake's cover was blown, he finished with the fact that Jake kept going back to the mess. Otherwise the stories were identical. By and large, the accounts from the various veterans of Regimental Headquarters Company were similar.

I have benefited from the fact that following the 1979 101st Airborne Division Reunion, the veterans of the company began to hold their own annual "get-togethers." At these they told and retold stories, allowing me to compare accounts and often gain greater detail. While Jack Agnew and Jake are reputed to have the best memories in the unit, their stories differ more in the details. Jack lives in Pennsylvania and Jake in Oklahoma. On average they meet once a year at the reunions and communicate a little more on the phone. Without a doubt this storytelling process by the group has had influence on the similarity of the stories and it has also helped validate the events. In some ways the telling of war stories at the reunions filled in lost details by others and performed the function of the long awaited group after-action review.

Jake's narration is not just another view of the war through the eyes of a paratrooper. Jake and the Filthy 13 played key roles in some of the critical battles of the war. At first it may be hard to believe that any one unit could have been in the thick of so much combat, but one must remember that the Filthy 13 was one of only three demolition-saboteur sections in the 506th Parachute Infantry Regiment. Unlike other infantrymen, they received special missions in accordance with their training, such as wiring or removing demolitions from bridges, or clearing mines and booby traps, all at the forefront of the attack. On top of that, their transfer to the Pathfinders and fortune would place these men in the path of even greater adventure.

After interviewing other members of his company, including two of his company commanders, Hank Hannah and Gene Brown, I found that Jake's reputation has if anything exceeded his personal estimation. Although he was but one of the many interesting characters in Regimental Headquarters Company—and for that matter, the entire 506th Regiment—he may well have been the wildest. This was in no small measure due to his sometimes anarchic sense of humor. In addition, almost everyone agreed that Jake was the toughest man in the company.

When comparing Jake's and other company veterans' stories with the official histories there are significant discrepancies. Jake's account of the fight on the bridges on the Douve Canal below Carentan differs from the official report compiled by the History Division under S. L. A. Marshall. Marshall, himself the pioneer of the group interview, has come under criticism for not being uniformly accurate in his research, particularly regarding the maelstrom of airborne melees during the Normandy campaign. Marshall admitted to historian Mark Bando that he did not use the group interview on the action at the Brevands bridgehead but instead referred to official reports. From the writings it appears that the officer who commanded the action at the bridge, Captain Charles Shettle, may at least have been consulted.

Shettle admitted that the demolition men reached the bridge first and wired it, but from there the stories differ widely. The official report says that Americans had crossed to the other side and established a bridgehead. All the demolition men who reached the bridge tell essentially the opposite story. The Germans held one side of the canal and the Americans the other. The paratroopers were pinned down on their side. Jake says that he never saw Shettle anywhere near the bridge. Jack Agnew says he saw him but Shettle never left his foxhole. He did hear that a lieutenant managed to get men across a wooden foot bridge further downriver from them.

The veterans are not certain whether it was the second or third day when the USAAF bombed the bridge. Shettle claimed it was the second day. The official history, veterans, and even a follow-up interview in the *Stars and Stripes*, differ on whether the planes were P-47s or P-51s. Jack Agnew and Eugene Dance knew the difference and agreed with Jake that they were P-51s. The report claimed that the men on the canal were relieved on the third day. The regimental journal states only that the 327th Glider Infantry was sent to relieve them on the third day. Most of the veterans do not remember being relieved by anybody and that they left the bridgehead some time after the third day. Jake is adamant that he spent five days on the bridge.

A turning point in the history of the Filthy 13 came after Holland when Jake McNiece, followed by most of the survivors of the section, decided to join the Pathfinders—the most dangerous job in the airborne. Typically, Jake analyzed this move pragmatically, saying that while he realized his officers were only trying to get rid of him, the war was nearly over so it was he who would have the last laugh. But then came the Battle of the Bulge, which the Allied chain-of-command hadn't expected. The role of the Pathfinders at Bastogne has in the years since been obscured. According to standard histories, the heavens parted and the planes found their drop zones clear on Christmas Day, 1944. Nearly everyone has heard the story. I have seen the official report by Captain Frank Brown, the roster of the jump, photo evidence—with one unmistakable photo of Jake McNiece dragging in a bundle—and read testimony by witnesses on the ground. The Pathfinders' drop was briefly mentioned by reporters at the time, but the hundreds of histories since have entirely ignored their participation. Along with the navigational skill of the C-47 pilots who dropped them in Bastogne, the Pathfinders were hugely instrumental in bringing in the resupply drops that saved the 101st Airborne Division from defeat. As for the courage of the Pathfinders themselves, one need only realize that after flying hundreds of miles from England, a missed drop of a hundred yards would have resulted in their immediate death or capture. Who would think that nearly sixty years after World War II there would be a vital aspect of the Battle of the Bulge that history has missed.

While I could have written the story of the Filthy 13 as my own interpretation, after having scrutinized the evidence, it would not have compared to the skill with which Jake McNiece tells it. Instead I have tried to preserve the art of storytelling by participants themselves. Each of Jake's stories stands by itself. As a writer I have arranged this collection together in a chronological manner and filled in the gaps with interviews to provide a more complete narration of the war and description of the characters. As a historian I have then added the corroborating evidence with my own interpretation as footnotes. In this respect it becomes a record of history. But this narration also seeks to convey a unique style of oral history. The main text is a war story. Its purpose is to entertain. I have deliberately retained some of the imperfections in grammar and style to preserve the feel as if Jake is talking to the reader. The art of storytelling is a gift and requires skill. For this reason I feel it should be preserved.

There are a number of people instrumental in putting this work together. On top of the list is Richard Sherrod, without whom this story may never have been preserved. I learned that other historians had written Jake or interviewed him but none fully realized the gold mine of information he had. I once asked Richard, how after all these years, I would be the lucky one to write Jake's story. He answered, "Because you were the only one who cared enough to take the time."

George Koskimaki is another who took the time to record everything he could about the 506th Parachute Infantry. Having served in the 101st Airborne Division, he had a special interest in preserving its oral history. He has published three books chronicling its exploits, which are mentioned in the bibliography. His research has been instrumental in filling in details.

Other veterans provided interviews, documents, clippings and photos as evidence of their experiences. One occasionally encounters people who claim to have been in places they were not or to have done things they did not. The survivors of the Filthy 13 are fortunately among those veterans who have amassed a number of documents to prove their incredible story, guarding against untruth. The veterans have been their own best historians.

Research would never be complete without the help of other historians and archivists. Jim Erikson provided letters and veterans' information from his research about his uncle, Lieutenant Charles Mellen. Richard Barone informed me of the wealth of firsthand accounts of battles written by infantry officers hidden in the infantry school library. Renowned WWII historian Mark Bando kindly reviewed the manuscript and provided rare details into the actions and personalities of the 101st. In addition, the Army War College Library staff has always provided more material than needed in any research project about which I have contacted them.

A writer often needs to impose upon friends to read his manuscript while it is still in the draft stages. They have to suffer through the unpolished work, sometimes several times. I began this work with a verbatim transcription of Jake's interviews. Dr. Doug Hansen provided the first valuable advice on which direction to go with a predominantly oral history, providing input as to how much of Jake's original language I should polish. (We should all read our own words as exactly spoken to appreciate this need.) It has been my intent to preserve as much of his original language as feasible while keeping the narrative readable. My mentor, the historian Gary Null, provided the best advice on how much of the language to change, simply saying, "Don't let the person telling the story sound stupid." Gary also provided the first critical editing. I was grateful for the input of other readers, Mike Van Bibber and Hagen, who verified that in these pages Jake's personal style has indeed been faithfully captured.

Richard Killblane

Introduction

JAKE MCNIECE

Only a few minutes remained in the fourth quarter and the ball was down. "Third and goal to go." The Ponca City High School football team withdrew into their huddle. They were tired. In 1938, the players played both offense and defense the whole game.

The Ponca City boys played their rival team of Blackwell. Both of these neighboring towns in northern Oklahoma had small industries that allowed them to recruit players. Ponca City had young men recruited from as far away as Texas, Arkansas, Louisiana, and Kansas. To get the best players the local businesses offered jobs to the fathers and in many cases the players themselves. Some of the players were as old as twenty-one and big! Many linemen weighed over two hundred pounds. With the teams evenly matched, this was the game of the season. Since Blackwell had won the year before, this game also became a grudge match and both sides played until the last drop of blood. Neither side had yet scored.

Jake McNiece, the team captain, looked at the young sophomore quarterback, C. L. Snyder. C. L. was a highly skilled quarterback but inexperienced at calling games. Jake had moved over from left end to offensive center so he could call the plays. "I'm going to shoot the ball right to you. You run right straight through my position, it will be wide open."

C. L. questioned his logic. At five-feet-eight-inches, Jake only weighed 155 pounds and he was lined up against the 295-pound Thurman Garrett.

But Jake guaranteed him, "There will be a hole there."

The team lined up with C. L. three yards deep. Jake looked straight at the giant in front of him and they began to exchange unpleasant remarks until Thurman finally looked Jake in the eye. With a wad of Copenhagen chewing tobacco packed into his mouth, Jake spit the burning juice right in Thurman's eyes. The big man screamed, grabbed his face and raised up. Jake snapped the ball and drove right into Thurman's gut, driving him all the way into the end zone. Because Thurman was so big no one backed him up. C. L. followed as directed and scored the only touchdown of the game.

With red, teary eyes and tobacco juice running down his face, Thurman pleaded with the referee. Nick Colbert knew Jake always chewed tobacco and confronted him. Jake had already swallowed the evidence and pleaded his own innocence. "Here look, I don't have anything." Colbert had no other choice but to let the play stand. Ponca City won the game six to zero. Decades later, this play was burned into the memory of those who witnessed it. To celebrate his victory, Jake puked his guts out in the shower after the game.

The story of the Filthy 13 begins with one man. The son of a sharecropper, nineteen-year-old Jake McNiece had made a small legend for himself on the playing fields of Oklahoma. He was a man who played to win and did whatever it took to come out on top. A few years later, the United States would enter a war against the toughest, most professional armies in the world and he would take that attitude with him. By the time the Allies invaded France, the Germans had been winning the war for over five years. The same traits Jake had demonstrated on the playing field would help him create an even greater legend in the army and on the battlefield.

James E. McNiece was born the second youngest of ten children on May 24, 1919, in Maysville, Oklahoma, the home of the famous Indian pilot Wiley Post. His parents, Elihugh and Rebecca McNiece, had immigrated from the farm country of Arkansas. Unlike the earlier legendary personalities of his state, Jake was homegrown—a true product of Oklahoma. His mother was half Choctaw, a fact that would play an important part in the later legend.

Jake grew up in rural Oklahoma, where not only was hunting and fishing every boy's birthright but almost an obligation. Food came from the land, not the store. He developed skill with a rifle and had tremendous peripheral vision. Later his wife, Martha, told how driving down the highway he could spot a deer up on a hill without taking his eyes off of the road. Farm life taught him to kill and prepare meat for the table. Field craft became a way of life. Rural living made young men dependent more upon themselves than others.

During the 1920s, the McNiece's lived well for sharecroppers and had the respect of the community. His parents were good Christian folk. Elihugh did not drink or smoke. Although not very well educated, they were very intelligent. Elihugh was a terrific farmer. In addition to his skill at raising crops he would also buy mules for next to nothing and have his sons break them. They would then resell them for a considerable profit. Elihugh's successful businesses allowed him to purchase the materials to build a ten-room house in 1928. By that year he had also put two sons through college. In pursuit of the American dream his hard work allowed his children the opportunity he had not received himself.

Just as things looked their best, disaster struck the next year. First, the McNiece's home burned down. The stock market crashed, causing many banks to close their doors. A chain reaction of events left no one untouched. Consequently, the owners of farms could not borrow money to buy seed for their tenants to plant. As sharecroppers in Oklahoma, the Depression of 1930 hit the McNiece family hard. While the McNieces descended into poverty, others shared the same misfortune. The Depression toughened Americans. Everyone knew they would have to work hard and work together to pull through the time of economic crisis. This experience fortunately brought families and people closer together. The McNieces remained very close.

Elihugh did not choose to migrate to California like other Oklahoma families. There were still ways to make money but they required the whole family to pitch in. Both parents and children cut broomcorn around Maysville, July through August. Elihugh then loaded the family in his Dodge car and packed the furniture in a four-wheel trailer to head for west Texas to pick cotton from October through December. Afterwards they cut maize and hi-gear corn until January. A season on the road earned enough money to survive the rest of the year in their rented home in Maysville. Consequently, ten-year-old Jake had to drop out of school in 1929 to pull his own share of the work. Boys had to grow into men. This migrant life cost the children their ticket to success—education.

Jake had lost two years of school until the family moved north to the oil town of Ponca City in 1931 to seek stable work. Ponca City provided the home for the Continental Oil Company (CONOCO) refinery and headquarters. The bust in the economy had also reduced the revenue people had to spend on gas. Consequently, the oil-driven economy of Ponca City likewise suffered. Elihugh was able to work out a deal with a farmer to clear his land of blackjack timber. Out of every two ricks they gave one to the farmer and sold the other at $1.50 a rick. Unfortunately, few employers wanted to hire a fifty-five-year-old man. Instead the McNiece children went to work to help.

At the age of twelve, Jake began driving delivery trucks. And fortunately, he was able to go back to school. He completed the ninth grade and demonstrated talent as a young athlete. Coach Jack Baker asked him to try out for the high school football team during the spring season. Jake informed the coach that he planned to drop out of school so he could work full time to help his family. His brother, Sidney, had already quit school to support the family since the other two brothers were gone. Football was huge in Oklahoma and the small Jake did not have confidence that he would even make the team. Ponca City had recruited some big bruisers and had some star talent. Wadie Young had just graduated Ponca City in 1935 and would make All-American out of Oklahoma University.

Coach Baker provided an incentive. He said if Jake could make the team he would find him a job. Jake had the speed, skill, and agility, and his toughness made up for his small size at the positions he played. True to his word, the coach found Jake a job in the evenings and weekends with the fire department, earning $35 a month. This good wage made Jake the major provider for the family. In the course of recruiting the coach found a number of players or their fathers jobs in the community. The fire department became a major employer of football players. One year as many as nineteen football players worked for it. In this sense high school football was semi-professional.

In those days teams were so small that the players played the entire game without a rest. Jake played both offensive and defensive end his first two years. He was a natural leader. In his last year, their star quarterback graduated and C. L. Snyder came up from junior high. He was highly skilled at passing, kicking, and handling the ball, but lacked the experience of high school football. The team elected Jake captain so he switched to offensive center in order to call the plays. He was fast and extremely athletic. What Jake lacked in size and weight he made up for in toughness. A man who had followed Jake's football career, Mike Landauer, said Jake "was not afraid of the devil and was always doing the unconventional thing." Jake would spit on the ball and when the opposing center picked it up to wipe the tobacco juice off, Jake would tackle him. The traits that Jake developed on the football field were those that he would need in the upcoming war.

As soon as Jake went to work with the fire department, Sidney moved out. Only a student in high school, Jake shouldered the responsibility of providing for his family. Fortunately the job paid enough for him to purchase the lumber so that one of his other brothers, who was a carpenter, could come back and build his parents their home.

While Jake had been baptized at the age of thirteen, his work on the weekends prevented him from attending church. He practically lived at the fire station. It was then that he picked up his three vices: drinking, fighting, and chasing loose women. Actually, Jake was not a bully. In school he would stand up for the underdog. "Honky-tonking" was the favorite pasttime for men in Oklahoma. One thing would always lead to another when drinking until a fight broke out. Jake, not one to back down, fought to win. Despite his size he won by getting in the first punch, knocking his victims to the ground where he could stomp them, or as he would say, "Put the ugly on them." Jake learned in fights that to hesitate was to lose.

Nonetheless, Jake was one of the most popular boys in his class. The smile that always spread across his face and his athletic prowess made him the kind of young man everybody liked. His nonchalant and friendly nature immediately put people at ease and made people feel like they had known him all their lives. He always wore overalls to school and thereby started a trend among his friends.

His reputation as a hell-raiser detracted from his better traits. He was mischievous but never malicious. He always played tricks while he worked at the fire station. Although he had a quick wit and great sense of humor, he did not play tricks on anybody at home. He considered himself not very well educated but he was a natural leader blessed with a great amount of common sense. He had the ability to find unconventional solutions for any problem. Friends said he was smart and did not have to study to get good grades. He was also very close to his family and loved old people. Graduating from Ponca City High School in 1939, he worked another year for the fire department. By this time Jake had refined the last traits needed for close-quarters combat in the years to come.

With war imminent, the mobilization created a wealth of government contracts and enough jobs to snap the nation out of the Depression. Elihugh found employment with CONOCO as a security guard, while most of the older children grew up and left home. The McNieces had survived the Depression. With his parents financially stable, Jake could pursue his own interests. He left for Houston, Texas, to work as a foreman in the shipyards. Five or six months later he picked up a job as a firefighter for the War Department in Little Rock, Arkansas. He then heard about a construction project in Southern Pines where he oversaw the construction of sixty bomb storage bunkers with Luminous Construction. Then on December 7, 1941, the United States entered World War II.

Jake participated in America's great experiment with paratroop units. He enlisted to have fun and participate in an adventure. He had no intention of being a hero. He liked to fight and the army was going to pay him to fight Germans. Unwittingly, he would create a legendary unit that would find itself involved in several of the most critical events of the Second World War.

In his narration, Jake hardly mentioned airborne training as a challenge but only as a chance to excel and prove himself the best. His officers recognized his skill and his peers considered him the toughest man in the outfit. Through a process of natural selection, Jake surrounded himself with twelve men nearly as tough as he was and who mirrored his own nature. The Filthy 13 would grow into a legend through the oral tradition of the war that leaked into the press. It was the smallest unit of reputation shaped around the personality of its founder to come out of the war. The stories of all the other famous outfits—Merrill's Marauders, Darby's Rangers, Frederick's Black Devils, Carlton's Marine Raiders, and Pappy Boyington's Black Sheep—have already become known to the public. Now, over half a century after World War II, the story of the last of the great legendary units can be told.

Jake always had a great sense of humor and a gift for storytelling that could make almost any event entertaining. He jokingly remarked that since nearly all the others are dead, he can tell the story of the Filthy 13 anyway he wants. With that remark, I will let his words speak.

1

Creating a Legend

Enlistment in the Paratroops

September 1, 1942

I was never really interested in the war until after the Japanese bombed Pearl Harbor. At that time I had been working as a firefighter for the War Department for quite a while. Then after Pearl Harbor there was a big project at Pine Bluff Perkins about sixty miles south of Little Rock, Arkansas. The Luminous Construction Company was constructing pretty near sixty long, storage arsenal buildings out there.

They would be fined $10 a day if they did not finish on time and they were falling behind. They had about 250 men from Arkansas, Louisiana, and southern Missouri working for them. The contractors could not get any work out of those boys or at least with any regularity. So my brother-in-law, Cam Steele, called me figuring that I could make due progress and asked if I would come out there and be a gang pusher for the project. I said I would.

Once there I kind of worked on the problem and changed the payroll to Wednesdays instead of paying them on Friday night. Before, the men would go out and stay drunk for three or four days and half of them would wind up in jail. Consequently, they would not show back up for work on Monday. After I changed their payroll, when time for a real tight-shoe night[1] came along on Saturday, they were broke. So they just kept coming back to work on time. I worked down there until I completed that project.

I had a total exemption from the draft because I was a fireman but I began to feel uneasy about not offering my services, whatever they might be. So I went back to Ponca City, Oklahoma, to visit my mom and dad for a few days. Then I got into some problems down there at the Blue Moon Tavern on South Avenue.

I was out carousing around one Saturday night doing the town up in good shape and fashion. Of course, I was drunker than nine hundred dollars and looking for trouble. There was one particular individual that I wanted to put the ugly on. Thad Tucker and I had always had lots of difficulties. Well, I wanted to whip him real good one more time, but I knew the minute that I stepped inside his joint he would call the cops. So I got a friend of mine to go down with me in his good clothes. He owed Thad quite a bit of money. Well he went in with a cock-and-bull story that he had just married an Osage squaw and wanted to pay him off.[2] He asked Thad to come on out to the car a bit. He would give him a big shot of whiskey then pay him.

Well, when Thad came clear out into the driveway, I walked up and went to work on him. I knocked him down and was putting the boots to him in that gravel driveway. I was so drunk that I lost my balance. When I lifted my foot to kick him, I kind of staggered back. He then jumped up and made a run for the front door of his joint. When he did, I scooped up a big rock about the size of a baseball and threw it at him. I was still in good shape and could throw pretty straight. I hit him right in the back of the head and it just peeled his skin. It nearly scalped him. He went down but by then I could already hear sirens blowing all over the place. Squad cars were coming in from every direction. So I thought, "I've got to get out of here." Then I took off and ran across the street.

This was back in 1942 and there were not many dwelling places on the north side of South Avenue. That was where the Hearst brothers had a big corral. So I made it over into that horse lot and tore out across the field. It had been raining. The mud and horse manure were just like soup, about ankle deep all over the place. In the dark I could just see the light-colored horses. While I ran I could miss the bays and the whites and the grays but I hit one of the black ones and tumbled down in that crap. I finally escaped out of there and went on home.

The cops had already pulled up in our driveway and talked to my mother and dad trying to get a fix on me. My parents said they did not know where I was so the cops left. My parents figured something pretty serious was wrong and were still up waiting for me when I got home. I watched them from the window. They were in the living room listening to the radio to see if they could hear any news. So I decided I would just sneak in through the back of the house, get in their bed and retire for the evening.

Well, Dad finally said, "Becky, we might as well go to bed. We might hear something tomorrow."

I had horse manure and barbecue all over me. One could smell me a quarter of a block away. So they had just come back into the kitchen, next to where their bedroom was, when Dad stopped and said, "Becky, I think Jake is home already." He smelled me.

The minute I got up the next morning, why I jumped up and beat a hard track straight for Oklahoma City. I knew if I could get signed up in the army, the local cops no longer had any jurisdiction over me, anyway except to detain me.

I had grown up in Maysville, Oklahoma, the home of the famous Indian pilot, Wiley Post, and had seen him make parachute jumps back in the late 1920s. So I wanted to enlist for parachute duty. That was the type of service for me.

It would be close-in, hand-to-hand combat. A paratrooper would look a man eyeball-to-eyeball fighting behind the lines. I did not mind the risk but I just did not want all that hanky-panky; policing up cigarette butts around the area or that close-order drill. I never saw any benefit in it. Well, the longer I live and the more people I talk to who were in the military, I can now understand and see some reason for close-order drill. It taught discipline to a lot of guys who perhaps needed to follow an order without any questions. This kind of discipline has some points that are good and it has some that are bad. In paratroop service, I thought it was absolutely futile and useless, because we were disciplined to act on assignments and orders in the absence of officers. So I never did go for that crap. I just did not want any of it and this would be the source of my problems in the army.

So I told the recruiter, "I don't want the infantry or tanks or artillery. I want to go straight into paratroop service."

This sergeant was not very encouraging. He said, "Well now, wait a minute. I want to tell you something. Not an awful lot of people are making it. A thousand men volunteer. We select a hundred out of them who are physically fit and ten become paratroopers. In the event you are not one of the ten, you will go into the infantry."

I said, "I don't have any doubts or qualms about being physically able to become a paratrooper, so sign me up."

He said, "You know they have an age limit on paratroopers. How old are you?"

I said, "Twenty-two."

He said, "If they catch you lying about your age, they will not accept you. They'll kick you right out into one of those other branches of service."

I said, "I'm not lying about my age. I'm twenty-two."

He said, "They have a limit of twenty-eight."

At the time I had already lost a lot of hair and had all these scars on my face and head. He said, "You may be twenty-two but your head looks like it has been used as a live hand grenade court and has used up three bodies already."

I told him that was the only deal I would accept.

So that is how I volunteered into the parachute service back in September 1942. It just kind of appealed to me. This was the kind of fighting that I preferred. I would not have to walk a hundred miles to get started. I would fly first class in a C-47 and jump right in the middle of them. It was more or less individual ability whether I was a success or a failure.

It was not like some of these ground troops that moved up. The higher headquarters would bring a division or regiment up about ten miles behind the lines. They would hold them there for a few days where they would see a few graveyards. They would then move them up another two or three miles where they would start seeing the live wounded and the hospital and the operating table. Then they would gradually work them up to see the shock of combat. This would kind of climatize them. In the meantime they would still be ten miles behind the lines when some Kraut threw an eighty-eight shell right there in the middle of them. There was no defense against an eighty-eight dropping in your shorts. The Germans would locate them bunched up in a group that size and then bomb and strafe them. Those infantry guys were pretty defenseless. I felt that if a guy wanted to kill me, I wanted to look him in the eye. That is why I enlisted in the paratroopers. I would be right there with them—eyeball-to-eyeball.

It is actually crazy to believe but paratroopers really had the advantage right there in the middle of the enemy. The Krauts could employ only so much back in the rear. If I was going to kill more Germans, it would be with the paratroopers. Anywhere a paratrooper looked he would have targets. If the Germans tried to pursue a paratrooper they would pursue him right past another little old squad or section of paratroopers. So really and truly we had the advantage. It was our personal ability pitched against that of the Krauts. We would not get bombed from ten thousand feet or gas thrown on us. So that is why I wanted it.

I signed up down there and the recruiters gave me twenty-four hours to report back in before we left for Fort Sill. So I came on back home.

CAMP TOCCOA, GEORGIA—BASIC TRAINING

Manual Cockeral and I were sent to Fort Sill in 1942. He was from Tulsa, Oklahoma. When we got down there to process in, they sent in these officers from different special forces. They addressed the whole auditorium full of enlisted and drafted people to give them their sales pitch about the advantages of the Rangers and airborne. Manual and I had talked some out there in camp and I told him that I was going into the airborne. Well, we talked back and forth and he said, "That sounds interesting. I believe I'll go in too." So he also volunteered for it.

We had to wait there a total of six days until we had seven volunteers for the airborne. Two or three of the boys were from up in northern Oklahoma. Because of my age they put me in charge and gave me meal and train tickets and all the stuff that goes with transportation. I saw that we were going to have a short stopover in Tulsa so I asked Manual if he wanted to see his family one last time. He said yes and I told him to call them and have them waiting at the terminal at the time on the tickets. When we got there they were waiting for us with lots of food and cakes. We were well treated.

We then took off for Toccoa, Georgia.[3] When we arrived, they put Manual in Regimental Headquarters Company, I think in the communications platoon. He goofed up in some way and they transferred him down to F Company. I did not see him again until the night we jumped into Normandy. We would remain at Toccoa for six months of basic training.

THE DIRTY FIVE AND THE WARSAW SEVEN

I went straight into the demolition platoon of Regimental Headquarters Company of the 506th Parachute Infantry Regiment, the day that I arrived. A demolition platoon had three sections, each assigned to support a battalion during training or a mission. They made me the acting staff sergeant for the 1st Battalion Section. Jim Davidson was the sergeant of the 3rd Battalion Section. Second Lieutenant William H. Leach was assigned as the officer of my section and First Lieutenant Gene Brown was our platoon leader.

They had regular army NCOs scattered over the regiment filling the top positions. Our first sergeant was Albert H. Miller. "Top Kick" Miller was one of the finest men that I have ever met. He had been in the regular army for twelve years. Times had been tough all over during the Depression and an awful lot of those Southern boys went into the army just to have a job. That is what Top Kick had done. He was real Georgia Cracker. He had also been in the original airborne test platoon that trained down in Panama. Afterwards they took the NCOs out of the test platoon for cadre for the 506th. I think every company had a man out of the test platoon.

He was a hell of a soldier and a hell of a man. He was a prince of a man both physically and spiritually. He had good morals but he had one vice. He loved to gamble. He also drank but outside of that he was great. He did not have much education but was smart, just shrewd. He knew human nature. If he saw some trouble growing, he could get in there and talk the man out of it. He defended his men against anyone up to Colonel Robert Sink.[4] If he thought they had a just cause or if recommending stressful punitive measures would be bad, he would just come right out and say so. Colonel Sink and our regimental executive officer, Lt. Colonel Charles "Uncle Charlie" Chase, would call him right in on their meetings and question him about how he would deploy men under this situation or how he would attack. They relied a lot on his advice. All the old regular army men were close.[5]

Leonard Leonitus Johnson was also regular army. He was my platoon sergeant when I first went into boot camp. He was a big ole heavy boy from northern Oklahoma and he had a speech impediment. One of the great sayings in the airborne was "Be Alert!" Well, he could not say "alert." He would say, "Be Alurk!" He was not real bright so we called him "Truck Horse."

When we first went into our basic training we were assigned alphabetically to five-man tents. It was the rainy season in Georgia. The tents did not have any floors in them. Our stuff sat on the ground and of course it was impossible to stay clean. We did not even try to stay clean. We were not disciplined at all. I had enlisted to fight Germans. The others began to call my group the "Dirty Five." It consisted of Charles Lee, Louis "Loulip" Lipp, Martin "Max" Majewski, and Frank M. "Shorty" Mihlan.

Charles Lee was a nice guy. He was a pretty quiet guy who would go to town with the four of us and drink and party. He washed out sometime after I was thrown in the stockade for I never saw him again.

Loulip was a German boy from somewhere up in Illinois. He was a big man, probably six feet one and real intelligent. He was so flat-footed he looked like a duck. He walked like this, clomp, clomp, clomp. You would think he was crippled the way he walked, but boy he was ahead of the class on anything that was physical. He could make a twenty-five-mile field march with full gear. He would never complain and was as happy as could be. He was a prince of a man and loved his whiskey.

Max was tough as a boot. He was one of the best football players we had in the regiment. He would fight anything that showed up but he was not aggressive or obnoxious. He just stood his ground anywhere.

Shorty Mihlan was not more than five feet four and an ex-pug[6] from Cleveland, Ohio. Boy, he was also tough as a boot. He was one of the oldest ones in there. Mihlan was a total blackout drunkard though. He stayed drunk all the time. He would always manage to get hold of some whiskey. Our regimental commander, Colonel Sink, made him his orderly. They were both alcoholics.[7] Shorty and I became and stayed good friends.

There was another group of guys in our demolition platoon called the "Warsaw Seven." Most of these boys were Polish and spoke the Polish language real fluent, although they were all born in America. They all had buddied together and were a pretty hard-headed bunch of kids to get along with. They adopted me as one of their own.[8]

Corporal Eddy Malas was a regular army man. He had tried to get me to do something stupid under orders one day but I told him to kiss my ass. He kept telling me that his rank was made permanent by Congress. I told him, "Look, Congress doesn't have a hell of a lot to do with me. I'll whip your ass right here and now." He answered, "You can't talk to me like that." He then took off.

They sent him out as cadre to train new recruits. They made cadre out of a lot of the regular army people at that time. They would train us to a certain point then they would ship out somewhere and end up in a whole new outfit. Malas was a book soldier—he did everything by the book.[9]

Most of these Polish boys were pretty smart kids. I think this kid named Edmund Lojko went into the S-3 (Operations). Frank Palys also was transferred up to the S-2 (Intelligence). There was another kid named Salinas. We called him "Deacon" because he was very religious.

George Baran was a young Polish kid from up in the Adams, Massachusetts, area. He was a coal miner and a bull of a man. He had lots of guts and was a good soldier. He was one of the original Warsaw Seven but he did not stay with us. I did not want him. He was not aggressive enough. One has to be the aggressor in combat.

Anytime a soldier becomes the defender he has had it. He was just a little bit slow on reacting. Another Pole was Joe Baranosky. I did not think he was much of a soldier either. He transferred to another stick.[10]

Joe Oparowski and Joe Oleskiewicz were two of the eight seventeen-year-old kids who enlisted in our company. Oparowski was killed during training. We were setting up a live-fire course to get the men accustomed to the noises of combat. We had a bunch of machine guns that were tied down set to fire live ammunition. We would get a bunch of guys started through there, then we would open up on them. We had nearly all the crossroads and bridges mined with trip wires. When they ran out into the timber behind us, we would blow the tops out of the trees just to give them the feel of combat.[11]

Oparowski was setting charges and laying out trip wires. He had taken the insulation off the trip wire and made a loop, then threaded it through the loop of another one. If anyone touched that thing it would pull the two loops together and Bang! He was up in one of those big pines down there in South Carolina. It was pretty windy that day. Oparowski had his charge all lined up. The wind started blowing that pine tree while he held the charge under his arm. The tree moved over far enough and pulled those wires together. It just blew his whole chest up.[12]

After Oparowski died, the rest of the Warsaw Seven were going to have a Catholic Mass up at the chapel. They invited me to go along because I was close to all of them. I told them I did not care for it much. Those things happen and it seemed like a big deal to go through all that ceremony. Of course, I did not know anything about mass.

I looked around and they were dragging out their bottles of whiskey and wine. I asked, "What are you going to do with all those bottles?"

They answered, "Well, we'll do some drinking at mass. That is part of our worship service."

I said, "Why, I've got a bottle of whiskey." So I went along with them.

When Joe Oleskiewicz came into the outfit, he was seventeen. He was just a kid. He came from a large family and was the youngest of about thirteen children. There were eight recruits that were just young kids. Herby Pierce was another one of them but Oleskiewicz was the best soldier in the whole bunch. He just had the guts for it. He never hesitated on anything. If you said you were going to charge into a building, he was step for step with you. He was kind of a short kid and he was a good physical specimen. Everyone of them Poles were good physical men.

Joe was a faithful Orthodox Catholic and attended the services all the time. Of course he drank some, but he was not much of a boozer. He was a big gambler though. Boy, he could rattle them bones. He could throw more passes with a set of dice than you could get grapes off a grapevine. He loved it. He would clean up every month on payday, four or five hundred dollars, then ship it right home. He would not touch a card, however. He did not know anything about cards. Joe was a first-class soldier. I made him a corporal and one of my squad leaders. I became very fond of him.

I got along pretty good with the Warsaw Seven. I had four sisters and two brothers who did not go to war. They and my parents would send me one or two boxes every week. Every box had the same thing in it: sardines, crackers, and Copenhagen. Every one of those guys got to know what the other was getting. Every package these Polacks received had kielbasa. It was one of the best Polish sausages that I have ever eaten in my life. I would swap with them some sardines for sausage. We always shared what we had.

We began to form into squads and platoons and companies and battalions. They put the Warsaw Seven in with my group. So the Dirty Five and the Warsaw Seven combined to form the 1st Battalion Demolition-Saboteur Section of the Demolition Platoon. I stayed with that platoon throughout the war.

My attitude was all wrong for the army but I was able to get work out of the men. When another sergeant had a paratrooper who was rebellious or did not give a hoot about courtesy or discipline, why he would stick him over in my section. The company segregated them so their attitude would not contaminate the rest. They would then be with others of a similar attitude and I could control them as far as I wanted to. I was grateful for them. Nearly everyone of them was an excellent combat soldier. The meaner the man, the better soldier he was, in my opinion.

The first six weeks of boot camp consisted of tough, tough physical training to weed us out. We got up every morning at 4:30 to run up the Curahee Mountain. After breakfast we went into physical training all day long. In the morning we carried and passed big logs around. We would fool around with those logs for about an hour.

Then we would run down to the obstacle course. We ran everywhere. There was no walking. We had obstacle courses that would nearly kill a man but we made a contest out of it. It crossed a river three times—on rope ladders, poles, and a swing. We would swing as far as we could, then hit belly first and scoot onto the bank. There were also ten-foot scaling walls. Each wall had a twenty-five-foot rope hanging from a beam that we had to climb hand over hand. At the very end of it was a half-mile sprint.

Other times they would divide the company in half and form a circle with a fifteen-foot diameter. When the whistle blew, a man from each side would charge in and have to throw the other out. When one was thrown out, another from that side would run in and take his place.

We also conducted two twenty-five-mile forced marches with full field packs each week. If the officers were mad at us we did three a week. We began our physical training from early morning and did not stop until midnight. They told us right out that the purpose of the training was to weed out the weak. If a man ran until he passed out, they would let him try again the next morning. If he quit in any part of the training then his ass was out the gate. This weeded a lot of those who were not physically fit.

Besides the physical training, we took technical training on demolitions and sabotage and various aspects of our field. We, being demolition saboteur people, had a large amount of primer cord. We had enough explosives of all kinds in our foot lockers to blow up the Empire State Building. We were supposed to turn it in but the ordnance people could not keep track of thirty or forty men out there.

Most of the demolition platoon wore primer cord around the shoulder of their coveralls just so people would know who we were. It was not regulation. We just did it. I imagine it started when someone came in one evening with it still on him when he had been setting explosives.

WHIPPING THE MESS SERGEANT

The first bit of trouble I got into was whipping a mess sergeant. I was only in the army about a week. They fed us slop, absolute slop. It was not just ill-prepared, it was ill-quality. They had fifty tables set up in a building attached to the mess hall. Then they would run the men through, a company at a time. We went in there one evening and sat down. I do not even like butter but our butter plate was on the table and empty. So this one kid said, "We need some butter."

So I hollered over to one of the KPs[13] for butter. He said we had had butter already. I said, "No, we have not had any butter. Just give us a stick of butter."

He called the mess sergeant and I told him, "Get us a stick of butter out here."

He said, "You've already had one."

I told him, "We have not even had a smear of butter. That was left on the table by the KP from the previous feeding."

He said, "That's a damn lie."

I jumped up and made a run at him but he got out of there. It was so crowded that one could hardly walk. We were ass-to-ass with everybody. Two nights later I saw him over at the PX. I whipped him. I just beat him like a dog. That was the first trouble that I got into.

Right after I whipped this mess sergeant, Colonel Sink was down there observing the obstacle course to see how the guys were coming along through it. I was always right in the first four or five people to finish the course. I was the first one to complete the course that day and Colonel Sink told me, "That is real good time. You did a good job."

I said, "Shit, that ain't nothing. If you'd given me a little butter, I don't know how fast I could have run this."

Of course he was very aware of the butter incident. You do not whip a staff sergeant without it going up the ladder. Sink just shook his head and I walked on off.

Smokin' Them Out

They decided to put me on extra duty, close-order drill, and all that for punishment. I went down the third night to do my close-order drill. Jim Davidson was the Charge of Quarters. I walked in and he said, "Okay, McNiece, I guess you're here for your close-order drill."

I said, "That's right."

He said, "You're the only one on extra duty."

I said, "That's okay. Come on, let's get this show on the road. I've got things to do."

Davidson said, "Okay, you just get out there and march up and down that street. We'll tell you when two hours are up."

I said, "Come on."

He asked, "What do you mean come on?"

I said, "You've got to have someone marking time all the time that a person is in close-order drill." I told him, "This is pretty good. This is one-on-one."

Davidson was just like me—sick of the army. He said, "Oh no, that's not right."

Ole Top Kick Miller said, "Davidson, that's right. You don't have to march with him but you have to mark time."

It was pretty cold. This was October at Toccoa, Georgia, up in the mountains. He said, "I'll tell you what McNiece. You build us a fire here in our stove and we'll use that as your punishment for extra duty for the day."

They were burning coal in those pot-bellied stoves.

I said, "Okay, I'll do that."

I got some newspaper and went over to get me a scuttle full of coal. I put a couple handfuls of that real fine dust in there. I found some sticks and made some kindling. I put that newspaper in under it and put the sticks in there, then I poured all that dust on top of that. I placed my coal on it, then I took another piece of that paper and stuck it up in that stove pipe. Boy, when I struck a match to that thing, it just blossomed up like nothing before. That paper and that dead wood really set off a charge. I jumped right out of there and ran across the street and crawled under a tent. You could hear them coughing, then the windows opened and smoke just poured out. The door opened and they were all cussing me.

One used to be able to beat those stovepipes with a broom handle or stick or get up on top and punch up and down to clear them out. Well, they were beating that pipe to pieces. They had one man up on top with a big long rod. He was poking and jabbing. They began cussing and calling for me. I laid there just dying from laughter but I never did get to build any more fires for them.

Boy, the airborne was a brand-new thing. The 506th Parachute Regiment was the first parachute regiment activated. They had only activated battalions before. Consequently, there was a dire and direct need for airborne vounteers to be successful. If they got hold of the type of people that they wanted, they tried every way in the world to keep them. So our punishments were going to be damned little. I do not remember one man in Regimental Headquarters Company ever being court-martialed. Very few of us even went to the stockade and we knew we would not stay in there very long. They needed us too badly. They were not going to sacrifice one of us who they knew was a good combat man.

Most of the time I just got light punishment for two or three days. Anyway the punishment would get me out of all that close-order drill and picking up cigarette butts. I enjoyed the stockade more than I enjoyed garrison life. I really had fun the whole time, making it worth it.

NATURE WORSHIP AND RETREAT FORMATION

When I first went in, the army felt that everyone had sisters or brothers or a wife or children that really needed some financial help. So after thirty-one days, they just automatically made everyone a PFC[14] and that raised their pay to thirty-one dollars a month. They anticipated that most of them would send an allotment of five or ten dollars back home. That was the general procedure.

I had not been in there much over a week until I whipped that mess sergeant. After that of course, I got a lot of details and this and that, and the longer I stayed the worse it got. At the end of the thirty-one days, why they were not about to promote me to PFC. I never made PFC the whole time I was in the army but I always remained an acting sergeant during training.

They had a stinking regulation back then—of course they have it now and always will. This reveille and retreat ceremony was the stupidest thing I ever saw in my life. We would stand there in formation and salute as they raised and lowered the flag while music played over the loudspeaker. What made it worse, they would bring us in out of the field about ten minutes to five o'clock and we were supposed to be shaved, shined, showered, and standing out there in formation for this retreat deal. This did not give us time to properly clean up. I thought, "This is stupid. I'll have no part in it."

They always gave a count just before we came to attention. The first sergeant would sound off, "Give the report!" Then each sergeant over each group of men reported to the platoon sergeant, "All men present and accounted for," or "Absent and unaccounted for." The platoon sergeant would then report to the first sergeant. If there was a man unaccounted for, he would ask him to give the name so he could go ahead and discipline that person.

Well, Sergeant Johnson, my platoon sergeant, reported me absent and unaccounted for. Top Kick told him, "You get with him and find out what the deal is."

So he asked me, "McNiece, I had to report you absent and unaccounted for at retreat today. Where were you?"

I said, "I was over at the PX."[15]

He asked, "What were you doing at the PX?"

I said, "I was drinking beer and eating peanuts."

He asked, "Why?"

I said, "I like beer and peanuts and I don't like retreat."

He said, "You think over that answer. There are about five million people in the military and they all stand retreat."

I said, "Well, this one doesn't. I don't stand retreat under any circumstances."

He asked, "What do you mean?"

I answered, "Well, it's against my religion."

He said, "What?"

So I told him, "You see my dad was Irish and my mother was Indian. Dad, of course, was Catholic. My mother was a nature worshiper. I adopted her religion. I'm a nature worshiper."[16]

He said, "What's that got to do with retreat?"

I said, "Well, it's like this. That flag you all run up out there that everybody salutes and pays tribute to. That's a handmade flag. Why don't you do it to one of these pine trees or something? It just won't work for me. We worship the sun and the moon and the stars, ants, and bugs and mosquitoes, lions, and tigers. Anything that's of nature, we respect. Not this crap on this handmade flag and organ grinder music you're putting out. That would violate every principle and scruple of my religion. Well, just count me out."

He said, "I don't think you've got the right perspective on this. You have to stand retreat. Everybody stands retreat."

I said "Yes, I have. I want to tell you something, Johnson. There wouldn't even be a United States of America if it wasn't for religious freedom." I said, "That's how this country got started. I have that right and privilege. I know it. I won't be at retreat."

He could not believe what he was hearing. He told me, "You better be there tomorrow night." Then he went back and told the first sergeant.

Well the next night I did not go out. Johnson kept heckling me. He cajoled me and threatened me and begged and pleaded for a week. Then he sent me into ole Top Kick Miller. Then he cajoled me and threatened me and begged and pleaded for another week. The third week they turned me over to this executive officer. He was a stupid little ole kid out of OCS and did not know any more about it. He cajoled me and threatened me and begged and pled and offered me different things for another week.

I told them, "I'm not standing retreat."

When they had all gotten through with me, I had repeated this story so many times that I had it down verbatim. It was just like reciting a poem. I had kind of begun to believe it myself. I got to where I would watch so that I would not even step on any ants.

Well, they finally sent me to report to Captain Hank Hannah, the company commander. He was an attorney out of Illinois and a very shrewd person.

I reported in to Captain Hannah, "Private McNiece as ordered."

The company commander's office was a little bitty room. Top Kick had his desk over against the wall with this executive officer next to him and then Captain Hannah. They were making out like they were doing all their work, but they were on the edge of their chairs just listening. They wanted to see how the captain was going to make out.

Captain Hannah said, "Private McNiece, I understand you're having a problem with retreat."

I said, "No sir. I'm not having any problem with retreat."

He said, "Let me put it another way. I understand you have refused to stand retreat."

I said, "That's right."

He said, "Why?"

So I gave him this whole big spiel about my religious freedoms and all this and that and how my religion of being a nature worshiper started. I told him, "I am a volunteer not a draftee. You can teach me to go over and kill Germans. I don't have any objections to that but I am a conscientious objector to retreat."

Hannah patiently looked at me and then he said, "You know what McNiece? We have nearly five million people in the military service today. As far as I can determine, you are the only one that has ever professed this religion."

I returned, "That doesn't surprise me. We are a very small group. There are very few nature worshipers left." I also added, "I don't think that should be a determining factor."

He said, "I want to tell you something. There are over several hundred regulations in the army and you have broken half at one point or another. I do not believe you have a speck of religion in you. So you will stand retreat this evening."

I asked, "You would give me a direct order and know, thereby, that you will violate and destroy every scruple of my spiritual life?"

He said, "Yes."

I grinned and said, "Well, that's all that I've been waiting on."

Top Kick Miller and that executive officer, they looked like they had been hit in the head with a club. Hannah was a fine old gentleman and I stood retreat that evening.[17]

I only stood retreat that one day in October. Afterwards we were so busy training that we never had to stand retreat again. Paratroopers were excused from all retreats from then on during their training period.

FIGHT WITH THE MP'S[18]

Our basic training was nearly over and we were getting ready to go to Fort Benning, Georgia, to make our five qualifying parachute jumps. The guys I tented with went with me into this little ole town of Toccoa the next night to celebrate. About half of the town was off limits, which was where we picked up all our whiskey and women. So we went into the off-limits district to get us a fifth of whiskey, then we went back up to where the MPs would not fool with us. We would drink our whiskey then go back and get another fifth. By about the third trip, we were pretty drunk.

This ole boy, who owned the joint and bootlegged this whiskey, was trying to get us out of there before the MPs came in and shut him down.

I told the guys, "Hey, we ain't even going to be able to get drunk tonight. We're walking it off faster than we can drink it. Let's just stay out here."

So they said, "Okay."

Every honky-tonk and beer joint used to have a great big gallon jug full of pickled eggs sitting up on the counter. Little Shorty Mihlan had to stand up on his tiptoes to reach in there to get him a handful of eggs. We were all drunked up and everything. Shorty would throw an egg up against the ceiling and holler, "Fifty dollars a month!" That is what our pay would increase to as a paratrooper.[19]

Then someone hollered, "MPs are coming!"

Well, Loulip, Majewski, and Lee ran out the back door. Little ole Shorty Mihlan was acting tough. He just walked out the front door to meet those MPs. It was about four or five steps down to the sidewalk. Well, Shorty stumbled and rolled down the steps just like an ole volleyball down into the gutter. I just proceeded on down the steps behind him.

When I got down there, why Shorty was rolling around trying to fight and hit someone. Those two MPs charged in on us. One reached down and picked Shorty up and Shorty started fighting. This MP took a swing at him with his night stick. I just stuck my hand out and warded it off.

I said, "Don't hit him with that stick. He's so drunk he can't hit the floor with his hat in thirty throws. He can't attack you."

He said, "I'll do anything I want to with this stick."

Then he reeled back to hit him again. When he did, I reached over and grabbed that stick and yanked it out of his hand. Then I whipped him and the other MP. Boy, I beat them right down into that gutter. After I climbed out of the gutter, I took their forty-fives[20] off of them. Of course, I was drunk as nine hundred dollars and started shooting up signs, not trying to hit anybody but shooting out street lights and neon signs, anything until I emptied their guns. I was just mainly trying to get rid of their ammunition. I just did not want them armed. Then I handed them back and said, "Now we are ready to go with you."

So they took us down and put us in the stockade. The next morning Captain Hannah came up.

He asked me, "McNiece, what happened?"

So I told him exactly what happened.

He said, "Jake, we're going to go in about ten days up to Atlanta from here by truck then we are going to make a forced march of a hundred and thirty-six miles, full field pack to Fort Benning. So that'll beat the record of the Japanese." The army wanted some unit in the United States to beat the record. He asked, "Do you think you can make that march?"

I said, "That would be no problem. Why, I could do that without getting a blister or change my socks."

Like a father talking to a son he said, "Well, I think you can. I'll tell you what I'm going to do though. I'm going to leave you in here until the day before the road march. I would rather they be watching you than me because I don't want to fool with you. They can control you better than I can. You'd be into a dozen different things. So I don't even want to hear anything out of anybody."

Captain Hannah was a fair man and treated everybody with equal respect. I told him, "Okay." So he left me in that stockade until the day before we left.[21]

CURRAHEE

The Currahee Mountain's base was laying almost in our camp. Every morning before breakfast we would run on a heavily graveled road up the mountain and back, a distance of three miles to the top and three back. Because of this big loose gravel, it was about as hard to run back down as it was to run up.[22]

Hannah was a good track man and a big fellow, tall, about six one. His specialty was the mile run. When we made this run every morning, Majewski and I would lay our toes down on his heels all the way back. When we got down to the bottom, within a quarter of a mile from camp, we would start hollering, "Heat! Heat!"[23] but he would not race. I believe Majewski or I or either one could have beaten him.[24]

The path that they ran up the mountain passed right by the stockade. The stockade was just about two hundred yards from the company street. It was just a barbed wire enclosure with five-man squad tents. When confined there I would stand there and grin every morning from behind the barbed wire fence as they came back past me. When they came by I would holler, "Heat! Heat! Heat!"[25]

Return from the Stockade

They left me in the stockade until the day before the march. Hannah sent word to the stockade for them to return me to the company. Three MPs armed with shotguns marched me down through the company street. I had on this stockade garb. It had two big "Ps" painted on the front and in the middle of the back of the shirt and a third on the pants of these blue fatigues.

Malcolm Landry, a kid from the communication platoon, later asked me, "Jake, do you remember the first time that I ever saw you?"

I said, "No, you did not come right in with the first batch. I don't know when you came in."

He said, "The first time that I ever saw you, I was standing out there talking and shooting the breeze and here you come up the street there with three MPs walking along with shotguns on you. I looked back and asked, 'I wonder who in the hell that is and what in the hell he has done?' One of the guys kind of grinned and said, 'That's McNiece and no telling what he has done. He's been in the stockade for ten days.'"

I started taking the dungarees off. The MPs wanted them back. So I started stripping them off and the other guys asked, "How come you get monogrammed uniforms all the time?"

I answered, "You can get one. The 'Ps' stand for Professionally Perfect Paratrooper. After you make so many jumps you are awarded these monogrammed uniforms."[26]

TOWARD EMBARKATION

ANOTHER FIGHT WITH THE MP'S

December 9, 1942

Third Battalion was dropped off by truck at Atlanta, Georgia, and we started our march from there. We completed forty-two miles that first day. Of course we mostly ran. A lot of the guys took their boots off that night and their feet swelled up so much that they could not get them back on the next morning. It was also raining and snowing. Oh, it was miserable. They had those "blood buckets" [ambulances] following right along to pick up anyone who fell out. An awful lot of the boys did fall out and only about seventy-five of our battalion finished. I did not have any problems at all. I did not even get a blister.[27]

There was a little ole kid named Arthur Hayes from Boston. He had buddied up with me. He wanted to be a Wild West, rootin-tootin, son-of-a-gun. So I called him "Red Gulch."

Hannah promised a seventy-two hour pass to anybody who could complete the whole march without falling out. We had just arrived in camp when I said, "Let's get our showers real quick then run down and get our seventy-two hour passes and get out of here."

He asked, "You feel like going out?"

I said, "Yeah, you bet. We'll be the first ones out of here before these paratroopers get in there and ruin the whole thing."

He said, "Okay."

So we shaved and bathed, then ran down to the orderly room and told Top Kick we wanted our seventy-two hour passes.

He said, "You know the passes are for tomorrow. So you can get one tomorrow."

I said, "I don't want one tomorrow. I want to go out before the rest of these idiots get into town."

He said, "Get the hell to bed and forget it. You're in no shape for a pass."

I said, "I'm all right. This has not bothered me at all."

Not very many guys wanted to leave that camp. They just wanted to bunk. Top Kick pleaded and begged with us but we kept heckling him until he gave us our seventy-two hour passes.

We went into the black district of Columbus to party and have a good time. The black folks recognized that we were paratroopers. They were real patriotic. They had one big ole woman there going around the room praying. She must have weighed three hundred pounds and she came over and kneeled down in front of Red Gulch. When she did, that dress was just as tight as a bow string right across her bottom. She was praying for us and our safety when Red Gulch reached over and patted her on the butt. As a result, Red Gulch had a word or two with some of the black men and then the brawl began. We went to work on them and whipped the shit out of those guys.

After the MPs brought us back, Captain Hannah called us in. He looked at me. "McNiece," he said, "I don't know what to do with you."

Red Gulch Hayes spoke with that real strong Boston accent and presented our defense. "Sir, let me tell you what happened." He began to talk but he was just drifting around giving the captain all this BS and crap. He was not even sober and I could see he was not impressing Captain Hannah.

"Wait a minute, Captain Hannah." I said, "You're missing the whole story. You evidently don't seem to understand that this was a bunch of black men we was whipping." I thought that all I had to say was they were blacks and that would wipe the slate clean.[28]

He said, "McNiece! I'll tell you something! There's no Mason and Dixon Line in the army! We're all one! It don't make a damned difference what they were. You think that's the whole solution but it isn't!" He continued, "McNiece, I can't believe you. I took you out of the stockade to get down here then you grab a seventy-two hour pass and you're in the stockade again before midnight. I give up!"

After he finished with me I was put back in the stockade.

Jump School

When we walked into training, the cadre tried to put us through the ropes. They would drop us for twenty push-ups and we would ask them if they wanted another twenty-five. Up to that time they had only trained recruits. We were the first regiment to go through jump school as a unit. We had had our physical weeding out process before we got there. When they saw what the score was they immediately sent us to the packing shed. Each one of us had to pack one chute by ourselves. After that we went right into jump training. We qualified as paratroopers after five jumps. It was a great day when we received our wings. We felt like we were top dog. Afterwards they gave us a short furlough.

Deacon Salinas was the only guy we lost out of our section at Jump School. He froze in the door on his first jump. Well, anyone who refused to jump, they usually just kicked them out immediately. Salinas begged and pleaded for them to let him go up for a second time. He said, "I made a contract with the army that I would make a jump from an airplane. Let me do that and I will then quit." They allowed him to go up a second time and he jumped. He landed bad and was bleeding from head to toe. He said, "Okay, I kept my vow," and we never saw him again. He was a good honorable kid.

BARRACKS BRAWL[29]

[Jack Agnew recalled how the section capped this phase of their training:]

Of course, we knew it was getting near time to go overseas. It just so happened that the medics had a party. The medics got to feeling pretty good and two of them started fighting. When one was knocked down, he would get up and knock the other down. "Dirty" Johnson was a tough little ole guy from a lumber company out in Washington. Johnson could not figure it out. He said, "Boy when we knock a guy down, you stomp him and don't let him get up or he'll beat you again."

So the next thing we knew, a lot of the fellows were carrying beer back to our barracks and they got to feeling pretty good. As a matter of fact they started throwing dish pans up and down the steps to the latrine. Communications platoon was downstairs and demolitions was upstairs.

Armando Marquez[30] *had started to feel pretty good. He thought we were going to Japan, so he took his knife out and was cutting the pillows all up. There were feathers all over the place. Somebody hit his brother, Mike, as he came out of the shower with a pillow and he had feathers stuck all over him.*

Someone else suggested throwing a bunk down the steps and everybody was pushing this bunk. Jake had seen Lieutenant Sylvester Horner coming. So he said to the guys, "Hey don't do that." But Jake was the instigator in the first place.

So Horner started coming up to raise Cain. Somebody was about to pull a knife. Kennedy had a pitcher of beer and pulled back to throw it on this guy but hit Horner right in the chest as he came up behind him. The beer was all over Horner and he raised all kinds of heck. He said, "I don't care if you guys are up to two o'clock in the morning. You are going to have a white glove inspection and clean this place out."[31]

So everybody was throwing buckets of water on the floor and cleaning the walls up but it was running down on top of communications. So they were getting mad. So the next thing we knew, we ended up in another fight. That all turned out to be part of the training.

CAMP MACKALL, NORTH CAROLINA[32]

February 26, 1943

We completed our five qualifying jumps at Fort Benning, then moved to Camp Mackall, North Carolina, right outside Southern Pines. That is where we became a part of the 101st Airborne Division. There we began some really serious tactical training as demolition saboteurs.

They named this camp after the first American paratrooper killed in North Africa. His name was John Mackall. They told us the demolition platoon was going to make a big jump to dedicate the field to him. They would have a bandstand set up with his family and several high-ranking military people there. We were supposedly going to land on that dirt. It should have been sodded but was not. It had been finely ground up with manure about an inch deep. They had some big runways there.

That morning when we woke up, the wind speed was about twenty-five miles an hour and just kept increasing. By the time they had us ready to jump, it was up to forty miles an hour. Since all these dignitaries and the kid's mother and dad were there they were going to go ahead with it anyway.

So we bailed out of those planes. I was lucky. On the ground I collapsed my chute immediately. Just bingo, I had her down flat. But I saw the wind drag men two hundred yards. It skinned and peeled the men and dragged them through this dusty manure, if they did not land on the runway. It wore out their reserve chutes until one could see the rayon threads. I had never seen such a debacle in all my life.

SECOND ARMY TENNESSEE MANEUVERS NO. 1

June 6, 1943

The Tennessee Maneuvers resembled any regular war maneuver. We were always considered the enemy unit and they used us for the element of surprise and checked whether or not we could accomplish the assignment that we had been trained for. We needed to leave proof of identification for everything that we destroyed. We made a total of four jumps in four weeks. The first week they dropped us on the west side, next week on the east side, then the north and south. Some real funny things happened down there.

Back in the hill country there were a lot of hillbillies. This one paratrooper was oscillating as he came down. He had no control of his chute and hit a chimney on a house that must have been about a hundred years old. There was hardly any mortar left in it. Well, he knocked that chimney clear off the building and it crumbled up in a heap down there. Boy, here came this hillbilly out of that house with that shotgun and demanded payment right then and there. Well, the guy did not have a penny in his pocket so the hillbilly was about to shoot him. The paratrooper talked and pleaded with him until some lieutenant came by and assured the man he would be paid, but not on the spot.

There was another kid who landed on the tongue of a wagon while an old man was cultivating with a pair of mules. Those mules ran away and he was still caught on it.

They had a lot of beehives in that country. Harold Scully landed on a beehive and knocked it over. His canopy then engulfed both him and the bees. He got stung hundreds of times and they took him to the hospital quick. They said he swelled up as big as a log. It was so bad that he was never able to return to parachute duty.

One time we were on a mountain so steep that one had to put his legs around something to hold his position. I looked over to where Lieutenant Leach was laying and there was a coral snake on a limb just about a foot from his head.

I said, "Leach, if I was you, I would move pretty slow over to my left. There is a coral snake right over your head."

He slid over and was just looking eyeball-to-eyeball with this snake. When he got himself to a safe position where he thought he could do it, he flung himself away from there. The snake never did strike him.

Tom Young and I went AWOL[33] into Nashville. Of course, we became drunk and were jaywalking and this and that. I staggered out in the street after dark and was hit by a city street bus. I bet it knocked me thirty feet. Of course, I was drunk and as loose as a dish rag. I rolled and tumbled. So the driver began to slow her down to a stop. I was already up chasing him. I ran up and beat on his door. It did not have a handle to where I could get in to him. So when he saw that I was still navigating he took off. He burned it out of there.

Tom and I went into a joint. I do not know what the deal was there but it did not take long before the bartender and I got into it. Then he said, "I'll just call the cops." He picked that phone up.

Tom, like me, always carried a heavy pocket knife. He had one of those big ole Cases with a four-and-a-half-inch blade on it. He just reached over and grabbed that phone line, doubled it up and cut it in two then handed the bartender his end of it.

We would steal a jeep or something out of a headquarters area, and drive it off and leave it. We did not have any business with a jeep in an "enemy position" where we were outnumbered a hundred to one. We had a lot of fun down there.

[Jack Agnew and Herb Pierce, who were in a different section at that time, remembered:]

One day an officer came in and asked for volunteers from the demolitions platoon, saying, "You, you, and you." Brincely Stroup and Joe Oleskiewicz were also volunteered. Ed Pikering was the medic for the operation. They had twelve planes to jump about fifteen men. Each plane kicked out five or six door bundles with parachutes as dummies to give the impression that the opposing army had dropped in an entire battalion. Their objective was to cause as much confusion behind the lines as possible. Brince and Jack served as scouts for the demolitions section. They cut their way through brush to a small barn on top of a little mountain. There they captured a communications jeep and its crew. With the radios they learned all the enemy's movements and sneaked down to capture vehicles out of the motor pool or at least steal the rotors out of the ones they left behind.

Herb Pierce asked the referees for permission to impersonate officers. So the demolitions men borrowed their bars and went down that night and lied their way into the command tent. They then sat in the back while the officers held their meeting. All the while a suspicious lieutenant kept staring at seventeen-year-old Herb. When the meeting was over, he came up and said, "You are too young to be a lieutenant." With that Herb figured it was time to do something. The men had spread out around the room and he told everyone they were captured. The major was mad as hell.[34]

FORT BRAGG, NORTH CAROLINA

July 23, 1943

After the Tennessee Maneuvers we went to Fort Bragg, North Carolina, to get ready to ship over to England. We spent the time getting our supplies and all the while we were training every day. We made about ten more practice jumps.

Down there, the authorities came around and said everybody had to get a GI haircut before we shipped out. Well, most of us did not want a GI haircut. We had one little ole kid in the company named

"Maw" Darnell. He had just transferred in from a chemical warfare outfit and they stuck him into my section. He was tongue-tied and a real Georgia Cracker. He was almost difficult to understand. Someone would ask, "Where did you come from Maw?" He would say, "Fow Fow Too, Chemico Wo-fare." He was illiterate. He couldn't read nor write. I wrote his folks for him.

He did not care what his head looked like. He would buy him enough Brown Mule chewing tobacco to last him a month when he got paid. Then the rest of it he would gamble off. He liked to gamble. When they put out this order, we had only two company barbers, a fellow named George Underwood and I think Frank Pellechia. So I got me a chair and an orange crate and set up a barber shop there. I sat Maw Darnell in that chair and started cutting his hair. Boy, he looked like a Halloween pumpkin. I was nearly through when Top Kick came by. Someone had told him what I was doing.

Top Kick said, "What in the hell are you doing?"

I said, "You want everybody to get a burr haircut. I'm just trying to help you all I can, Top." I said, "There's nothing I won't do for the company, you know."

He looked at that kid and said, "I'll tell you, it will cost you five dollars to get your hair straightened up. McNiece, if you cut hair off of another head anywhere while you're under my command, I'll send you to prison."

I did not get any punishment out of that. He just chewed me real good. I thought I would give them all a burr haircut.

STOLEN TRAIN AND BLOWN-UP BARRACKS

Service Company ran a short school that taught us every minute detail about operating and disabling tanks, trains, dozers, and stuff like that. They figured if we came across any equipment like that behind enemy lines we should know how to operate them.

Trains only had two gears. If a man would just watch the temperature and water level then all he would have to do was go forward or backward. But one had to be awful careful. The engine had a fire sheet in there that the engineer kept red hot. If the water dropped to where that sheet was exposed, the next time that the engineer shot water in there it would blow that thing a million miles high.

They taught us if a train was in motion and hit a torpedo (kind of like a firecracker with a band that would crimp around a rail) it would indicate that there was another train on the track or that trouble was ahead, a bridge was out or something. The engineer would have to slow the train down to a caution speed. After he hit two of these then he would proceed a little further and see a flare, kind of a Roman candle. The flare had a spike that would stick down in the wood.

Well, they taught us this to avoid collisions behind the enemy lines or our own lines. I think they issued each one of us three of those torpedoes in Normandy. I kept mine in my musset bag and placed them on any track that I came across. It was a deterrent but not effective for firepower. It would delay a German train so they would have to send a group of men out ahead to see what the danger was. This would allow other American troops to destroy the train.

While we were down at Camp Mackall, I had gone into town one night in Southern Pines and got hooched up. They had those two-and-a-half-ton trucks or six-bys that would come into town and make a shuttle back and forth out to our barracks. All the trucks had left out of town and I had missed my ride. There was a cafe down at the railroad yard. So I thought I would jump down there and get me some drinks and eats.

I kept watching these goats (that is what they called these small engines that work inside the yards) trying to figure out what was happening there. Those firemen and engineers and brakemen were in and out of there all night eating. Those guys would park their engines and come in and eat a sandwich and drink some coffee. They would just leave a spot fire. At that time all locomotives had a big fire plate on the bottom and the water would be under it boiling for propulsion. They had put what they call a spot fire on that plate which kept the steam from reaching a certain level. When they were ready to take the goat out of there, they had enough steam to move with. They would then crank that burner up and build up a good head of steam.

So I kind of watched this and became familiar with the operation, and then this engineer and fireman came in. They ordered a pretty good-sized meal. I then went out to look the engine and throttles and everything over. That locomotive was a very simple piece of machinery. It just had the throttle and release and the gauge there on the oil burners.

So I climbed in there, cranked her up and threw that throttle, whipped her down to the end, threw the switch and took off out of there about thirty miles back to camp. Away I went.

I did not know if I was on the right track or not but they had a box of safety equipment there. It had flares and torpedoes. I did not want anyone to get hurt so when I stopped I walked out and put out these poppers on the track up and down there and in back of it. Then I put flares out just like I was taught.

So when I got back to Camp Mackall, of course, the railroad people were already sending out messages and alerts for other people on that track. Of course, the next morning there was hell to pay. Boy, they were mad. Our officers were questioning every one of us and particularly they were questioning me. I just denied any knowledge of it all together.[35]

They put my company under arrest of quarters and we had to stay in the barracks. We could not go to a show or anything. This was just before we shipped overseas. It did not bother me but a lot of the guys' wives, mothers, and dads and relatives had come in to enjoy a few last days with them. The guys could not talk to their mothers and daddies or anything. Boy, they were a mad bunch of soldiers. They were ready to revolt. I thought, "Well, this warrants a little activity to see if we can change that line of thinking."

In the demolition platoon everyone of us stole explosives, caps and detonators, primer cord and everything else. Everyone of them had a foot locker full of it or they hid it up under the barracks. The front of the barracks was at street level and the back of it was on a grade about four feet down from the floor of this barracks.

So I was sitting out there on the back steps of my barracks and they had a guard just walking. I kept watching and timing him and this and that. There were some big ole pine trees around the camp that were about a foot and a half in diameter. So I went in and asked the men for explosives and rigged up a big charge on the opposite side of this tree from where this guard walked so it would fall away from him. The bulk of the trunk would protect him from danger. Then I made me a trip wire like we had done before.

Boy, he came through that area right on schedule. He must have been mechanical or something because his timing was perfect. He came around there and hit that trip wire. When he did, that charge went off like a clap of thunder. It cut that tree down. That ole boy was scared to death but he was not hurt. I made a run into the barracks and told the other guys, "You better get in your bunks."

In just a minute here came that, "Ten-shun!" Everybody rubbed their eyes and looked around and yawned. We got up out of our bunks. The officer said, "All right. Which one of you blew up the tree?"[36]

Nobody knew anything. He said, "It's funny that you all could sit within twenty feet of that tree and be sound asleep when we've had calls from Southern Pines wanting to know what was happening down here."

I said, "It's probably because you all work us too hard with this fatigue."

He said, "McNiece, you were awful close to that tree when it blew up."

I said, "I was in here asleep."

So they just raised Cain but they never could prove it on me. Each individual was later questioned by Lieutenant Charles Mellen,[37] Staff Sergeant Earl Boegerhausen, and Platoon Sergeant Johnson. They interviewed and interviewed and interviewed, and finally Lieutenant Mellen asked me, "Would it be plausible that noncommissioned officers could have been involved in this?"

Sergeant Johnson added, "If you would change that around just a little and include acting NCO, would you say yeah?" Of course I was the only acting sergeant at the time.

I said, "I want to tell you boys something. Listen good. I didn't come in here to kiss anybody's ass. I'm going out the same way but if you all make an accusation against me on this and you can't prove it, I'm going to demand a transfer. I'll go to an outfit where they appreciate a fighting man. So just take your pick."

Well, they never did accuse me. They never did charge me with it but they were all convinced that I did it. Of course they saw that it was futile to keep everybody under arrest. Everybody was ready to go AWOL. The next day we blew up a corner of the barracks. They began to fear what we would do next so they lifted the restriction on passes for Regimental Headquarters Company. The guys got acquainted with their women and mothers and dads. I did not care whether I was there or in town.[38]

PFC?

August 29, 1943

We finally loaded up and shipped up to Camp Shanks, New York,[39] our port of embarkation. That place was top secret. After we arrived they put us in a one-room gymnasium. Boy, it was like a prison. They had armed guards on the doors and walked every inch of the perimeter. It was almost impossible to get out.

While we were there they had people go through our records real good to see if our insurances were in order and that we had specified next of kin. They went over our records with a fine-tooth comb. I guess every guy in there grabbed a file and just checked a certain section, then handed it on to someone else.

Well, they called Browny and said, "You have made a mistake in McNiece's records." Lieutenant Brown had become the acting company commander right after Hannah was promoted to the Regimental S-3.[40]

He said, "No, I have not made a mistake in McNiece's records. They're correct."

They said, "Well, you've got him listed as a buck private."

Brown said, "That's what he is."

They said, "This is a disgrace to think that you have had a man in the airborne units for thirteen months that never made PFC. That won't get it at all. We've trained him for a year and a half and got him ready to ship over there and get killed maybe and he is still a buck private."

Brown said, "I don't care if he's been in here thirteen months or if he's been in here thirteen years, he'll still be a buck private. He is not the type of person you would promote to PFC."

They said, "Well, that won't work. We're sending his papers down there and you will make him a PFC tomorrow."

He said, "Well, it is against my desires and wishes and better beliefs, but I'll do it."

So he called down to Miller and said, "Top Kick, send McNiece down to the orderly room. I've got to talk to him."

Top Kick had already missed me. He had figured out that I had gotten out of there and gone to New York. I had professed to be sick that morning. I wanted to go on sick call. Well, after I left for sick call I managed to get on out of that building. I took off to New York City which was just a short distance away.

Miller called down to sick call and they said no, they didn't have Private McNiece. So he knew I was AWOL and we were going to ship out the next day.

Top Kick said, "Browny, I don't see him. I don't know where he is exactly right now."

Browny said, "He's in that room with you. You get busy looking for him. I want to have him in my office right now."

Top Kick answered, "I'll call you when I get him located."

Browny said, "You're going to locate him right now. I've got orders. I've been chewed out from the colonel on down for this deal. We've got to make him a PFC."

Top Kick said, "I don't know if I can get hold of him right now."

Browny said, "Wait a minute. Is he AWOL? He's got to be AWOL if you can't locate him in two buildings."

Top Kick finally admitted, "Jake's got out of here some place. He's not here. I imagine he's down in New York City getting drunk."

Browny said, "I can't believe that Jake would do that knowing that we are shipping out."

Top Kick said, "I guarantee you he'll be here in the morning. He's not trying to get out of anything. He is just as anxious to get overseas as the rest of us."

Browny said, "You send him in to me the minute he gets here."

I came back the next morning and got all my stuff together. Top said, "Go in there and talk to Browny."

So I went in there and he told me this conversation he had had with the hierarchy about making me a PFC. He said sternly, "I'm going to tell you the truth, McNiece. I'm going to write up exactly what has happened and tell them I refuse to make you a PFC even if they threaten to send me to Leavenworth!"[41]

Years later at a reunion, he laughed and told the other guys, "Jake said, 'Well, Captain Brown, I really appreciate that. It would tear me up and change my whole disposition to be working under that kind of responsibility and authority of a PFC.'"

I was an acting sergeant the whole time during training, and when I jumped in behind the lines I was automatically promoted to staff sergeant. When I came out, why I would get busted in very short order back down to buck private. I never held PFC at any time I was in the service.[42]

Top Kick always interceded for me whenever he could. Colonel Sink and Uncle Charlie Chase kept telling him to get rid of my ass but he said, "No, no. McNiece isn't really hurting anything. There will be a day when you are going to be awful glad to have McNiece around. McNiece will do you a good job."

2

FUEL FOR THE MYTH

THE VOYAGE

September 5, 1943

We left the United States on September 5, 1943, bound for England. There we would put the finishing touches on our training and continue to have our own brand of fun. The company did everything it could to keep our reputation from getting out.

We shipped over on the SS *Samaria*. It was in the Star Lines, the same class as the *Queen Elizabeth*. We loaded the whole regiment on that thing. They had all kinds of rules. We could not smoke on the deck. Every man was issued a life preserver and if we were out of our quarters we had to have it on. Herb Pierce, however, would not wear one and he would smoke wherever he felt like it. Herb was in another demolitions section.

I told him one time, "Get your equipment on. The first thing that you will know, if we get hit, you are going to cause about a hundred people to lose their lives out here with you running and dashing and grabbing and shucking. Don't do that. You are going to get a bunch of people like yourself in trouble."

He said, "Well, okay."

The next thing I knew he was over there leaning against the wall smoking a cigarette and his life jacket was not within a mile of him.

When we arrived at Liverpool on September 15, 1943, the commander issued a three day pass to the entire Regimental Headquarters Company. I told Top Kick Miller, "Don't you give Herb a pass." And I explained to him why.

He said, "Okay."

Well, Herb came up to me about ten minutes later. Boy, he was mad. He was just a kid, one of eight seventeen-year-olds who came into our company. He became real excited when he was mad and just went to pot. He told me, "McNiece, I will kill you when we get there in France."

I kind of grinned, "Herb, that is a two-way street down where I come from. We kill one another. I'll be ready for you." The funny thing is I would actually end up saving his life.

THE FILTHY 13

The demolition platoon had one of the highest ratios of sergeants and officers of any outfit. We had a platoon leader and staff sergeant in charge of the platoon and three lieutenants, each in charge of a section. A demolition section was composed of a staff sergeant and two corporals. Each one of those corporals was responsible for a squad of six men and the staff sergeant was responsible for a section of two squads. This added up to thirteen men per section. Occasionally we would get extra men assigned to us for a particular mission. Our platoon also had a platoon sergeant and two or three Tech-5s, bridge foremen-carpenters.

Of the original Filthy 13, I still had Joe Oleskiewicz, Loulip, and Maw Darnell. Max Majewski had transferred up to regimental S-3.[1] I would also loose Darnell. My section would receive several more new faces by the time we invaded Normandy. Every time a guy came into the outfit that another sergeant could not handle, they would put him over in my group and isolate him. They knew there was no discipline at all in my section.

Corporal Johnnie Hale was just a little bitty guy.[2] The other two sergeants did not want him. I told them, "I'll take him." He was a real serious kid when he was on duty but after he got off duty he was just a wild man. He spoke squeaky-like, just like a chicken; peep, peep, peep. So we called him "Peepnuts." I made him one of my squad leaders. Brincely R. Stroup was the other corporal. He was a little bigger than I and all muscle. He was a quiet guy, very unassuming. I would lose him on a training jump.

Jack Womer came in from the 29th Rangers about three months before the invasion.[3] Our company picked up three of those Rangers when they disbanded the outfit. One of them, William Myers, was made sergeant in charge of the second demolition section. The officers had reduced Johnson from platoon sergeant to a corporal in Myers's section. John Klak also came in from the Rangers to our platoon. I saw Womer was a first-class soldier as soon as he came in. He had the best eyes in the outfit. He had eyes like a hawk. He never missed a thing. He could see anything within ten miles. We called him "Hawkeye." I always kept him to the flank on the left. He was also as neat as a pin, clean-shaven, and always kept his uniform pressed. Jack Agnew was a man with a lot of principles and disliked Womer for it. Jack Agnew and Robert Cone were real close friends. The later fight between Womer and Cone increased the friction between him and Agnew. After Womer was promoted to corporal I would put him as the last man in the stick.

Jack Agnew was a couple years younger than I but he was a bull. He was born in Ireland and raised in Pennsylvania. He was the best qualified combat man that I had ever seen. He could fly a plane or run any kind of big boat. He could also repair a boat. When we were down at Zell-am-See, Austria, after the war, he became Colonel Sink's big motor man. He could just about do anything and he was an all around good soldier.[4]

Jack had been assigned to Davidson's section but considered him a brown noser. He did not want anything to do with that and asked to transfer into my section while we were in England. Of course I pushed for him so they let me have him. I figured he would be a good soldier to have around for what we would have to do.[5]

Robert Cone was a real interesting individual.[6] He was an ex-pug from Cincinnati. He was a short and stocky Jewish kid. He was probably five-five weighing a hundred and eighty pounds and nothing but muscle. He was as tough as a boot. He wanted me to work out with him with the gloves. I went out there and he was hitting me ten times for every one time I hit him. He threw a hell of a punch. It hurt. So when I had about all that I could stand, I said. "Let's get these gloves off and go knuckle busting."

He grinned and said, "I'm not going to do that, Jake. You'll kill me."

He was an awful good soldier, but not too much of the garrison type. He was the type of guy who would have been a terrific soldier if he'd had an even or close break in combat. He did not lack for guts. He did not drink much and I never saw him get drunk. The Catholics and the Protestants were big drinkers but the Hebrew boys were not. He was not an Orthodox Jew and did not live according to any doctrine that I had ever heard about. He usually took an order real well, if there was any sense in it. But if it did not make any sense to him, why he just canceled it out and did not give a hoot why. He was a nice guy and got along well with everybody.

He received the name, "Ragsman," because he would not take care of his clothes. I do not think he ever washed a set of fatigues from the time we hit England. He would wear them until they would just be all torn up, ripped, and tattered. It would finally get so bad that the company would issue him a new set but he would not wash them either.

George Radeka was a kid from Joliet, Illinois, up around Chicago. He picked up the name "Googoo" on a field problem one night in England. We could not see very far at night because of the fog, so we kept close contact with one another. We were going out through a pasture when Googoo tripped and fell down into a fresh cow paddy. After he got up, he led the rest of the column off at an angle. Later he explained, "If you'd have found that googoo like I did, ain't no telling which way you would have went."

Googoo was a pretty nice guy. I received him because he could not get along with the other two sergeants. He was kind of dumb in a way but he was pretty smart in combat comprehension. He never gave anyone any trouble. Anything we would try on the officers in the barracks, why he was right in with it. He did not flinch an inch. If we wanted to put pornographic pictures up, he did it. He hated that mess hall, so he was right in on all the deer killing. He was a good man and I enjoyed having him.

Roland "Frenchy" Baribeau was from up in Massachusetts.[7] He was married and had a son just before he signed up. I did not know much about Baribeau even though he had been in the platoon a long time. I do not even remember how he arrived. He may have come in as a replacement. I do not remember him being under any of the other sergeants. He was a real boozer though and one tough, tough cookie.[8]

William Green had been in Sergeant Myers's section. Myers was tough and smart and he did not want Willy. Willy was a good soldier but he was young and slow-thinking. Willy could not make a decision so the platoon put him over in my outfit. If I told him what to do, he would do it but he could not figure anything out on his own. I think he had completed some college. He was a real nice, clean-cut kid and I do not think he even had to shave but about once every three days. He did not curse and was not a troublemaker but he took care of anything that came his way. He was a fighting dog. This army life was totally new to him. He fell right in with the barracks life though. He kind of just rolled with the flow.

I guess he had never had any experience at all with women before he arrived in England. Piccadilly Circus was about a two-square-mile "red light" district in London. There were about ten thousand whores and a drink at every turn. Of course, when he found out about this red light district why, he just went crazy over it. He never went anywhere else while he was over there. Every time he had a day off, he just took right off to London with a pocket full of money and two or three cartons full of cigarettes. One could sell a carton of cigarettes for two hundred bucks. He would go in and really have a ball. If he did not get a day off soon enough then he just went AWOL and came back grinning from ear to ear. So we began to call him "Piccadilly Willy."

Chuck Plauda was a real young kid but he was very hot tempered.[9] He started out in the second battalion section. He was always going to knuckle junction with someone over this or that. They finally said, "If you like that knuckle junction deal then we'll put you over there with McNiece." So they sent him over to my outfit about a month before the invasion. He was a good soldier but he was not very dependable. You could not tell what Chuck would do next because he was just too immature to make the correct decision. As long as someone would show him or tell him what to do he would do it until he caught one between the eyes.

They called me "McNasty." When the thirteen of us all got together, one of us had an idea working all the time. We did not salute any officer nor did we call them "sir." Instead we called them by their nicknames. We called Brown "Browny," and Lieutenant Shrable Williams "Willy." We respected each man for his own ability. With few exceptions I had a good relationship with my company officers.

In England we got in a new captain named Daniels. He was a Louisiana Cajun who spoke French fluently. He wore those riding britches and carried a riding crop. We called him "Dapper" Daniels. I had lots of trouble with him. He and I did not get along for shit. I got into so much hell over there in England that when news of our antics became known outside the company he did not like it at all. Just before we jumped into Normandy, he transferred into the Office of Strategic Services (OSS) to better use his talents.

Lieutenant Leach was a sorry officer and everybody hated him. He could scheme up some of the most improbable missions that ever entered a man's mind. They were useless and the end result would have been nothing. He came from a rich family and was arrogant. During a break on one of those forced marches back in the States, I told him, "You know what my primary objective will be when we get in behind them lines, Loot." Then I gave him a grin. He knew I intended to kill him if I got the chance. I guess he remembered what I had said as we were getting ready for the invasion. He pulled strings to transfer up to S-2 on regimental staff.[10]

Second Lieutenant Charles Mellen took his place as our section leader. He was a good officer but contrary to the article written in *True Magazine*, he could not have whipped any of us. Any one of my guys could have whipped him without much effort.[11]

When we arrived in England, the subordinate units of the regiment were billeted in different locations. Regimental Headquarters Company and Service Company moved into Quonset huts on Sir Ernest Wills' manor place near Littlecote.[12] He was the cigarette magnate of England. The Quonset huts were outside the walled courtyard. In England we put the finishing touches on our combat training to prepare for the invasion of Europe.

Our training was more of the same thing that we had back in the States. It was physical, physical, physical. We did everything on the double. We continued to do field marches but we had no obstacle courses. We also practiced marching on an azimuth.

We conducted advanced infantry training while there, along with several tactical war games. They taught us to take into account tactical positions, how to deploy, use terrain, and seize the high ground. England was also a finishing course for demolitions. We learned about calculations, bridge piers, and such.

Jump Collision

While in England we made three or four more practice jumps. When we jumped, the air force flew those C-47s in nine plane formations. Every three planes would fly in a "V" formation and the three "Vs" would form a larger "V." The whole demolition platoon would jump in three planes, each section to a plane. It was easy to observe what was happening all around us. So we had a contest to see which section could empty their plane the quickest.

One time we were shuffling to the door and Oleskiewicz was right ahead of me. I was pushing him and pushing him and crowding him. I had got up even with him so that he and I went out of that door side-by-side. The door was right behind the propeller. That prop blast would shoot a man like a bullet right under the tail. Consequently, the pilot would usually drop the nose down just a enough to raise the tail to give us a better chance of making it without our chutes tangling on it. When we went out of there, that prop blast hit both of us. I was a little bigger than Joe so it had more of me to grab hold of and it shot me on past him. Our chutes opened and collapsed. Then his opened again but he was tangled up in my shroud lines about halfway between me and the canopy. So he was slipping my chute to one side and I was losing air over on my opposite side. Boy, we were coming down like a bullet and we were not jumping from very high. My chute also began to steal air out of his canopy which began to wilt and fall down all around us.

Joe hollered, "Jake, what'll I do?"

I said, "Hell, take your jump knife real quick and cut yourself loose."

He said, "Like hell I will!"

So we fell together and I landed on a rock fence line. I just slammed into it like a ton of bricks. The minute my two hundred and fifty pounds[13] were released from the pull of his chute, Joe, who probably was about ten feet off of the ground, came down easy and just walked on in.

In May 1944, our division practiced an invasion rehearsal. My section conducted a night jump to secure a bridge. We lost fifteen percent of the division to injuries. We normally jumped at 500 feet under combat conditions but we were flying over rolling hills, kicking some of the guys out at 200 feet. Corporal Stroup broke his ankle and would never jump with us again. I promoted Jack Womer in his place.[14]

FIGHTS

The guys would fight at the drop of a hat. It was their way of having fun. There was an ole boy who had started out in Regimental Headquarters Company named Chuck Cunningham. He was constantly fighting. He was kicked out of Regimental Headquarters Company over some AWOL situation or a fight or something. After he wound up in a line company, he kept trying to retain his original relationship with us in Regimental Headquarters Company.

Well, they had a little ole shack maybe five hundred yards from our Quonset huts where Sir Ernest Wills used to entertain guests. It was a pretty nice little place. We used it for our own pub. We kept it stocked with beer and whiskey and stuff just for our own entertainment. We even took women in there.

One night we had a big blast of a party. I do not know what happened between Cunningham and Baribeau, but they got into a heft of a brawl. Cunningham cut him up pretty bad. I went looking around trying to find Baribeau but I could not find him. I knew he had gotten cut up pretty bad so I went back to the barracks. I found him there loading up his M-1.

I asked, "What are you doing?"

He said, "I'm going to kill that son-of-a-bitch."

I said, "Well, that would not be very smart. I don't see anything wrong with it except that it is not very smart, Baribeau. You're liable to get in a bunch of trouble. We're going to get the medics and get you patched up." He was as drunk as nine hundred dollars.

"Well," he said, "I guess you're right."

So I got him over to this doctor and they fixed him up.

I said, "You get to bed and we'll figure out a way that Cunningham gets what he needs."

He then crawled into the sack. I then went back to the party. When a bunch of us left, Cunningham came out and stomped off to our barracks with us. He was mouthing off and telling us how tough he was.

I said, "I want you to do something for me, Cunningham. You get your ass out of here. We need some sleep. We're not going to get it while you're standing here raving. You get on out."

He kept jabbing, "I am tough. I can whip any man in this Quonset hut."

I said, "I'll tell you what. There are thirteen of us in here. You pick one. Pick any one of us."

He chose Agnew and Agnew whipped his ass, then threw him out on the asphalt walk along those barracks. He continued to whip his ass until it was pathetic. Then he put a choke on him. Cunningham was a reddish-blond-haired type. His damn face was turning blue and I said, "Jack, you can kill him if you want to but there is probably not much profit in it. I have never tried to clear out a murder case. Why don't you turn him loose and drag him off to the side."

So Jack got up and drug him off to the side. The next morning Cunningham was gone. I never did see him again. He was just a brawler. If he had gone to a Catholic mass, he would be in a fight before he had gotten out of there. That is the kind of guy Cunningham was.

[John "Dinty" Mohr recalled how Jake was considered the toughest man in the company:]

Jake McNiece was the sergeant in our hut in Liverpool, England, and I had gone on a three-day pass of some kind and I left a towel on a bed and he took that towel and threw it in the stove. I asked him what happened to that towel and Jake said he threw it in the stove. I met him the same day down in the latrine and I says, "So ya threw my towel in the stove, huh Jake?" and he says, "Yea, Dinty I did." And he grabbed me and there was a big long pee trough there and he tried his best to throw me in that pee trough, and he was supposed to be the number one guy in our company to fight, and he had me a certain way but I couldn't get ahold of him very good. He had me up too high or too low. He couldn't throw me in there. I finally got my arms down where I could get ahold of him and then I had him over a barrel and I had more strength than he did. But then he quit, and I shouldn't have let him quit. I should have throwed him in that pee trough.[15]

While back in Toccoa, Georgia, I was in a joint one night with two other guys and three girls. This one paratrooper had a bitch with a soup jockey who was serving our table. That paratrooper was rank and foul. I told him, "Look trooper, I know you're a little teed off, but get it out of our booth. I don't want you talking like that in front of these young ladies."

He said, "I guess you're going to have to stop it."

I said, "Yeah, I imagine I can."

So I stood up and busted him right in the puss and knocked him clear across the room. It was a small "hole-in-the-wall" cafe with a jukebox and beer and that sort of thing. The minute he bounced off of that wall, I had him by the throat just beating him to death. About that time two other paratroopers bailed in there with him. One of them was a first sergeant from up in F or G Company. Then two more joined in. So those five went to work on me and these two idiots that were with me took the women and left. Those five boys really put a bunch of ugly on me and whipped my butt pretty good. Since my section was assigned to 1st Battalion and they were in the 2nd or 3rd I never did see them again in the United States.

When in England, I went into this London pub one night and recognized one of those guys who had piled in on me back in Georgia.

I walked over and looked at him. He and his buddy had two of those English "split-tails" [girls] with them.

I said, "Hey, why don't we step outside here. We've got some unfinished business to settle."

He looked at me kind of funny, then he recognized me and said, "Let's don't have any trouble. That was probably wrong the way you were treated but let's forget it."

I said, "I won't ever forget that. Come on and let's get outside. It won't take but a minute. Let's get this show on the road."

He would not do it. So I just kept drinking beer and whistling around there. I missed two dozen women while keeping an eye on him. I finally saw him and the girls get up to go out. When they did then I filtered right on out too. I started beating him and kicking him and stomping him on that cobblestone. I could hear all this racket and noise as a pretty big crowd gathered around.

Lieutenant Gordon Rothwell had just walked up and said, "Private McNiece, if that soldier is badly injured we'll nail you to the cross."

I said, "Hop to it, Rothwell. I have had my fun. You have yours."

He said, "One paratrooper doesn't stomp another."

I said, "I never knew of five paratroopers whipping the butt off of another paratrooper except one time and it was this bastard and four others. Him and four other paratroopers ganged up on me while we were in Toccoa, Georgia. This is the first time I have had the pleasure of making his acquaintance again. You have your fun. I've had mine. He's not injured. He is pretty badly bruised but he ain't going to die from it I guarantee you." So I just took on off. I never heard another word about that incident until we jumped into Normandy.

Well, we were out on a field problem one day in England. Jack Womer had just made corporal and told Cone to do something. I did not even hear what it was.

Cone said, "Blow it out. I ain't going to do that."

They got to arguing back and forth and then Womer called Cone a Jesus killing son-of-a-bitch. When he did, the situation exploded. They started fighting like a couple of mad bulls. Both of them were just perfect physical specimens. Jack and Ragsman were really in a brawl out there. The minute one knocked the other down why he started putting the boots to him. Then one would get up and have the other down.

We were in sheep country. Those sheep fences were pretty low, probably not over two feet high with one strand of barbed wire across the top. Those two fought back and forth over this fence. Their clothes were so torn up, they were almost naked. I believe Lieutenant Edward Haley, a lieutenant in another demolition section came by and asked, "What's going on here?"

I said, "Nothing."

He said, "What do you mean nothing?"

I said, "They've had a disagreement and are trying to iron out some orders or something. There is a misrepresentation of the stated condition. They are kind of settling it and coming to a determination."

He said, "Well, they can't fight out here. That's a private fighting a corporal. So that's against regulations. You've got to stop it."

I said, "The quickest and easiest way I can stop it is to tell you to get your butt out of here. They have a dispute going on here and they're going to settle it. When we have a problem in this section we settle it right here. We never go outside on it. I want you to just get lost."

They fought, I guess, for thirty minutes. By then they were both so tired that one could not knock the other down. Neither one of them won nor lost but they were both cut to ribbons on that fence. And boy, their knuckles were bruised. They finally shook hands and went on back to their business. They fought side-by-side from then on.

JAKE'S BAR AND GRILL

They were feeding us slop. This was from the day we went in the army back in the United States until we got out. But that grub in England was the sorriest, filthiest grub that we ever had. We were having stewed tomatoes, brussel sprouts, and carrots for breakfast, dinner, and supper. It was terrible. I think they fed paratroopers in such a manner so they would be so mad when dropped behind enemy lines that they would attack anything that was available.

Of course, I realized they were using a lot of their transportation for men, equipment, and supplies running back and forth to the coast. But I thought they could do better than this. It did not improve. It just continued.

Sir Ernest Wills had a pasture with a fence around it about two hundred yards from our barracks. This pasture must have contained close to a square mile. It had around a hundred Silka and Fallow deer, which are pretty small. In England all the wildlife belongs to the king. Only the lords and ladies are allowed to hunt and fish on the manors. This did not stop us.

At night I would go out there with a flashlight and walk in among those deer until I would pick out a set of eyes—then I would blow its head off. I would clean, skin, and dress him, then take him back. There was a big old hollow tree up near the camp that must have been three feet in diameter. Well, I would hang this carcass up in there and let it cure for a couple of days. Later we would eat it in our barracks. We were eating deer like you never saw.[16]

We never did eat in the mess hall. Back stateside we just sneaked out of town or stole food out of the mess hall. We had a little pot-bellied stove in our barracks in England. I believe we were on a ration of one scuttle of coal a day but there were all kinds of dead trees in those hedgerows. One could gather up a truckload of burnable material. So we just cooked those deer on top of that stove with grease right out of the mess hall. We had one guy in there who had a tie-in with the mess hall where he could get all the bread and butter he wanted. He was providing the bread and the butter and I was providing all the meat. We ate right up there in our barracks all the time.

I then found out that there were rabbits all over the place. They were great big rabbits nearly as big as Belgian hares. They were wild, not domesticated, but they fried up real good and real quick.

I asked Maw Darnell, "Maw, did you ever hunt rabbits?"

He said, "Yeah."

I said, "Well, let's go get a bunch of rabbits."

He said, "All right."

We walked up where they had dug holes in those hedges. We did not take any guns. We just took clubs with us and clubbed those rabbits. If we missed one, it would run back in its hole.

Back in west Texas, every Sunday, when we were not pulling cotton boles, eight or ten of us kids would get on horses and each one of us would take a piece of barbed wire that was ten to fifteen feet long. We would spread it open to where it would fork on the end. We would then roll it up into a six- or eight-inch coil. We would just hang it from our saddle horns then take off and run down those rabbits. Of course we had guns and if one would stop, well we shot it. Well, one could not hit very many of those jack rabbits on the run. If one ran in a hole why we just piled off of those horses and took our wire and uncoiled it. Then we twisted it real easy until it snagged the rabbit in its hole.

I told Maw, "Let's get out here somewhere and find us some barbed wire and we'll get us some rabbits."

I don't know where we found the barbed wire but I armed ole Maw Darnell with it. He was a patient fellow though. It never became too difficult to where he would quit. He would sit there and work and work and work and twist that thing whenever we had seen a rabbit run in a hole. Why, we returned with a whole sack full of rabbits.[17]

So Maw Darnell and I went out there one day and I got to watching this creek. The River Kennet ran through Sir Wills' big estate. Those little rivers over there were not even knee deep but as clear as tap water with rock bottoms. One could walk out there and not even discolor the water. There was not any silt in it at all. It rains constantly in England but never to the point to have a runoff which would muddy a stream with silt. This creek was full of salmon and trout.

So I went down to the mess hall and stole myself two of those big aluminum forks that were sixteen to eighteen inches long with two prongs on them. I got myself a file and filed two barbs on each one of them. Afterwards I would go out there day or night, any time I wanted when I was not on some kind of assignment, and gig those fish.

I went down there one day and someone told me, "Why don't you get your fish out of the hatchery?"

I asked, "What hatchery?"

He said, "Over there on the other side of this house. He has diverted the water out of this creek and let it run through these two hatcheries and on down."

They really were not the kind of hatcheries where he raised fish.

It was where he trapped and kept them. He had thousands in those two ponds. So I would go down there of an evening. I wore a jumpsuit with all those big pockets. I would just gig until I had every pocket full of fish.

Boy, that jumpsuit smelled and I never washed a pair of those britches either. We even slept in them at night with fish slime and blood and guts all over them. We were filthy but we ate good.

There were also pheasants there all over the place. We tried to eat pheasants but they were not any good. They were tough as whang leather[18] so we gave up on them.

One boy would go in every night and get us a bunch of beer. We were just about a mile from the town of Hungerford. We also had another source for beer.

The officers would go into the town of Swindon, which was about thirty or forty miles from our camp. I will never forget the name of the beer. It was Simon's Brewery who put it out. Anyway, they would go in there and buy those little kegs for the bachelor officers quarters. I always found some way that we could steal one of their kegs of beer. We had a rack set up in our barracks with their beer setting right on it. Every man just served himself.

Browny told me, "Jake, we have made a run into Swindon to pick up some beer. We've got a party coming up. We've got five kegs."

I said, "Why that's real nice. Hope you enjoy it."

He later admitted at a get-together, "We had actually bought six kegs. I thought if I told you we had five kegs, you would come down and steal one and leave the rest of them alone."

He said, "The next morning that sixth keg was gone. I thought I had won a victory over you by making you not bother the five I told you we had."[19]

We were having beer and deer and rabbit and after I got all this fish we really had us a good supply. That is the way we lived there. We had good food and beer all the time.

The 9th Troop Carrier Command was just a little ways from us. If we had an opportunity we would kill those deer up there in their pasture. We would then throw the heads and horns and all that stuff over on the air force base. We knew a "day of reckoning" was coming because the size of the herd was going down pretty fast.

Sir Ernest Wills came out there on an inspection tour. We had a big dump out there. He got to looking around and saw deer heads, rabbit fur, hides of all kinds, and remains of fish that we had thrown away. Boy, he just hit the ceiling. He claimed that he had all this stuff inventoried and knew how much he had. Then he inventoried what was left and demanded that the government pay him several thousand dollars in restitution. It came down through division headquarters to Colonel Sink and on down to Regimental Headquarters Company. Well, the officers had not eaten a bite of it but if they could not pin it on someone they were going to have to pay the bill. Of course we did not have any money. We spent every penny we earned.

So "Dapper" Daniels fell us out and began to question us and make accusations. He said it was going to cost so much. We did not care how much it cost. They were not really doing us right by the lousy food we were getting. So nobody confessed to anything. The officers were trying to get some enlisted man to admit that he did it without the oversight of officers. No one would make any announcements that they had been involved.[20]

After he finished pleading and begging and harassing and so forth, he had gotten a lot of the guys to admit they had eaten meat in my barracks but they did not know what it was. When it came down to it, he got no confessions out of anybody.

He then walked right up to me and said, "I'm going to tell you something Sergeant McNiece. This shit has stopped as of now! There will not be another deer killed. There will not be a rabbit taken and nobody even gets close to those hatcheries. There are going to be armed guards on that hatchery from now on."

I said, "Well, Captain Daniels, this cuts me to the quick. You are addressing me just like I was involved in this sort of thing that was going on. I have had nothing to do with it. What you ought to do is find the guy who was involved and be talking to him. I am free as a breeze."

He said, "That's a dirty lousy lie! Shit McNiece, they can put me in the back of a two-and-a-half-ton truck and blindfold me at night and drive it around here within a five mile area of this camp for two hours and I can step off of the tail gate of that truck and walk right straight to the door of your barracks."

In England during the blackouts on dark nights when it was foggy, one could not see his hand in front of his face. One just went around by feel. It was just about that kind of night there that night.

I said, "That would be a pretty good chore, Daniels. How would you propose to do all that? We have guys get lost between barracks here. You could not find your way to the latrine from here right now. How could you do that?"

He said, "I would just follow my nose. That barracks of yours smells like a damn hamburger and barbecue joint twenty-four hours a day. I can smell you! I better not smell you any more. That shit is going to quit!"

I said, "I certainly hope it does. I hope this whole outfit does not get penalized over some man's hunger and greed."

The officers finally had to pay Sir Ernest Wills several thousand dollars. It was assessed to their pay. After that they began to put guards on the fish hatchery at night. Shorty Mihlan would tell me when and where they would put a guard. He knew all that.

I went in there one night and gigged trout. When I got my cargo pockets all filled up why somebody on guard hollered at me to halt. So I took out. I ran down and around this damn stone wall and got back to my barracks. I slipped my jump suit off and threw it up under my bed on the brick floor.

We were a small unit. Headquarters Company and Service Company were all that was there. So I knew most of those guards. They come running and charged into our barracks. Of course I was in bed. All the other guys knew something was happening but they did not know what.

The guards came in and screamed, "Attention!" We all fell out of bed. "McNiece," they said, "you've been down there in that hatchery gigging fish."

I said, "Bullshit! When did that happen?"

They said, "About ten minutes ago."

I said, "I was lying here in this bunk sound asleep until you all came in here and started screaming that shit about attention."

Meanwhile those fish were flopping under the bed, flap, flap, flap. So I started moving my feet around and tried to run their asses out. "Get out of here. Nobody in this barracks has been involved in gigging a fish," and those fish were just a flopping under there. I could hear those jump pants of mine, splat, splat, splat. I would move around and bump into bunks and everything else. We got rid of the guards and they did not find a fish we had.

FILTHIER

We slept on mattresses filled with dried dirty cornshucks over hogwire frames. If someone hit one a cloud of dust would raise up just like a sandstorm. Well, if someone took his clothes off and slept on it, the next morning he would be covered with a fine coat of black dust. My boys were so dirty and nasty that we would jump in there with our clothes on and come out feeling pretty good. So we slept in our full uniforms, seven days a week.

We were under a ration and they issued us only one scuttle of coal a day to do our washing. We used it instead to do our cooking. We did not wash our clothes. What good would it do to wash them in that filth that we were in over there.

Neither did we clean our barracks. When we had an inspection, we just told the officers to go on and help themselves. The floors were brick and a half inch from level, just like a road. We did not clean anything. We did not take any trash out. We had fish skins and heads and guts laying all over the place. It just smelled like the city dump. The platoon assigned the platoon sergeant, Staff Sergeant Charles "Chaplain" Williams, to our barracks in the hope that he would inspire us to clean up but he could not.

Well, this group of boys that were with me did not shave, shine, nor shower, not even for inspections. We were under restriction all the time but we did not care because we went AWOL everytime there was a moment or a chance to take it.

We were a filthy bunch of people since we were only permitted one bath a week because of the water shortage. Sir Ernest Wills had six or seven cars and limousines that he washed every day down there out of this water supply but we could only take a bath but once a week and that was set up for Saturday. The shower was a cold water deal and we had to get in line for it. So it would take two or three hours to get a shower. Come Saturday I wanted to have my coon dog right in the middle of that Red Light district in Piccadilly Circus in

London. I did not want to be standing in line waiting for a bath.

As soon as me and my boys got passes, each of us would just grab one set of those ODs[21] and put them in a sack and away we went. We would go in our junk clothes into one of those Red Cross buildings over there in Regents Square in London. We would go in and get us a shower, shave, and shine, change clothes and boy, we had one or two women before any of the others even got into town. We would then raise Cain until Monday morning.

So they were getting to call us the "Filthy 13." Thirteen men was the number of men in a demolition section.[22]

Tom Young's Barracks Display

We had a big general inspection there one day. Of course my section did not do anything to get ready. Our clothes were just stacked here and there and the beds were not made.

Tom Young, Burl Prickett, and Sergeant Myers were in the next Quonset hut. There was about ten yards between each Quonset hut. Of course they were going to make their section look really great, especially compared to mine. There were a lot of loose bricks around there. So they went out and got some of these bricks and arranged them up in this circle that was about two feet in diameter. They found a bazooka shell and painted it white then stood it up in the middle. They then went back out in the woods and picked them a bunch of leaves and wild flowers. They constructed this display halfway between our barracks.

I saw this going on and of course I knew what was happening. There was a wall that ran right along our barracks. It had a hole in it where we stepped into this long latrine that had been a stable. It had those "honey buckets." They were just like coal scuttle buckets. This latrine had a platform on it which we used for bowel or kidney movements. We could not flush it so that stuff kept accumulating in the buckets. These scavenger wagons would come through once a week and pick up all those honey buckets. By the time of the inspection those honey buckets were just about full.

So I waited until just about two minutes before they called us outside then I ran in there and grabbed me one of those honey buckets. I came back and just dumped it all over the flowers, bazooka shell, and bricks. My people were in the barracks laughing their heads off. When Tom, Prickett, and Myers heard this commotion, they looked out and there I had this honey bucket just pouring it all over their display. You never saw such a mad scramble in your life. They did not even get close to cleaning it up before someone blew that whistle and we all had to fall in. The general was mad but there was not anything he could do. We were already under restraint all the time.

Tom Young was a big ole boy from down in Texas. He and his brother and I jumped into Normandy. His brother, Kaiser, was killed almost immediately. Ole Tom kind of took a shine to me in the absence of his brother. So we became very, very close friends.

Queen of the Filthy 13

Someone put out a stupid order that we could not have any cheesecake pictures over our bunks. Of course cheesecake then was where a lady had on a short dress or a pair of shorts that came down to the knee. Those were our pinups back then. He said no one could have anything on their wall except a family portrait.

So I sat down and wrote Eleanor Powell that I was in charge of the Filthy 13 and we needed thirteen uncensored and assorted photos, none of them alike. I told her we were going to have a big contest to elect the queen of the Filthy 13 and I would appreciate if she would send me pictures so that I could let the boys know who they were voting for.

She was a great dancer and famous Hollywood star. In about a couple weeks or so I received this big envelope and it had thirteen of these pictures and none of them were alike. So I told the boys, "Now take your pen or pencil or something and write down on the bottom of it, 'To Peepnuts from your loving mother,' or 'to Tom from Aunt Sue or Sister Lil' or something like it. Have that on each one of them and we will hang them up." Since she had signed the pictures, we just penned in the messages.

So when the officers came in to inspect the barracks, why they just hit the ceiling. They said, "Get them off the wall!"

I said, "No, you can't get them of the wall. We are allowed one family portrait."

They said, "These are not family portraits. They are all the same woman."

I said, "These guys are related to a lot of people. Read those captions on them. Some of these are from grandmothers, some mothers, some sisters." They said, "These are all from Eleanor Powell."

I said, "That's beside the point. She may be related to everyone of these guys. You've got us limited to one thing above ground."

They finally just gave up and said, "Well, forget it."

We kept those pictures up. When we jumped into Normandy, some of the boys took those things down off the wall and put them in their helmets and jumped with them.

Pre-Invasion Party

In the first part of June, I was under arrest of quarters. The previous week I had decided to go to London. I had gone down by the Service Company quarters to see if there were any vehicles available which there were not. I noticed this captian had come over in a jeep and was talking to Colonel Sink. So I confiscated his jeep and took off to London. When I returned I was placed under arrest of quarters until they figured out what charges they wanted to bring against me.

We were going to have a big demolition platoon party one night just before the invasion. The officers went over to arrange for our use of an air force hangar. They were going to schedule music and dancing. They would send two two-and-a-half-ton trucks into town to pick up girls. They had it all decorated and this and that. The officers also wanted a fifth of whiskey per man. There were fifty of us. So they needed fifty fifths of whiskey.

Lieutenant Shrable Williams[23] came to me and said, "Jake, I know you buy whiskey by the fifths. Where do you get it?"

Well I said, "It's in London but it wouldn't do me any good to tell you where I get it. You couldn't find it anyway even if I told you. Besides they wouldn't let you have it." I said, "But I'll tell you what. If you'll give me a seventy-two-hour pass, and have every man in this platoon give me a five pound note, I'll go to London and get you that whiskey."[24]

He said, "McNiece, what do you mean a three-day pass to London? I can't even get you to the mess hall."

I said, "Well, we'll have to figure out something because it is not available to you people. Why don't you put me on three days of detached service to 3rd Battalion to instruct them in mines, booby traps, and explosives."

He said, "Jake, can't you see you're not worth flying down there to Lankensbere."

I asked, "Do you want the whiskey or don't you? That's the only choice you've got."

Each one of them gave me a five pound note and I left to buy fifty bottles of booze. I checked in at the Red Cross motel there in Piccadilly Circus. However, I did not have a very good means of conveyance of all this whiskey that I was buying. I would go down to this gin mill that I knew of and buy me ten bottles of Scotch or Bourbon or whatever they were holding at the time. Then I would take them back up to the Regents Palace, which was a hotel mainly just for GIs. I had a security lock on each cubicle. I would then go down and get me ten more fifths of whiskey in a duffel bag then take it back to my room and lock it up. Later I would go out and party the rest of the night on my own. So I had to make a total of five trips.

I had made three or four trips back and forth and was coming out of there one evening during a blackout. I was not drunk yet. It was early in the evening and I had just gone back and gotten me ten bottles of bourbon. I then saw this officer approaching. He was a lieutenant. He was looking at me and really giving me the eye and then here he comes. I thought he was a lieutenant looking for a big salute.

We got to probably within fifteen feet or so when he said, "I don't believe you recognize me?"

I slid my whiskey down real easy on the cobblestone so I would not break any. I said, "Yeah, I recognize you. You are a first lieutenant in the United States Air Force and you're wanting to be highballed. You met the wrong boy at the wrong place and the wrong time. I don't salute."

He said, "I didn't mean that Jake." He called me by my name. I thought that was odd. I hesitated hitting him until I figured out why he knew my name. He asked, "Don't you recognize me? I'm Truman Smith." It was Truman Smith from Ponca City.

[Truman remembered it this way:]

I'd gotten away from the base rather late without lunch or dinner and it was well into the blackout when I felt I was approaching my target, the S&F Grill, about a block from Piccadilly Circus. I say "felt," because the blackout eliminated the sense of sight, leaving touch, smell, taste and sound.

It was crowded. I could feel the bodies and they felt me as everyone jostled and groped each other. Then I finally felt a non-body.

What in hell was it? It wasn't soft, yet it was moving along in the flow. It kind of rattled like a Coke truck full of bottles—and it felt like a bunch of bottles—in a canvas sack.

A little bit of light came from between the blackout curtains in the doorway of a bistro and I saw that it was a GI carrying a duffel bag—and I recognized him.

"Jake!" It was Jake McNiece from my hometown.

"Friend or enemy?" Jake challenged in the dark, having not recognized me.

"Truman Smith, from Ponca City, Oklahoma."

"Well, howdy boy," Jake responded in a little cheerier tone. "I'd like to say its good to see ya, but I can't see a bloody thing in this blackout."

Having reached the S&F Grill, I steered him inside where we could see each other.

Jake was about four years older than I and had been one of my idols when he played high school football. And being senior to me, I was pleased that he even recognized me.

"Well, son, it's good to see ya, even though you're wearin' a Lieutenant's uniform. I don't like Lieutenants . . . Good thing I didn't see that uniform in the blackout, or I'd-a knocked the hell outa ya just for the fun of it."

He was smiling and I hoped he was kidding, because Jake was known as a fighter and a hell-raiser. That was his character and his charm: friendly, smiling, easy-going, one hundred and seventy pounds of impulsive "dynamite." It was no wonder he was in the 101st Airborne. Although I was a bit puzzled that he was still a Buck Private.[25]

Truman had just been a little ole pudgy kid. I am probably five years older than him. I had left home just before he began to change into a young adult. That was why I did not recognize him at first.

We shook hands and I said, "Truman, I'm sorry. I didn't recognize you at all. You've changed tremendously since I saw you previous to becoming a young man."

He asked, "What have you got in that sack? You sound like a pop truck."

I said, "I've got ten fifths of whiskey."

Well, we went out and had some dinner and I asked, "Let's go out and party."

He said, "Jake, your attitude shows that you are kind of looking for trouble already and being kind of antagonistic. You don't have anything on your sleeve to lose but I've got a bar. I don't want to sacrifice it for one night with you!"

We had a good long talk and I could not pull him off.[26] I wound up with fifty fifths of whiskey in a duffel bag and grabbed the trolley back to camp. I drank three or four bottles but only broke one.[27]

Well, the next day we threw a party up there like you never saw. There were men and women having all kinds of sexual affairs out on the dance floor and around the sides. Others would run and jump and catch parachutes hanging from the ceiling and swing back and forth. The enlisted men were fighting with the officers. The air force provost marshall came in there and asked our officers if they wanted some assistance to quell this mob.

One told them, "You'd better go ahead and get on out of here or you'll be the next victims. We're just having a party here and nothing is wrong."

The provost marshall said, "You've got officers fighting enlisted men. You've got indecent exposure all over the place."

He said, "Well, you just get on out. We'll take care of these boys. They're ours."

The next morning we went in and were all still drunk. Well, this provost marshall in the meantime had contacted Colonel Sink and told him what a terrible thing had happened there. So Colonel Sink very quickly called out the demolition platoon. Then he was raising Cain, raising Cain, and raising Cain. When they finally located

Lieutenant Williams in his room in the officers' quarters, he had all these women in bed with him.

Colonel Sink commanded that we do close-order drill for a certain period of time. Tom Young was corporal and was supposed to drill us out there. He was just marching us up and down the field. He then had us running and gave a "to the rear march." We just piled up like a herd of cattle in a snowstorm.

I never did object to any physical conditioning or training with equipment or explosives. That is what I was there for. I was not there to engage in all that military discipline. I could not see any reason for an enlisted man saluting an officer under any condition other than just respect for that person. I always figured that ought to be a two-way deal. An officer ought to salute an enlisted man just as quick as he saw him. Why, he is the guy who is making his bread to begin with.

Preinvasion Religious Service

D–1: June 5, 1944

For the Normandy jump, I had been assigned to the 3rd Battalion. We did not know any of the officers. We were locked up in this marshaling area. One of the officers came around and said, "All the Catholics will meet in this apple orchard here and all the Protestants will meet out in the field there." They were going to have a religious service. This was about six or seven o'clock in the evening. So everybody just picked whatever area they wanted.

Well, everybody else went out to these deals. Most of my boys were Catholic. Cone was Jewish and stayed with me in the tent. We were just talking, cleaning up our guns, sharpening knives, getting ready, and checking all our equipment. The tent door flew open and in walked this lieutenant. He asked, "What are you doing?"

I said, "Nothing."

He said, "You've got to go to service. We've got a Catholic priest here and a Protestant priest there. The Catholics are meeting in this hole and the Protestants are meeting out there."

I said, "I don't believe I care to join in on it."

He said, "What do you mean, you don't care to join in on the religious service?"

I said, “I have not tried to be a Christian. I don’t believe in deathbed repentance. Count me out.”

He looked at Cone and asked, “Why aren’t you going?”

Cone kind of grinned and said, “You don’t have any ‘rabbit’ for me.” He laughed, “Do you think I would go to one of them stinking services out there. If you have a rabbi, I might consider it.” He said, “I won’t take part in this.”

So the old boy said, “Listen, you don’t have to go but it would be real convenient if you did. After the services are over, we are going to all join together and then we will be addressed by Eisenhower and Field Marshal Montgomery. We don’t want to have to be running around here hunting up stragglers for this.”

I kind of grinned. I said, “I’m not real sure I am interested in listening to that horse cock.”

He then said, “It sure would be a good accommodation for me if you would.”

I said, “Okay.” I told Cone, “Most of our guys are Catholic. Let’s go in there.”

He said, “Okay.”

So we went over there. Chaplain John Maloney was talking in Latin and all these guys were thumping or kissing their head and crossing and this and that. They had these guys in rows just kneeling and sitting on their heels. We walked over and knelt right down by Loulip. Finally this chaplain got through with all his rigmarole and said, “Okay, fellas. Let’s get down to the nitty-gritty. We’re going to be jumping in there about eleven o’clock tonight. Look to the guy next to you. You or him are not going to make it. We’re going to loose fifty percent. So in the case of imminent danger of death, I can administer extreme unction to you.” That is a very important part of their religion. “I can do that right now. If you get killed, you’ve already got it done. I may be the first one killed. So you can’t tell. If I am, you all get this little ole box off of me. You can give it to one another. All of you but me.”

So he just started down the row with this box which had a vessel of wine and was full of white wafers about the size of quarters. No one is allowed to touch it but the priest. That is actually supposed to be the body and blood of Christ. So they were kneeling there with their hands behind their backs as he was walking along. Every time he got in front of a guy, well he reached out and gave him a cracker.

So we were back in the third row and I was kneeling right beside Loulip. Joe Oleskiewicz was next to him and then Barinowski. I looked at Loulip and asked, "Should we take one of them?"

He said, "If you want to, go ahead and take it."

Joe Oleskiewicz heard me and asked, "Do you believe this?"

I said, "Joe, I don't believe one word of it."

He said, "Then don't take it."

I did not go in to insult anyone's religion but neither did I want to acknowledge that I believed any part of it when I did not. So they were talking back and forth and reaching a decision whether me and this Jew boy were going to take it or not. This ole chaplain was getting closer and then he got to the end of the line and headed toward us. I looked over to ole Ragsman. I said, "Ragsman, you can stay if you want to but I'm getting out of here." So we both got up and walked out.

> [Mike Marquez remembered:]
>
> *General Eisenhower came over to review the Hundred-and-First one time while I was standing at attention between two big, husky soldiers, typical Euro-Americans, on either side of me. Eisenhower approached one of them on the left side and said, "My what good looking shoulders you have. You are sure going to give those Germans a hard time." Then he looked at me and didn't say a word. I guess he figured I was too small and wasn't going to be dangerous enough or maybe he didn't like little Mexican people. If I remember right, he used to read a lot of Western stories. In the Western stories the Mexicans and Indians were the bad guys. Anyway, he passed on and complimented the next soldier. Later I never forgot that. When he ran for president, I did not vote for Eisenhower and not because he was a Republican.*[28]

Mohawks and War Paint

D-1: June 5, 1944

Of course every war they ever had over there in Europe has been filled with body lice and head lice and then they came out with a new one called scabies. These scabies were I don't guess bigger that a pin point, if that big, but they would get on the skin and bore down underneath and infect it. There was not much of a way to doctor or cure them. When totally infected with these, why the medics would give a good bath then coat a person's whole body with a white liquid like a lotion or ointment or something. That would seal all the pores of the skin so those scabies would suffocate.

I did not know about them before we jumped in but of every war I had ever heard tell of by guys who were actually in them, the most miserable thing over there was the lice. All that country that those Germans occupied was lousy. Boy, one could just see them crawling on the clothes. I knew it might be days or months before I ever got a bath or got another chance to clean my head, face, and body. So I thought, "I'm going to shave my head so at least I can wash the sides of my head and maybe not get those lousy lice."

Back in Georgia I had professed to be an Indian nature worshiper and a "gut-eater" and did not like their regulations. So when we got ready to jump into Normandy, I shaved me a Mohawk scalp lock.

So the others asked me about my haircut and I told them, "This is a custom back home like you've got your St. Christopher's medal." Nearly all the boys of mine were Catholics and they all had little ole chains around their necks with a medal on it called St. Christopher. He is supposed to be the patron saint of travelers. Boy, they would not be caught dead without that thing on them.

I said, "We wear scalp locks down there in Oklahoma. Whoever kills the other'n gets that scalp lock as a trophy. This is an Indian custom that we've always observed. To me it is kind of like your St. Christopher's medal."

They said, "No kidding?"

I said, "Yeah."

They just did not see how it would work.

I said, "It doesn't necessarily work but I will tell you the truth, I'm cutting mine off because of the lice we are going to be in. There will be lice there under every leaf. There ain't no telling whenever you will get a bath again if you ever do, but this will help you fight the possibilty of lice covering you. It will be a safeguard against the lice."

They asked, "What're you painting your face for?"

I had mine all painted and said, "We're going to be jumping in over there in about four or five hours. It's just camouflage. I don't care about sticking a bunch of leaves and grass on my helmet." We had netting on our helmet for camouflage purposes. "I don't care about looking through a brush pile every time someone is trying to kill me. This will act the same way, exactly. You'll blend right in with any kind of foliage they've got anywhere in Europe."

They said, "Why I believe that's a good idea."

I asked, "You want me to cut your hair."

They said, "Yeah!"

I cut all of them a scalp lock and painted a bullseye on nearly everybody's cheek. I had every part of their faces painted. To me it was just common logic.[29]

Up until that time our officers had tried to not let our reputation get out of the company. They had a pretty good deal going. They knew that we were pretty good soldiers. They needed us. I did not know it until I started seeing the pictures in books after the war but the army had Signal Corps men taking motion pictures of us getting ready for the invasion. Neither did I learn about the *Stars and Stripes* and other articles until after the war. The pictures of us with our Mohawks were seen everywhere.[30]

3

A Bridge in Normandy

The Mission

Carentan was the hub of transportation networks leading in and out of the Cherbourg Peninsula. General Maxwell Taylor wanted the 506th Parachute Infantry to blow all the bridges below the Douve Canal, then seize and hold the main bridge. This was strictly a 3rd Battalion mission.[1]

Colonel Sink was a little afraid that Davidson would not be able to get the job done so he asked me to volunteer for it. I had never jumped with the 3rd Battalion before, since I'd trained with the 1st. Our original 1st Battalion assignment was just to lend support to Colonel Sink and Regimental Headquarters Company. Regiment instead wanted me to clear out the passages, roadways, and bridges from near St. Come Du Mont on up to Carentan and then hold that bridge if we could. I said I would.

They then asked if I would have any problems working with his section. I said, "I got along well with everyone in the demolitions platoon and would have no problem." But I also told them, "I would rather take my section though."

That is what they wanted anyway. They were hoping that my section would volunteer for it. I asked my guys and they did. They wanted to go anywhere I went.

This Normandy deal was going to be tough so I told Regiment that I would need more men. I anticipated losing half of them on the drop.[2] I asked for another squad of demolitions men. They said yes, and added six boys, giving me a total of a twenty-man stick counting Lieutenant Mellen. I remember them giving me Charles "Trigger" Gann, Clarence Ware, George Baran, and Thomas E. "Old Man" Lonegran.[3]

On the bridge I also needed someone with a little more instruction than the average soldier. I asked for Andrew E. "Rasputin" Rasmussen. Rasmussen was our T-5 bridgeman. He was a pretty clean-cut kid from a military family. He once told me he had his dad's discharge papers and cavalry spurs. He was a spit and polish soldier. He kept his hair neat and his uniforms clean and pressed. Boy, he changed those socks every day. He was a good soldier. He never cursed or used bad language, but he boot-legged whiskey all the time in the company area. So he always had his eye out for another dollar. Some way in the loading schedule at Exeter, however, he was pulled out of my stick and someone else was sent in his place.[4]

NORMANDY JUMP

11:45 P.M., D–1: June 5, 1944

We left England just before 11:00. They were using nearly 1,000 C-47s to convoy in the 82nd and the 101st. Third Battalion took off down around Exeter and flew directly across the Channel.

It was really a pretty night with moonlight, lots of moon. There was scattered rain but we had clear visibility. When we hit the coast, all these people were loaded up and ready to go across and hit the beaches the next morning. Of course, I grew up in Oklahoma and had never been around any big ships. I had only seen a few down in the Houston area on the intercoastal canal. Those big ships were so thick that they were just bow to stern all the way from Southhampton to sixty miles or eighty miles across the English Channel. It looked like a bridge, like someone could walk from one ship to the other and it was just as far as I could see on either side. I never imagined there would be that many ships in the water. Then as we neared the Jersey and Guernsey Islands, we began to see these huge balloons with cables hanging down to the water near where the boats had passage. It was really a beautiful sight.

We hit our first antiaircraft fire over the Jersey and Guernsey Islands. They really opened up on us. It was a real bugger. We were going to go in above them, then circle back to our drop zones. When we reached those two islands the pilot turned the red light on, then we stood up and hooked up.

At that time the Germans did not have very good radar. They could not pick up a plane under four hundred feet. If we were higher they could put that radar on us and really bust us apart. So we flew across the Channel at four hundred feet. Neither did they have any time-delay fire that would burst below four hundred feet. They had smartened up though. They began to shoot a flat trajectory far out with the hope that it would burst under a plane. Not a lot was successful but they did hit some. Boy, they sure riddled us with the automatic fire though.

Those Germans were firing ammunition up at us that went all through the plane, our chutes and things like that. Those stinking automatic weapons had tracers about every fifth round. It just looked like a string of fire coming up at us. I did not know that there was any other color of tracer than orange but it looked like the greatest display of fireworks that I ever saw in my life. It was beautiful. They would have a blue one then a couple of red then a couple green. There was every color in the rainbow rising up to meet us. We lost several planeloads of paratroopers but the greater part came through it.

I was joking with the guys in the plane. I needed to. Those guys were sitting there looking at each other, eye to eye, figuring the other would not be there in the morning, which was more than true. We laughed and talked. We just exchanged messages and went over the plans of exactly what we would do when we got on the ground. I kept instructing them on how to jump, how to assemble quickly and then just as soon as we located our objective, well we would go to work on it. We were all in a mood ready to go.[5]

If a paratrooper did not have fun in there he would not last. I had soldiers in my section, right there, who had trained for two years through all kinds of difficulty. But no one knew how many of us would survive after the first splurge. If I could get them in the proper frame of mind then they would fight better.

If a bunch of guys go in there half scared to death, they are whipped before they jump. We did not have that. We believed we could accomplish any assignment that came our way. I do not know if I had any man who was more physically fit than I, but they were probably better soldiers. I did not live because I was the best soldier. I think I lived because I took advantage of everything that I could. If a soldier is not aggressive, he is going to get killed.

Our division jumped in about 11:45 that night. Then in the early morning hours, they began to reinforce us with glider troops. That was a massacre. These little ole fields were small, about two and a half acres. Five acres was a pretty good-sized field. Of course these glider pilots tried to land in those fields instead of the hedgerows. But the Germans had gone out and put telephone poles up in there. Then they ran a cable from the top of that pole to the bottom of this one, then from the bottom of this one to the adjacent bottom of that one. They would just crisscross the wires. They called them, "asparagus fields" and boy they slaughtered those glider boys.

General Don F. Pratt rode in on one of the gliders. They had sent in a jeep for him to ride. It was in the back and he was sitting in the front seat on top of a reserve parachute. When that glider landed in one of those asparagus fields, it got tangled up in the wires and lost all control. It ran up into the hedgerow, which was a mound of dirt two to four feet high. I mean when it hit that, it just stopped dead still. That jeep came loose from its moorings and when it rammed forward the general was sitting up so high it just took his head off.

My stick was supposed to jump with the 3rd Battalion about two or three miles from the three bridges at Carentan, but as we were going in, the Krauts were tearing our ship up. We began losing altitude. The pilots were supposed to feather engines and drop the nose so the tail would come up to give us room to clear it. But once that plane starts losing a little altitude at four hundred feet, a guy had better bail out regardless if he is a hundred miles from his drop zone.

So when we started losing altitude I yelled at those in the door, "We've got to get out of here! Let's get out of here!"[6]

Piccadilly Willy was right behind me in the plane. My stick pressed together like a coiled spring, toe to heel. There was not any space between us. As we shuffled to the door, a big chunk of flak came up through the belly of the ship right between Willy and me. I had just stepped past it when he stepped into it. It did not hit my backpack but instead hit his belly reserve. It blew the cover and everything all to pieces but did not draw a drop of blood. The plane was so full of air from the holes and the open door that his chute blossomed out. He could not go out the door with it, so he gathered it up in his arms.

The C-47 had a cable that went clear through from front to back. A paratrooper hooked his snap fastener to the cable. When at the door, he would throw it past then jump right on out. I managed to clear the door. Well, Piccadilly Willy was trying to gather up his chute and keep moving. He ran on past, still gathering up his chute to clear the door for everybody else to exit. This delayed the last squad about a minute before they could exit. Those planes fly about a hundred and sixty miles an hour. So with the hesitation of one minute, the second half of my stick was dropped down the road about two miles.[7]

In other words I was the last man out in the first half of the stick. I had one squad of nine men. Chuck Plauda was the last man out. He later told me, "Jake, I wasn't out of that plane three seconds till it blew up." I never heard of Piccadilly Willy again.[8]

I had nine behind me and ten to the front. I always jumped in the middle of the stick instead of pusher or lead man. A section was made up of two squads. I always placed a corporal in the front of the stick and a corporal in the back. I jumped in the middle of it and had the men assemble toward me along the flight of the plane. When they hit the ground, they would look up. If the plane was going toward me they would follow it, if it was going away they would double back. Not any one of the eighteen assembled on me.[9]

I landed in an open area about two miles from Ste. Mere Eglise. This place was just about eight miles from our bridges. It turned out to be a Kraut bivouac area. The Krauts were dug in just like a checkerboard and I landed right in the middle of them. Boy those Germans were just boiling out of there like ants. Everywhere I went there were a jillion of them. Joe Oleskiewicz fought out one side of it and I fought out the other but we could not get together. All the others were gone. No way could we assemble.

On all the combat jumps that I made, the parachute harness had these old straps with big hooks and snap fasteners. When I got on the ground, the first thing that I did was reach up and grab those risers and cut them off.[10] I fought until I got a break, then I took the rest of the harness off.

General Bill Lee was the father of airborne units in America. He had been the organizer and inventor of it but somehow he got disabled. So the command of the airborne passed on down to other officers. In preparation for this invasion, they told us that when we jumped out the door, instead of screaming "Geronimo" or something like that, everybody would scream "Baseball and Bill Lee."[11]

Loulip jumped out of the plane ahead of me and landed on a blacktop road. It was very tough to distinguish between a clean, hard, coated surface and a stream of water. Lou landed on a roadbed there and I guess it broke his back. He never even got out of his harness. Lou lay there when I passed by, but I could not get to him. He was beyond help anyway. He was just moaning, "Baseball and Bill Lee, baseball and Bill Lee."

BREAKOUT

D-Day: June 6, 1944

It was a hell of a feeling to be by myself in the middle of a foreign land surrounded by enemy soldiers. I had been by myself for two hours and had not seen another paratrooper other than Loulip; nor had I heard the sound of an American rifle. I was beginning to think they had canceled the entire invasion and I was the only American down there. It gave me a hell of a feeling. It was a pretty lonesome feeling. One thing about it, combat kept me so busy that the anxiety soon left me and it became a matter of either kill or get killed.

In France, they have these hedgerows along every road divided into little posts. There were a bunch of Krauts in every hedgerow and they had me pinned down in the junction of three hedgerows that formed a "T." Every time I felt like they were moving in, I would shoot at them. They would cuss and threaten me, then cuss each other. They would back off, then another side would try to close in. I would shoot at them and then another side would try.

There was a dugout across the road, a gap in the hedgerow. The Germans cut these gaps in those hedgerows where their vehicles could go through. They would also have a dugout manned right there at the opening. Back at the opposite corners of these little ole farms, the Germans would also have machine-gun nests set up. If someone started to approach it, a Kraut machine gun would shoot his ass off.

There was one of those right across the road from me. I kept thinking, "There's a man in there." I could see him. His shadow was a different color. All the time the other Krauts were making a little more progress toward me and I thought, "I've got to get out of here or they'll kill my ass." I had jumped with a M1 Garand and bayonet. I finally decided that I was going to have to get across there and eat him up or I would be killed right there.

We jumped with little ole toy crickets.[12] So I gave him a cricket and received no reply. I cricked him again and still did not get any reply. With all the roads over there, I decided that the only way I was going to get that boy was root him out with a bayonet. So I got set.

When we jumped into Normandy we had a challenge, a password and a reply. We used "Flash" for halt because the German word for "Halt" is "Halt." Then we used "Thunder" for our password because even if they knew it they could not say it. They cannot pronounce the "th." They would have said, "Dunder" or "Tunder." And they cannot pronounce "W"s. They are all "V"s to them. So we used the reply of "Welcome" because they could not say it. So if a paratrooper had handed them a note and told them what it was all about, the Krauts could not have been able to use it.

When I made a run at that dugout, this ole boy came up out of there screaming, "Flash! Flash! Flash!" Of course I knew it was a paratrooper. I had that bayonet right on him—boy I was going hell bent for leather. I jerked it up over him and slid right down into that bunker with him. I just missed him by an inch. I asked, "What in the world are you doing?"

He said, "Boy, you better be careful about running at these dugouts. They're full of Krauts. Right across the lot they've got two machine guns."

I said, "Well, I found that out already tonight. This isn't the first one I've been in. I wasn't the one who was about to get killed, you idiot! If you had waited one more second, I would have had your ass on the end of this bayonet rooting you across this field. Why in the world didn't you answer my challenge?"

He said, "Well, I had been watching that mess going on across the street there with you and these three hedgerows of Germans. I really thought you were a Kraut putting on a show to get me to open up.[13] If I had answered your challenge and you had turned out to be a Kraut, do you know what I'd of had to have done?"

I said, "No, I don't. What would you have had to have done?"

He just picked up a belt of machine gun ammunition and said, "I would have had to jump up and run across the road and beat you to death with this belt of machine gun ammunition." He was a machine gunner out of some heavy weapons platoon. He said, "When I got my opening shock, me and my machine gun parted company. This is all in the world I've got left to fight with."

I said, "You're pretty poorly equipped. I'll tell you what. They've kicked me in and out of every hedgerow over here. I had begun to think that the invasion had been called off and that I was the only man in Europe. You look like Coxy's Army to me and I'm going to give you a couple of grenades. You follow me. We're on the attack now. We'll have no more of this damn running."

So he took a couple of my grenades and threw away that belt of machine-gun ammunition and then we took off out of there. He was the first guy that I met after I landed in there. All I had was thirty-six pounds of Composition C-2, a thousand feet of wire, blasting caps, and a ten-cap detonator and not a man in my demolition section, but I headed toward my objective.

I heard a noise, motioned him down and then we squatted there. We were right on the edge of this landing that the Germans had flooded. This noise kept getting closer. It was three soldiers out there in this water walking along, laughing and talking and bullshitting. They got up a little closer and I thought, "They can't be Krauts.

That's got to be paratroopers," although I could not hear their voices distinctly enough to make that determination. I told him, "There's three paratroopers. I want to holler them in."

He said, "Oh no, no! Don't do that. They might be Germans!"

I said, "No German would fight a war like that. That's got to be three stupid paratroopers." So I hollered at them and they came on over immediately.

One of them was this kid named Manual Cockeral. He was the kid from Tulsa, Oklahoma, I had enlisted with down there at Fort Sill back in 1942. I had not seen him since that time in Toccoa, Georgia. He was the second American that I met. Out of twenty thousand people to jump into an area of combat and confusion, I bumped into someone that I personally knew.

It was a pretty tough go in there. Those hedgerows usually had small brush and trees that were fifteen to twenty feet tall all along them. They were so close and so dense that a lot of the boys became hung up in those trees and were killed. A bunch of them even drowned in the fields flooded by the Douve Canal, but in spite of that the drop really turned out to be a successful operation.

I picked up three more guys from our demolition platoon. They were Jack Agnew, Mike Marquez, and Keith Carpenter.[14] I just gathered up all the demolitions men I could find. Of course, any troops we passed we asked to come along. If they did not we would at least ask them for their demolitions. I even got three men from a mortar company to go along with me. I did not tell them where we were going or anything else about the mission. I just told them to stick with us and we were going to make it out okay. The mortar men carried six rounds of mortar ammunition. I grabbed all the explosives I could get.

I had rounded up about ten paratroopers along the march, just piecemeal here and there. Demolitions men jumped with two eighteen-pound satchels of Composition C-2. We had electrical blasting caps, wire, and primer cord. So my little demolition squad was re-forming.

GERMAN CP[15]

Along the way we accidentally ran into a big German military headquarters. It was possibly a regiment or might even have been a division. We knew that because a lot of big brass were there. It had never been mentioned as a target in our training. We did not even know where we were. We were just as surprised as the Germans were. All we did was blast them from every side then scattered.

This was a beautiful part about paratrooping. It was a commando-type operation. If we bumped into a company of Krauts marching along through there, why two of us would just lay in and kill fifteen to thirty of them and then we were gone. They could not interrupt an operation just to hunt down two paratroopers. That is what we did to this headquarters. We just went right on through them, just like a bunch of bobcats.

COLONEL JOHNSON[16]

When we passed Ste. Mere Eglise, we ran into Colonel Howard R. Johnson. He was the commander of the 501st. He had established his headquarters between me and my bridges. Well, when I reached his command post, I think I probably had up to ten men. I went to tell an officer who I was. I had three bridges to blow up out there beyond him about six miles. Of course, he was glad to see anybody who could squeeze a trigger. He was desperately short of men and needed firepower. So this officer told me that he was assigning us to his unit.

Then Johnson came up and said, "You take up a defensive perimeter out there in that area."

I said, "It's not right. Johnson, I've got another assignment on these bridges. I have a job assigned to me and a lot of lives depend on me accomplishing it. You can't use me out here as just a line man. No, I won't do it."

He said, "That's been rescinded. You're part of this position now."

I said, "Evidently, they thought it was important that those bridges be destroyed or held."

He said, "That's the way it is. You go out there and establish a perimeter defense right in that section."

I said, "Okay."

So I took my little group and headed out to the sector where he wanted a perimeter defense. It was night and we could not see but ten feet. Of course when we got there, I just kept on going. One of the guys, I think it was Keith Carpenter, said, "McNiece, isn't this where he told us to get? Where are you going?"

I answered, "Yeah, but don't you remember I told him that this is not where we were going to be, that we've got bridges down there to take care of."

He said, "Well, the colonel gave you orders to stay here in this area."

I said, "I'll let the colonel figure that out later. We're going to the bridges."

He said, "Okay."

We took off and I do not think we had gone a hundred yards until ole Keith Carpenter was shot through the calf of the leg. He looked like Hercules, a big man, not enormous, but he was built like a brick shithouse. That bullet went clear through his leg and exited out the other side and did not touch a bone—not a bone! We just poured a bunch of sulfur powder in it and he was okay. So we took off.

WARE GETS HIT

The jump in there was pretty tough because the Germans had undone the locks along the Douve Canal and flooded some fields as wide as four hundred to five hundred yards. In some places out there the water was as much as ten feet deep. A lot of the guys landed in that with their chutes and military equipment and drowned.

By then, somewhere we had picked up of Clarence Ware. I was picking up stragglers here and there. They had no idea what had happened to their outfits. They had all been killed off except maybe one or two. I had about thirteen men by the time I finally reached the bridges.

Of course, I was older than most of the kids in there. Jack Agnew was really just a young kid himself. He was amazed at all the things that I had done and gotten away with in garrison. I had kind of become his hero. It was his ambition to be like me.

I always led point on every patrol. I would have a guy follow close enough so that he could determine anything I said with hand signals, then he would pass it on back. When we were going across that flooded area, Clarence Ware was walking right along beside me. Agnew was the first man behind him about ten or fifteen yards, straggling through this water with the rest of the pack. The rest of the squad was marching in a wedge formation. About halfway across, one shot rang out. Ole Ware went down like a lark. I stopped to check him out. They had hit him right between the shoulder blades and it went clear through his chest.

We were only two hundred yards from the front edge of the flooded area. So I figured there was only one place from where they could possibly have shot him. It had to have come out of that little old farmhouse, right there in the middle of that bog off about seventy-five yards behind us to one side. It was just a little frame country shed or building.

So I put everybody down, then went over and checked that house out. I went all through it and checked every room. I could not find anything. I did not even find any sign of recent occupancy. So I went back, picked up the guys, and took them on down to the bridges.

After the war was over, Jack Agnew told me, "Jake, when that shot rang out, I saw Ware go down. I thought, 'Oh, hell. The war is over! They've killed McNiece!' It just scared me to death. I thought, 'What in the hell will we do now?' Then I got on up there and saw it was Ware."[17]

DOUVE CANAL[18]

We came to this flooded area and started out across it to reach the bridges. I went out there about seventy-five to a hundred yards. I was walking in water ankle deep and then suddenly I took a step and was over my head. I knew there were ditches in there. So I went right on across about six or eight feet to the other side.

The mortar men each carried six rounds of mortars in a vest, three in the front and three in the back, that slipped over their heads like an apron. It was so heavy that it took two people to lift it up and put it on them. One mortar man stepped right behind me into that ditch before he saw what had happened. Those mortar rounds pushed him right down. The water was just bubbling as he tried to fight his way back up to the surface. I grabbed him and dragged him on out, then we went back to work.

The farmers had cut ditches through their farms about every seventy-five to a hundred yards. With the fields flooded we could not see them until we stepped in one. When I got ready to step up to the next one, I would tell him to step up behind me about two or three steps. Then I would help the mortar man across each ditch.

My primary assignment was to blow the two wooden bridges up stream. One was just a foot bridge that did not show up on the map. Then we would move on up and place charges underneath the girders of the big bridge at Carentan.[19] I was to hold it if possible and not to blow it unless the Germans started across it with armor. The Allies wanted to hold that bridge so they could make an exit out of the Cherbourg Peninsula en masse. But if the Germans started to cross it with tanks, we were supposed to wait until they got two or three tanks out on it then blow the whole thing. We were to keep the Germans from reinforcing their men down on the beachhead.

When we reached the bridges about 3:00 that morning, I think I had about thirteen people. Most of them were demolitions men that I had picked up along the way. I also had three mortar men. I used those mortar shells for explosives. We wired those bridges for demolition. We blew the supports out from under the two wooden bridges, then moved on up to the bridge on the main thoroughfare. We got in and wired it up under the cover of darkness where and how I liked it. The bridge was unguarded since the Germans were not anticipating anyone being in that deep behind the lines. We had it wired up and ready to blow before daybreak. After daylight, we began fighting in there.[20]

The Douve Canal was fairly narrow and had real high causeways running the full length of it. The dike on both sides of the canal was probably ten to fifteen feet high. We could walk back and forth behind it. We had plenty of cover so none of us dug in. We just laid on the banks of the causeway and fought back and forth with rifle fire across the river. There were Krauts right behind the other causeway just across the river but they had the high ground. It was still dark enough that they could not see us but they knew we were in there. Of course, we did not know what the picture was behind us at all.

I was soaking wet from my toes clear to the top of my head. When we jumped in I had on long handle underwear, a full set of ODs and then my jump suit. After I got those wool ODs soaking wet, I could hardly move around. They were heavy.

It was just getting daylight. The first thing I did, when I got a break, was take off my jump suit then rip the ODs off. Once wet they were going to need some air and sunshine or they would never dry. They were wool. So I took them off and laid them right beside me. I just laid them out flat where I could dry them one side at a time.

I did not have them off ten minutes when the Germans dropped one mortar round from back across the water and it landed right in the middle of those clothes, right in the middle of them. There was not a piece of them left that could have been used as a handkerchief.

That mortar shell also knocked sand and stuff in my eyes. I lost my vision. I just had a very misty look. Everything was burning so I reached up and wiped my face. I looked at my hand and could definitely see that it was covered with blood. I thought, "Boy, this is one heck of a way to be, in here blind, fifteen miles behind the front lines surrounded by ten million Krauts." That was the most helpless and frightening time for me during the whole war.

I was blinking my eyes and they began to water. This washed the sand out. My vision just cleared right up, which was great news. I had been hit up around my eyes and across my hand. It turned out most of the blood came out of my hand.

It is almost ridiculous to think but I went clear through that war from the day before D-Day till the end and I never got hit bad. I never did go to the aid station on account of that wound in Normandy. It just healed up by the time we got out of there. There were a lot of real fine pieces of metal though, that looked like little short needles, in my face above the left eye. They would work their way out long after the war was over. Those in my hand went clear through.

The first thing I did after that was dig me a standing foxhole. I dug one six feet deep in about two minutes. After I got down in that hole, I thought I needed a good big shot of that Copenhagen to calm me down.

When I had gotten ready to load on that plane, I put on all the gear I could. I stuffed all my demolitions gear in my musset bag on my back. We did not have any room for a blanket or shelter half. The rest of our personal gear like razor and razor blades, cigarettes, whetstone and K Rations were stuffed in the pockets of our jump jackets and cargo pockets on our pants. Why, I just had these two front pockets left and they were pretty big pockets. They were about half full so I put everything over in one pocket. Then I had three of those K Ration boxes. They were about the size of a kitchen match box. I also had two cartons of Copenhagen. They were paste board outside and inside they were lined with wax. I thought, "I can't take them both with me. So I'll throw this food away. It won't ever get so tough in there that I can't find something to eat, but it may be a long time before I have a chance to get some more Copenhagen." So I threw my three boxes of K Rations out on the ground and stuck the two cartons of Copenhagen in the big pocket on my side.

When I reached down in my jump suit pocket to pull out a box of that Copenhagen, those boxes had just dissolved and come apart. We had been in the water for three or four hours getting to that last bridge. I had also fallen down and landed on them. I just had two big pockets full of mud, water, and sea weed. The whole thing was ruined. I did not have a thing left in the way of Copenhagen. I just pulled out a handful of Copenhagen and seaweed. It would be thirty-six days before I would get another box of Copenhagen.

I finally got straightened around there after I was hit. Jack Agnew was off about ten yards down the causeway from me. He asked, "Mac, what've you got to eat?"

"Nothing. What've you got to eat?"

He answered, "I've got one can of cheese." (They were about the size of a shoe polish can.) "You want a piece of it?"

I said, "Yeah, throw me one over."

So he just broke that thing in half and threw me half of it. That is all we ate that morning. The first day or so I was very hungry and then after a while I was not hungry any more. But once I got thirsty, it was terrible. I could not get any water. I could hear the water running in the canal all night long right in front of me but the Krauts kept flares up in the air at night. If someone tried to get in the canal they would kill them. We had nothing to eat or drink for five days and nights.

AGNEW AND THE GERMAN SNIPER

That day we just fought back and forth from across the canal. The Germans had one ole boy who was a crack shot. Boy, he was a sniper. He hit a lot of our men. There were only about fifteen of us in there at first and he killed four or five of us.

Jack Agnew and I put our heads together. I told Jack, "The only place that he could be shooting from is that two-story building. You get your eyes wide open and watch and knock him one."[21]

That German shot three more men. Jack leveled down on him and just cut him in half. He jumped up on the causeway and said, "I got that son-of-a-bitch." I think it was the first man he had really killed.

I grabbed him by the ankle and jerked him down. His head did not clear that causeway an inch before there came a burst of machine-gun fire that just ate it up.

> [Jack Agnew remembered:]
>
> *"The Germans could see us on the other side of the embankment from the church steeple. If we stuck our heads up the Krauts would blow them off. Every time someone would come in from behind us, they would wave as soon as they saw us. We were trying to tell them to get down and the first thing you know, a sniper must have picked off about sixteen of them before they reached us. We lost a lot more after that."*
>
> *Agnew said that after he killed the sniper, "I was so glad when I got that guy that I jumped up on that dike. Jake pulled me back over just before they shot it up."*[22]

FIGHTING

We were supposed to hold the bridge if we could. We could do that unless they came on there with armor. We did not have anything that could stop a tank, except a bazooka and satchel charges which were not very good choices. The bridge was seventy-five yards across from end to end. If troops got on that bridge, we could kill them off as fast as they stepped foot on it.

The Germans did try to cross that bridge with infantry that first morning.[23] We killed them as soon as they got on the bridge. The next day they tried again to move troops out on it but we also blew them away as they assembled. The Germans never tried to cross that bridge again. Aside from that there was not too much activity. We just waited until we heard some activity then we would peek up over the embankment and shoot at them.

Every time I raised up, I threw a burst into them across the river. I would then duck back down and go on over to another spot because they were watching the other one. This is how the fighting took place over the next few days. This way we did not expend too much ammunition. We also gathered up ammunition from the dead.

I was moving around and shooting. I looked over at Mike Marquez and he had not moved at all. Mike was a big Mexican kid from El Paso but not too smart. He was a good soldier though. He never was frightened of anything.

Well, he was lying on that causeway and just stayed in the same position all the time. He would raise up and fire off a burst then duck back down. I thought it would just be a minute or two until they leveled in on him. I looked back over because I was going to tell him what to do. He had just laid his rifle right there against the causeway where it would be handy for him. The barrel of his rifle was sticking up in the air higher than the causeway![24]

I went on over there and told him, "You idiot, why don't you just stand up there to where they can see you? If you want to commit suicide, do it quickly." I said, "Move around once in awhile. Don't come up in the same place two or three times."

He said, "Okay." He was not offended at all.[25]

Meanwhile there had been different guys scattered all over this area. The air force had started dropping men from the tip of the Cherbourg Peninsula and had been trying to work back twenty-five miles this way. There was just one, two, or maybe three paratroopers who were left out of a stick of ten or a platoon of twenty men. They just kept straggling in.

They heard us in there firing those M1s and knew we were paratroopers. They could identify the sound of our rifles. There was a world of difference between the sound of an M1 and a German rifle. So they thought, "Right down there, there is something going on. That must be the best place to be." They would then work their way into us, sneaking in at night. They would then take up a position on the line. The second evening about dark a lieutenant came in. From then on we directed the stragglers to him. I guess by the third day, we probably had from forty to sixty men, just leftovers from different groups. I do not know how many exactly but we had a pretty good bunch of men.[26]

P-51 MUSTANGS[27]

The invasion forces on Utah beach were supposed to have reached us at that bridge by dusk the first day. Well they did not make it on the first day and they did not make it the second day and they did not make it the third day. We did not have any contact or communications with anybody outside the bridge area. I am sure they did not think it was possible for anyone to be in there for three days and still be moving around. I guess they thought that we had been eliminated because late in the afternoon on the third day, here come these four P-51s.[28] They circled and came in on us in single file. I thought, "We're screwed." The first one missed the bridge and the second one hit it, man, just head on and blew that thing sky high. At first I was filled with a surge of anger. We had been guarding that bridge for three days and three nights against terrific odds and then our own air force came in and bombed it.

The air force had an order that they were not supposed to return and land on the runway with live bombs because an accident might destroy ten other planes. So they had the understanding that after they accomplished their mission, they would expend their bombs on a secondary objective and get rid of their ammunition, then fly back home.

Well, when the second one hit it, the other two peeled off. They were so low that they could see us in our foxholes and the Germans in their foxholes on either end of the bridge but they just figured we were all Germans. So they circled around, split up and two of them took the Germans and two of them took us. They came in and dropped the rest of their bombs, then strafed us with machine guns.

I was overcome by a great sense of fear to be under that bombing. Then I had a sense of calm. There was nothing any of us could do but wait for the bombs to fall. One ole guy had dug a seven-foot standing foxhole. A big chunk of that bridge came right down in that foxhole and drove through his head. After the planes flew away I was shocked at the loss. Out of the forty men we had in there, we probably lost fifteen to our own air force. So we did not have anything to do. We did not have a bridge to worry about anymore. It was gone. No tanks were going to come across there, so all we were dealing with then were those German soldiers. In that respect we were still in good shape.[29]

A KRAUT BATTALION[30]

The Americans were pushing these Krauts back to us. We were in a defiladed area from the causeway back to the high ground over on the other side, about five hundred yards. About every one hundred or seventy-five yards, not exactly but pretty regular, the farmers had dug ditches out there about six feet deep and eight feet wide to drain that meadowland during the rainy season. We were sitting there just on our hind end fighting a little. When they would lay it in on us, well we would fire right back at them.

The Germans from the beach had retreated and retreated and retreated until the afternoon of the fifth day they had come right up to the edge of the water. Every time they would show themselves, we shot at them. When they realized what our situation was, they sent an officer and a sergeant in there under a white flag and demanded that we surrender. They knew there was not very many of us in there.

I do not even remember our lieutenant's name. He said, "What in the hell do you mean, us surrender. You've got to surrender to us. If you stay where you are, those Yankees coming from the beachhead will eat you up. You've retreated up to here already. If you come out in that water we will kill you like a bunch of ducks. If you would all like to surrender intact, stack all your rifles and all your weapons over there and just put up a white flag and surrender to them boys coming in."

This German officer, I believe he was navy, said, "Why we would not surrender to thirty or forty people. I've got a whole battalion."

Our officer said, "Well, get your ass out in the water and come right on out here!"

The lieutenant came back and told us, "You let them come out in the water and cross the first ditch. When they get halfway to the second ditch, I will blow this whistle and we will all open up. Then you pick out the thickest bunch of them and shoot into them. They will not have anywhere to go or nothing to get into."

We had two or three light machine guns and mortars. The rest of us were mostly demolition saboteur people. I think we still had one bazooka in there. Anyway we were a lightly equipped bunch of people.

So the Germans charged right out in that water firing everything they had. We did not fire a shot until they got right in between those two ditches. Then we went to work on the bastards. We cut them down by the hundreds with the first salvo, then we just picked them off one-by-one. All they could do was get down in that water. The water was anywhere from calf to knee deep. Some of them tried to make it back to the original ditch. There were a few of them close to that second ditch who made a dash to get into it. Once they got in they could not get out of it. When they did we just zeroed in on some old boy and waited for him to come up for air and then we just blasted his head off. We killed off nearly the whole bunch. They did not have a Chinaman's chance.

When the Germans on the other side of the river saw this happen they did not know what in the hell was going on. There was very little fire from across the bridge. Within fifteen minutes this American unit that had pushed the Germans to the bridge saw what happened and then they began to lay a heavy covering fire on that town of Carentan.

After we finished rubbing out the Germans we went out and combed the field. A lot of the wounded laid there and played dead. We walked out through there killing the ones that were just wounded or hiding.

Jack Agnew and I worked together. He had a Colt forty-five. A chaplain named Captain Tilden McGee went up with us and signaled for us to stop. I signaled for the other guys to stop, then I moved on up. I saw this Kraut in one of these deep ditches. Just his head and shoulders were above water. One of those machine gunners had tore his chest clear up. It was like a sponge. He was laying there trying to breath. He was pumping that blood and foam out in that water.

I said, "Here he is," and they walked over there.

Chaplain McGee said, "Give him a shot."

I looked over at Jack and said, "Agnew, you've got that forty-five. Blow his head off."

Agnew shot at him and missed him. Then he kneeled down and put that Colt against his temple and just blew his head clear off of him.

That chaplain just screamed. He said, "You knew I didn't mean to shoot his head off. I meant to give him a shot of morphine."

I said, "I'll tell you what, Chaplain, you do anything you want to with your morphine. There will be a thousand paratroopers all around here that will need a shot of morphine. We are not wasting it on these Krauts. You're going to kill him anyway. Do it quick and easy in his sleep."

When we got together later at some of these "get togethers," I asked Agnew, "What are you doing now?"

He answered, "I'm retired now. I work with the NRA all the time."

I said, "What are you doing with the NRA?"

He said, "I run the rifle range and the target practice and teach these people how to shoot."

I laughed and said, "You must have improved a hell of a lot since I last knew you, Jack, and what I saw in combat." Of course we were sitting around with the others and I kind of grinned and Agnew blushed. Then someone said, "Come on, tell us what you are talking about." So I told them about Jack missing that German while standing over him, then having to kneel down and stick it to his temple before he could hit him. I said, "And now he is a range instructor up there in Philadelphia."[31]

A JUICY STEAK

D+5: June 11, 1944

We got out of there on the night of the fifth day.[32] We knew the Americans were right behind us so we walked out in that field and called out so they would know we were paratroopers. After linking up we headed on back to join our unit. It was five or six miles back to regimental headquarters. They directed us to this little old village. So we went down there and reported in. I had five or six demolitions men with me from Regimental Headquarters Company.[33]

Most of us had had nothing to eat or drink for five days. A lot of cattle had been killed over there by bombs, gunfire, and artillery. The

French saw how things were developing. When we got out of the water and among those Frenchmen, they had cooked up a big ole pot, nearly as big as those army kettles. They had gone out there and cut meat off of those dead dairy cattle. They cubed it up and added some greens and potatoes and onions in it. They boiled that thing up and had it ready. They also baked that big ole heavy French bread. They fed us that soup and it was the best soup that I ever tasted in my life. My belly had shrunk up so much that I could not eat much of it. But it was real good.

The next day we went back and joined our unit. They were just holding a perimeter defense at the time about eight miles west of Carentan. The first thing that I wanted to do was lay down and get some sleep, then eat. I found an empty barn about fifty yards from the Regimental CP.

Little ole Shorty Mihlan came running up to me wanting to know what all had happened. He was still Colonel Sink's orderly. I explained what we had done. He then asked, "Jake, how would you like a big steak?"

I said, "I'd like a steak pretty good."

So he came back in, a little bit dirty and grubby. He opened up his field jacket, reached in and pulled out a big, thick steak. Then he gave me the rest of his bottle of cognac and said, "I've got plenty of it." I was exhausted and had had hardly any sleep for five days. I laid my rifle down at the base of the ladder and crawled up there in that hayloft and began to work on that steak and cognac. I could not eat all of it but I ate most of it and really enjoyed it. When that hot steak hit my belly and that cognac warmed me up I just passed out like a light. The next morning, Mihlan woke me up thumping me on the chest with another bottle of cognac. We got to talking and he asked, "How would you like a steak?"

I said, "Boy, good."

So he took off and in probably twenty minutes he came walking back, looking at everybody and watching everything. He came up and pulled another steak out of his jacket just as big as the first one.

I said, "Shorty, these steaks are delicious but you can overdo a good thing. Let's don't kill the goose that lays the golden egg."

He asked, "What do you mean?"

I said, "From the amount of this meat that you're bringing me, Colonel Sink is pretty soon going to figure it all out. If he sobers up, he's going to know we're stealing his steaks."

He answered, "This isn't his steak."

I said, "It's illegal some way because you're sneaking around doing it." I asked, "What do you mean these are not his steaks? Where are you getting them?"

This was the seventh morning after the invasion and those dairy cattle the Allies had killed were just laying around all over the place. That was what the guys were eating, but on the sixth day the medics put out a big order that we could not eat them any more because that meat would be contaminated. The weather in June was fairly cool. I imagine some of it might have been contaminated but if they were taking it off of the hindquarters, it would not be. That is what Shorty was feeding me.

He said, "I'm getting it off of them cattle."

I said, "The medics put out an order that you could not eat that any longer."

He just flipped his cookies [vomited] when I told him that.

I ate that steak, then rolled out of bed and started down the ladder. I looked down and there was that boy I had whipped back in England. I had my trench knife in my boot but I did not have a gun. He was standing down there looking right up at me with an M-1. He was not aiming it at me but I did not know whether to jump on him from the ladder or just climb on down and make an attack.

He backed away from the ladder and said, "Well McNiece, we did you a real bad deal there in Toccoa, Georgia. I can understand your attitude toward me because of that. I think that you pretty well evened it up back there in London. How about us shaking hands?"

I said, "That sounds like good news to me." I only had a knife but was fully prepared to fight him. He was a pretty nice guy but was killed not too long after that.

SEVENTH DAY: ATTACK ON CARENTAN

D+6: June 12, 1944

The 501st and 502nd had tried to take Carentan but failed. The Krauts were dug in pretty good and held the high ground. I had rested for a day before the 101st finally decided to send the 506th in on a direct frontal attack. It was the only way we were going to get those Germans out of there. Regiment decided that Headquarters Company would fall in with the 3rd Battalion. We would move in there during the dark hours of morning as close as we could and then throw incendiary mortars in to pin the Krauts down. We would then rush them in a frontal bayonet assault.[34]

So we started out from near St. Come du Mont about midnight.[35] We traveled about four miles and would attack from the south, just two miles past the main bridge. We went out through this flooded area where I had been seven days before. Sergeant Bruno Schroeder, who worked in the S-2, was leading this column of men from Regimental Headquarters Company.

I told Lieutenant "Willy" Williams, "Schroeder's off the beaten path. We're lost. He's missed our gathering place."

He asked, "Are you sure?"

I said, "Yeah, I'm sure."

He asked, "How do you know?"

I said, "I've spent five days and nights down here."

The first thing we knew, the Germans started eating us up with machine-gun fire up at the front where Colonel Sink was. Colonel Sink and all of his staff were right up at the head of the column. He sent a command back for Willy to send a couple demolitions men up there to knock out that machine-gun nest. I heard it passed along. Willy was on one side of the hedgerow and I was on the other. Of course, I knew who Willy was going to send.

Willy whispered, "McNiece, McNiece."

I said, "Hell, I can't hear a word you are saying, Willy."

He said, "Come over here."

I started climbing over the hedgerow to where Willy was. It was more than three or four feet high. I had a musset bag on with two or three bottles that Shorty had given me just before we started out. When I climbed up, the bag became tangled up in a wire strung along the base of the hedgerow. It just rattled like a pop truck. There was a machine-gun nest within about forty or fifty yards of that point. When they heard the noise they just began to mow that hedgerow. I bet I tore up a thousand feet of that barbed wire before getting on down to the ground.

I told Willy, "Willy, I heard the orders come back. Why don't you just send him a quick sweet reply and tell him to take care of the machine guns up there and we'll take care of ours back here. We're completely surrounded. I told you that Schroeder was lost long ago. We are in the middle of the outskirts of Carentan right now."

The thrust was not supposed to start for about two hours. They had not even laid the phosphorous mortars in on them. So Willy told them, "We are surrounded. We've got machine guns back here looking us right in the eye. You all take care of the front and we will take care of the back."

They had us pinned down tight. We could not make a move. The hedgerow probably was not over two hundred yards at the widest point. Yet, it really did not stay very hot once we start laying in on them. Every time we saw a flash we shot at it. Finally we killed them inside that hedgerow with rifle, grenades, and machine-gun fire. Once we killed everything in there, we had a hedgerow to fight out of. Schroeder had led us clear into the town on that deal. He received a battlefield commission for leading us into this trap.[36]

Colonel Sink then put us into a perimeter defense and we just hunkered down. I just laid down and went to sleep. Lieutenant Sylvester Horner came along, kicked me and asked, "What in the hell are you doing?"

I said, "I'm getting some sleep. What do you think I'm doing."

He asked, "Why are you sleeping? You're supposed to be looking over this hedgerow to stop anything that moves."

I said, "Why do you think they would attack in here tonight when it's dark. When all they have got to do is wait until it gets daylight and start picking us off like ducks? Nobody's coming in here. I'm going to get me some rest. You've got about two more hours to get you a nap if you want it. When they get a little more light, they're going to shoot us like we were a bunch of ducks. I'm going to grab me some sleep while I can."

Well, in about an hour and a half, around 5:30 or so, we started throwing phosphorous in and pinned the Germans down. Then we started breaking out. I was on the left of this road. There was a deep cut, probably anywhere from twelve to twenty feet in the hedgerow, for the road to go through. I started moving to it when this ole boy opened up on me with a burp gun. There was a little defilade area and I jumped into it. I was not twenty yards from that guy with the burp gun. I could feel those bullets impacting into my musset bag but they did not touch me. It was a hell of a feeling to lay there with a burp gun pointed at me dead center and ripping my bag apart but he could not hit me. But I could not move. He shot up all my cognac and that made me mad.

I reasonably knew where he was. I could see the flashes from his stinking gun. So I kept listening to the number of rounds he was firing. I was not fifteen feet from this bank. I just waited until I thought I had a chance. After he ended a burst I then made a run back down into that road. I just came right on up behind him through this cut up the road. I climbed up over a hedge that was about eight feet high. I could not see anybody. I then moved on up to this tree. I found the burp gun but I did not find anybody. So I always believed that it had been a French civilian. No German would have abandoned his weapon.

The others were fighting up this street. So I just moved on up the road and took up the fight. We had fixed bayonets but the Germans would not fight us that close. These Germans started retreating the minute we started in but there were pockets of them left in the confusion. We just mopped them up house to house. It took us until noon before we wiped the Germans out.

> [Tom Young fought alongside Jake and remembered:]
>
> *The next morning after we attacked Carentan, Jake and I were together. We heard this, "clompity, clompity, clomp," coming down the street. This German had put on wooden shoes to make us think he was French. That bastard was shooting at us. I had dug a little foxhole but could not get down deep enough. He shot a hole in my canteen. Jake was cussing him. After the German emptied his grease-gun, Jake jumped up before he could reload and swung his rifle butt at him like he was swinging a baseball bat. He knocked that German down and his helmet went rolling up the street.*[37]

STUMP JUICE

After we had taken Carentan, we were laying around in this building. A small bomb had nearly destroyed it. Right next door, there was a music shop with guitars, fiddles, and such. So we took all of them. Hell, everyone of us had some kind of instrument—a fiddle, a guitar, or some kind of stringed instrument or a horn and we were laughing and whooping it up. Only a few of the guys could play any music but we could have been heard ten miles away. We were just having a good time.

Meanwhile Tom laid down by a fireplace to get some rest. He looked up in the chimney and saw a box. He messed around, then jammed his legs up in there and dislodged it. It turned out to be a whole case of cognac. There was also a box of wine up in there. So we really started to work on it when Tom laughed and said, "The Colonel will send you a guy immediately." Since we were in Regimental Headquarters Company, he was in the same area.

Pretty soon Shorty Mihlan walked in and said, "Colonel wants a bottle of that stump juice you've got there."

I told Tom, "Give him a bottle of that wine."

So Tom said, "Okay."

He gave Shorty a bottle of wine and he took off. He was back in five minutes and said, "You can have this damn wine. The Colonel wants some of that stump juice you've got hid. He does not have any stomach problems. He just wants something good to drink. He said he would take a bottle of that."

Tom said, "Tell him we don't have any."

Shorty said, "I ain't going to tell the Colonel that. He's up there in that second story window with a pair of field glasses that can read the labels on that stuff ten miles away. He knows what you've got. He's been watching you. So do you think I'm going to go back there and tell him that you don't have any schnapps."

Tom said, "Okay, he can have one bottle. We've got a whole platoon here drinking out of this and he won't get any more than that. He'll have to get out and hunt some himself."[38]

Colonel Sink was a real drinker. He was a great soldier and a fighting dude though. He knew tactics. He stayed in and made two-star general.[39]

Two or three hours later, someone came up and told me I was on guard up at the CP. Boy, I was drunker than nine hundred dollars. So I went up there and stood guard. I still had a bottle of that cognac in my jacket. Lieutenant Horner walked up and asked, "Jake are you aware of the new orders out that any paratrooper who is drunk will be disarmed?"

I said, "Yeah, I think I've heard about it."

He asked, "What have you got in your jacket there?"

I said, "I've got a fifth of cognac."

He said, "You're already drunk and you're standing here guarding Colonel Sink's CP. I don't know what to do."

I said, "Okay, I'll tell you what. Let me give you this gun and you stand guard and I'll keep the cognac."

The second day in Carentan, a sniper had killed four or five paratroopers right down there in this one area. We had to be awful careful because there was so much sniping over there. The civilians would snipe at us just as much as the Germans. France had been under occupation for four years. A lot of those women had married German soldiers and had one or two kids by them. We had a difficult time with snipers because there were so few of us left in that town.

Most of these paratroopers had been killed within a twenty-yard radius. I searched all over for any doors or windows that it might have come out of. I concluded it was not coming out of the houses because someone would have detected it. Basically it could only have come from the big Catholic church.

I took four or five boys with me and went in and met this priest. He could not speak my language and I could not speak his but I made him understand what we wanted and asked him to lead. He kept saying something about the Geneva Convention and religious freedom. I could understand what he was talking about, so I told him, "No. We're going to clean this place out. You just get on outside."

We went right on through it. It had a balcony going up into this steeple. So we started through there. We opened every door we came to. We were looking it over and made no headway finding anybody. So the closer we came to the top the more I was convinced we were going to run into something but we did not find a damn thing.

Well, there was not a whole lot left for us after we took Carentan. It was really the first town of any importance that was taken by the 101st. We did not stay in Carentan very long. We held it for about ten days, then were relieved by someone in the 83rd Infantry Division. They moved a line infantry regiment in where we were and took over. Then they withdrew us and pushed us on out south and east of Ste. Mere Eglise. They just put us in a defensive position. From then on there was not a lot of fighting out there.

AWARD CEREMONY[40]

June 20, 1944

They moved us back to a holding position. We had suffered such high casualties that we did not have the combat strength left to do any fighting. So they had us up there on outpost duty in an area that was not threatened. Then someone from division came around and issued orders with a list of all the personnel who they wanted to go into Carentan for an awards ceremony. So we assembled and went in there.

Tom Young and I were together. The first thing we did when we got into town was break loose. We decided that we would go find us some women and whiskey. Tom wanted to get a haircut. So we took off from there and fooled around for quite a while and then came back. We could see that things were finally moving into shape. They had a big podium there with six or eight men on it. I believe it included General Taylor, General Higgins, Colonel Sink, and Uncle Charlie Chase. That area was kind of like a triangle and not even a block in size.

Well, Tom and I just worked our way up into the formation. Meanwhile, Maxwell Taylor was talking. He was reading off his spiel about what a tremendous job his division had done. He was proud of them and he was going to issue a bunch of awards, ribbons, and medals. Boy, then three 88 shells just dropped in that triangle. At the first, the boys started breaking their ranks. Taylor yelled, "ATTENTION! Stand where you are!"

Me and ole Tom had already backed up in a doorway when the Germans dropped three more right in that square. There were bodies all over that street. Tom and I just kept moving back in between ranks. Just as quick as the Germans could they had thrown in six rounds which landed in that square every time. After they finished, Taylor went ahead with the awards ceremony. Since we were down to such a strength, we could not be used as a combat unit.

Leach Sends for a Prisoner

After Carentan we occupied a section of the front. The Germans occupied a hill overlooking our position. We were just eyeball-to-eyeball with them. Lieutenant Leach was in the S-2 and making these wild selections for missions.

Leach wanted to send me with about four or five people out into the German main line of resistance. He wanted us to bring back three Germans alive so he could question them. He wanted to know their unit identification and strength. Ninety percent of our interrogators spoke German fluently and most of them were Jewish. Boy, they got the information out of those Krauts. They did not fool around. Leach was Jewish and that was what he was wanting to do.

I told him, "Well, I don't care anything about going out there and getting my head blown off just to get someone for you to talk to. You know what their strength is already. You know what they've got up there and I do too. If you want to send me out on a search, kill, and destroy patrol, I'm ready. But I'm not ready to go out there outnumbered a hundred-to-one just to get you any prisoners. I won't go." I looked at him, "I'll tell you what though. If you think that information is so important, I'll take you with me so you can see that it is done right."

Well, he was not even about to leave the safety of that CP under any circumstances. He remembered the threat I had made to him back when he was in my platoon. He knew I would kill him if he went out there. Of course he did not go, nor did he send me out chasing down any German prisoners.[41]

Policing the Dead

After we came back from Carentan, Tom Young and I ordered a croissant in a little village. That was dairy country down there. There were thousands of cattle killed by bombing and strafing and a jillion dead Krauts and paratroopers were just laying all over the place.

That ground was just covered with them and maggots were climbing out of their guts. We could hardly take a step without sliding down because of the maggots. It got to where one could not hardly stand the stench of it. I would be eating a can of K Rations and look down and there would be fourteen flies.

So Browny told Tom and I to go down in that one area and clean out those dead bodies; all of those cows, Germans, paratroopers, and civilians. Anything that was dead we were to get rid of. So Tom and I went down to a village and found two of those Frenchmen in that little ole village who had ox carts. We told them that we wanted to put all those people that we found in those bomb holes. There were these great big bomb holes all over Europe. They could have anything they wanted off the corpses except the dog tags. Tom and I collected the dog tags off of every paratrooper and Tom had a helmet full of them. We reported what we had done to intelligence since airborne units did not have graves registration people.

The Frenchmen loaded the bodies up in the ox carts and hauled them over and threw everything—the cows, the paratroopers and the Germans—in the same bomb holes. Of course they were glad to get all that clothing, money, watches, and rings. We just kept them busy down there. It took them all day to clean that mess up. Some time after that we began to move back to the landing to get ready to return to England.

[Tom Young remembered:]

Jake and I were the only ones at this apple orchard. Captain Brown came up and asked us to gather up all the dead bodies. He said there were some trucks coming up later that we could load them on. He told us there will be a cholera outbreak if we did not. He told us to load up all the Americans first. I went down to a town and found a Frenchman who spoke good English. I told him we needed some help and asked if he had about five men who could gather up the bodies. He said, "Yes." We told them not to touch anything on the Americans but they could have anything they wanted off of the German bodies. The Germans had some good boots. Jake and I did not touch a body. The

Frenchmen loaded up all the American bodies in the trucks. He asked, "What do you want us to do with the Germans." I said, "I don't know." I thought there would be some trucks to pick them up later. The Frenchman said, "I know where there is a big cistern, where we can dump the bodies." That is what they did.[42]

There was a PX set up there for soldiers who were exiting. I bought me a big ole box of Copenhagen. I had been without Copenhagen for thirty-six days. We also had a mail call and I received two or three packages from my brothers and sisters and mother and dad. They all had Copenhagen in them. I sat down on the back steps of these German barracks that we had taken. I packed my head just as full as I could get it. I just thought I was in hog heaven. In about two minutes I was so dizzy and sick that I could not see. I hung on to the stairs until I could not stand it and then I laid out on the ground and just puked my guts out. Afterwards I took a little chew of it and started working back into it. It took me a couple of days before I got to where I enjoyed it again.

WHAT HAPPENED TO THE OTHERS

When we finally came out of there, I had five men out of the original thirteen left. After we hit the silk, I did not see Joe Oleskiewicz, Max Majewski, Chuck Plauda[43] nor Jack Womer until I rejoined my company. Jack Agnew was the only one of the thirteen who fought with me on the bridge. Many of the guys never lived to see the sun come up.

[Jack Womer remembered his experience:[44]]

Jack Womer jumped as the sixteenth man in the stick. He landed in a deep ditch of the swamp and nearly drowned, but the "wind of the Lord" caught his chute and pulled him out, then dragged him into shallower water. He could hear Krauts screaming all around him. He figured that they were evidently more scared than the paratroopers.

Jack moved to high ground but ran into wire. He then retreated back into the swamp where he met up with a lieu-

tenant and nine other paratroopers. Since he had been out of the swamp they asked him to lead them down a road where they might link up with somebody else. He walked point. When a twenty-millimeter cannon opened up on him, Jack walked back and told the lieutenant that a drainage ditch would give them protection. They decided to continue down the road with Jack about twenty yards out in front of the scouts. A voice warned him, "What are you doing out there?" So he jumped into the ditch. The others came up and the lieutenant decided to flank the cannon. About that time the Germans sent up a flare. The paratroopers froze as they had been trained, then the twenty millimeter killed nearly half of the party. The rounds sprayed dirt on Jack's head. When the flare burned out, Jack ran out into a wheatfield with three other guys. He was crawling on his hands and knees when a mortar round landed right next to him. It blew him backwards. When he checked himself, to his amazement, the explosion had only singed his left sleeve.

At daylight, he found a bunch of 501st guys walking up the road. He warned them about the twenty millimeter, then wanted to go and check on the wounded up the road. A captain told him instead to go back down the other way to find others. As he started walking back a voice again warned him not to go down that road. He stopped just in time as the enemy fired down the road. He then continued in the same direction and passed a paratrooper with a broken leg. He asked for a medic and Jack assured him that he would return with one. As Jack continued he came across a bunch of paratroopers waiting in a ditch. He asked if any of them were from the 506th. He felt it would be safer to have some company moving through the countryside. About a dozen men stood up and followed him to a house where a captain had established a defensive position. Jack then put his men on line.

Jack found a medic and headed back to the paratrooper with the broken leg. As he jumped over a drainage ditch he looked back and the medic was gone. About halfway through the woods he ran across a man wounded in the arm and leg. He found other paratroopers, only to learn that the man with the broken leg had been killed. He then led that group of paratroopers back and recovered the other wounded man. He placed them in a defensive line, then assumed responsibility for the 506th men at "Hell's Corners" near la Barquette. On one occasion he was sniping on German positions from a tree. Suddenly an eighty-eight shell narrowly missed him but knocked him from the tree.

On the second day, the 1st Battalion of the German 6th Paratrooper Regiment approached unaware of the paratroopers. The Americans held their fire until the Germans were close, then they surprised them with an ambush. Over a hundred Germans surrendered. The Americans herded the Germans out onto a road along the dike. They had them strip off the camouflage smocks which they wore over their blue uniforms. About that time a German mortar barrage landed among them but the Krauts could not run because GIs were dug in all around them. The mortars killed nearly all of the Germans. Jack saw one wounded German who looked fourteen years old. He read the fear in his eyes so Jack picked him up and took him back to the house for treatment. When others asked why he was out on the road, Jack just told them he was the runner.[45] *The wounded were still lying everywhere moaning.*

After six or seven days of fighting, an officer came over and told Jack that the 506th was coming up to relieve them. The officer said he had kept a record of what Jack had done and that he could go back with them for a rest instead of going right back into action with his unit. Jack followed the 501st back.

Lieutenant Mellen was the officer who took us in. Someone reported to Regiment that he had been wounded as many as three or four times because he had lived long enough to bandage his wounds. Joe Oleskiewicz had seen him before he was killed. Another boy said he died trying to knock out three machine-gun nests, which was not very good odds. They found his body the next morning.[46]

Baran was hit very soon in Normandy. The Germans shot him in the head with a wooden bullet. They were made of hard wood that would splinter easily. They could shoot someone right between the eyes with one and it would not kill them but the splinters would go all through the head. The red, green, and black dyes in them would cause a heck of an infection that required a lot of care. The Germans used them to occupy ten men for every wounded man.

Baran was hit in the temple right above the eye. It just shattered and went all over his head. That green dye stayed with him forever. It looked like someone had taken a tattoo needle and jabbed him all over his face. It was still visible after the war was over.[47]

Peepnuts Hale had jumped out with the second half of the stick. He was killed attacking his third machine gun nest. He wore a size four and a half boot. Before we jumped into Normandy they issued everyone of us a brand-new pair of jump boots. The quartermaster would not issue one boot of an odd size like that. Instead they would issue six pair at a time. Peepnuts received six good pair of size four and a half boots and the rest of us only received one pair. He was killed and I wore my one pair all through the war. I wore the soles out and had to stuff paper in it.[48]

I found out about the others from some people who had seen them. The stories got out from graves registration and filtered back into the company. Nobody knows what happened to Googoo Radeka.[49] They just found his body. I do not know what happened to Baribeau either. I was surprised Baribeau did not last any longer than he did because he spoke fluent French. He was tough. I figured he would come through that whole show without a scratch.[50]

All anyone ever found of Ragsman Cone was his dog tags. Back then the army designated one's religion with a letter on the tag. "H" stood for Hebrew, "P" for Protestants, and "C" for Catholics. I guess Cone did not want to get caught with that "H" hanging around his neck.

[Cone related his story:]

Cone jumped in the middle of his stick and landed in the hedgerows with another paratrooper from his squad. The two fought off Germans armed with machine pistols. During the fight, the Germans sprayed the hedgerow and hit Cone below the right shoulder, breaking his arm. One round hit the other paratrooper in the head killing him instantly. Wounded, Cone could no longer fire his M1 Garand so he made his way out of there to a French farmhouse. Afraid the Germans would kill him for being a Jew, he pushed his dog tags into the ground. After Lieutenant Alex Bobuck turned in Cone's dog tags, he was listed as killed in action. His parents even received payments on his insurance policy.

Cone had the farmer hide him. After two days the farmer turned him in to the Germans. They treated his arm, then transferred him to a prison camp. A fellow prisoner was released and informed the army that Cone was still alive. His family gladly returned the insurance money. Cone spent the next eight to nine months in three different prison camps. The Russians liberated the American prisoners at the Kristin camp. Most of the Americans fought with the Russians hoping to link up with the Americans. The Russian offensive had stalled. Cone had struck up a friendship with another paratrooper. After a week fighting with the Russians they decided to make their way back to American lines on their own.

With Polish money they had picked up from the prison camp, they made their way through Poland and Rumania and finally reached Russia. Without any identification papers, the Russian authorities put them in jail until the American government sent word to release them. They sailed through the Dardanelles on a British ship to Port Said, Egypt, where they reached an American air base. They were thrown in jail because of a report that a mutiny had occurred on the British ship. A lawyer arrived to question the two and cleared them of any charges. They made their way to Naples, Italy, then on to Boston. Cone was sent to Fort McPherson, Georgia, where they took the bullet out of his arm. He went down to Fort Benning to make one more jump to keep his jump pay and was finally discharged on October 7, 1945. Until he called Jake McNiece on June 5, 2002, none of the men of the 506th knew he had survived the war.[51]

Rasmussen survived. Those C-47s always had a pilot, a co-pilot, and a crew chief. In flight, the crew chief looked at Rass's flamethrower[52] and asked, "What are you doing with that thing? Are you going to jump with that thing on your leg?"

Rass said, "Yeah, I've got a cotter pin here." It was tied to a rope which was attached to his belt. "When the chute opens I'll just whip that key out of there and it will drop down to the end of that rope. That will take that hundred and five pounds off of me as I land."

Rasmussen pulled the key out and showed him how it worked, then he tried to put it in. He had so much crap on that he could not. So the crew chief said, "I'll put it in," but he put it in backwards.

When Rass jumped out and that chute opened, he tried to release that flamethrower but he could not pull out the cotter key. So he landed with it on his leg. He sprained both of his ankles. To walk he had to balance himself with both his hands outstretched. He was trying to work his way out of there to a ditch and there were Krauts all around him just shooting up a storm. One bullet hit him in the elbow and it ricocheted down to his belly.

He and Trigger Gann landed together. They were about four miles from where we landed. Trigger poured a whole bunch of sulfur powder on his arm. Then he told Rasmussen, "Rass, I'm going out of here. I'll give you a couple of shots of morphine and I'll come back. I've got this job to do and need to get out of here."

Trigger went off to fighting around there and the Krauts just pushed him in and out of every hedgerow in there. By the time it quieted down he headed back to take care of Rass but he never could find him.

To this day Rasmussen hates Trigger Gann with a purple passion because he feels that Trigger deserted him, which I do not think is the truth. Trigger was a boy from Birmingham, Alabama, about six foot one. He was not afraid of anything. They called him Trigger because he was a hair trigger. If you said the wrong word he would just bust you in the mouth. Trigger told me, "Jake, I went back and tried to find him."[53]

Rasmussen did not join back up with the company for about four or five days.[54] He told someone that he had this bullet in his belly and it was hurting, not all the time but if he made a quick move or he sneezed or coughed or hit the dirt quickly it was pretty painful. He said, "I would like to see this officer who is examining all these wounds. I would like to get that thing cut out."

They asked him how it got into his belly and he told them, "I don't know."

We had this doctor who was out of a field hospital about two miles south of us. Rass told him about that bullet in his belly.

He said, "Let me see your belly."

Rass pulled his shirt apart and the guy looked it over. He said, "I don't see any bullet holes, son. I don't even see any discoloration."

Rass said, "I got hit in the elbow."

The doctor asked, "How did it get in your belly?"

Rass said, "Look, I'm not a medical man. I don't know. It's right there. You can feel it."

The doctor then asked, "Is it getting too tough for you up here, son?"

Rass answered, "I want to tell you, you son-of-a-bitch, if it was too rough for me up here you wouldn't be around asking me any questions. You would have been long gone. It ain't too rough for me. I've got this bullet in my belly and I would like to get it out. It's painful."

The guy said, "I'm going to send you back to the field hospital. They've got X-ray equipment down there and you had better have a bullet in your belly."

Rass said, "That's no problem. Just get me down there to where I can get it taken care of."

They took him down there and X-rayed him. They could see scars and bruises on these bones up his arms and into his shoulder. It stopped down there in the wall of his stomach. They told Rass, "The bullet's there. We can operate and take it out but if we do, this will cut a bunch of nerves and muscle tissue. You might have trouble with it the rest of your life. If you just want to leave it in there, if it is not too painful, probably in another three or four weeks you won't even know you've got it."

Rass said, "If that's the medical analysis, I've got to take your word. I don't know."

They sent him right back to duty that very day. He never missed a day of combat and still has that bullet in his belly to this day.

Wilbur Shanklin had gone all through Normandy. He was a good soldier. He had taken a horse from somewhere. He had a bunch of prisoners and they told him to take them to a POW pen somewhere for interrogation.

When we got out of there and back to our barracks in Littelcote, he was cleaning his rifle. We had been laying in that mud and water for thirty-six days. He shot himself through the foot. They were going to court-martial him. They thought he did it on purpose but Shanklin was not afraid of anything. He did not make the next jump because his foot had not healed up enough but he rejoined the outfit and soldiered good.

Out of the Regimental Headquarters Company, Maw Darnell was captured along with Burl Prickett, George Smith, James "LaLa" Leach, and Lieutenant Carl Bedient. The Germans took them clear up into Russia.

RETURN TO ENGLAND

July 13, 1944

We had stayed in France for thirty-six days. When we got back to England, Division issued us new clothes and decorations.[55] We had two months' pay coming along with all the loot we had stolen in France. They gave each one of us a seven-day pass for which they had an ulterior motive. They knew we were going to be parading all over Piccadilly Circus with these medals hanging on us advertising parachute operations. The airborne divisions needed a bunch of replacements and they wanted to show off paratroopers and get other people excited enough to volunteer for it. We had lost over 65 percent. We needed troops real bad.

They had these six-by trucks driving right up and down the wharves where these people were loading boats to join the fighting in France in about two days. They drove up with big bullhorns saying, "Anyone on that boat who wants to transfer to the 101st Airborne just tell your commanding officer and come down the cat walk." Airborne had the highest priority for troops in the army at that time. Of course they had preplotted and planned it with the naval people. It worked. Men just started piling out of those boats like drowned rats.

Of course those boys on those boats had figured, "We'll be fighting in there in twenty-four hours." But they thought, "If we volunteer for paratroops, why it would take them a year or a year and a half to train us to make five practice jumps and then so many training jumps to learn their type of warfare." To them it looked like they would have about a year of relief. So they just loaded up by the thousands and came out of there. The rest of us celebrated.

After about three days on pass in Piccadilly Circus, Majewski had a premonition that something was wrong so he went back to camp. He checked in and Lieutenant John Reeder stepped up to him and said, "Max, you've got a telegram up at the message center. Do you want to know what it is?"

Max said, "No, I don't. I'll go up to the message center and read it myself."

So he went up and there was a telegram for him from the War Department. His wife had been killed in a car wreck about nine miles east of Phoenix, Arizona, at 9:30 in the evening. There was also a captain in the S-3, who had received a telegram that was almost word for word the same. His brother had been killed, nine miles east of such and such at 9:30 in the evening. If someone had just took the names off of the telegrams and handed them back to one another, they would have read exactly the same. So Max realized that his wife was out hanky-pankying with this captain's brother back in the United States. The Majewski's had a small child about two years old at that time. Max went downhill from there on and he never was the same after that.

FIRST SERGEANT RETURNS

Top Kick had jumped in right close to Colonel Sink and Uncle Charlie Chase, the bigwigs. He had just barely gotten on the ground when the Germans were on him with a machine gun and shot up his legs. They did not hit anything vital but he lost a lot of blood. The army had come in and picked him up on a stretcher, put him in an ambulance, and ran him back to a field hospital. So he was still in the hospital getting patched up when they gave us those seven-day passes. I had not seen him yet.

When my seven days was over, I still had a bunch of money and was not worn out or anything so I stayed and kept drinking. The next night I came back. I had overstayed and was AWOL. When I came in my Quonset hut I just walked over to my bunk and went to bed. The next morning a guy shook me and I looked at him. I did not know who he was. This barracks was full of guys I had never seen before. I had lost most of mine. They were all replacements who had just arrived from the States. This guy asked, "Are you Sergeant McNiece?"

I said, "Yeah."

He said, "They want to talk to you down at the orderly room."

I said, "I more or less suspected that they would. Yeah."

I went down to the orderly room. It was a horse stable and I knocked.

"Come in!"

I recognized Top Kick's voice the moment I heard it. I went through that door. That stable was just full of officers and noncoms who were replacements. I did not know a one of them. I stepped through that door and said, "Top Kick, it is good to see you back. How are you doing?"

He said, "I'll tell you something, Private McNiece." All those guys sitting around there were just ogling him, his purple heart, invasion ribbon, and all that crap he had on. "You have violated AR such-and-such and AR such-and-such and AR so-and-so." And he just kept reading those army regulations off. "If you had been in the regular army, do you know what would have happened to you?"

I said, "Let me tell you about the regular army, Boy! You're regular army aren't you Top?"

He said, "Yeah."

I said, "You were in twelve years before I got here, remember?"

He said, "Yeah."

I said, "I'm just a little ole peacetime soldier from Oklahoma who came over here to fight a war. For the twelve years that you were in here, I was working my ass off picking cotton and cutting broom corn and bailing hay and anything that I could find to do paying taxes to support you." (This was a lie. Nobody was taxed back in the thirties.) I continued, "You jumped in there the other day and you did not last thirty lousy-ass seconds. You never fired a shot. I jumped in there and fought for thirty-six days. I killed every German I could find and anyone standing close to him. If the United States was depending upon you regular army people to win this war, they'd be in a hell of a shape. So don't even mention regular army to me ever again."[56]

He said, "You get in your quarters, Private McNiece. You're under arrest of quarters."

I said, "Well, thank you. Why did you bother to call me in here to tell me that."

Long after that, we were down at Tom Young's ranch and sitting around chatting. Top said, "McNiece, you are a liar."

I kind of grinned, "I ain't a liar Top. I never told you a lie in my life. Every time I was caught at something I would just say yeah. I didn't lie to you."

He said, "Yes you did. Do you remember when you went AWOL there in England after the invasion."

I said, "Yeah."

He said, "You know, I ordered you to report to me there in the orderly room."

I said, "Yeah, I did."

He asked, "Do you remember what you said?"

I said, "Generally. I could not quote it verbatim. Yeah, I know what I said."

He asked, "Do you remember telling me that I jumped in there and did not last thirty seconds and never fired off a shot?"

I said, "Yeah. That wasn't a lie. That was the gospel truth."

He said, "No, it wasn't! When they put me on that stretcher, I throwed my Thompson over in the ditch. I took the clip out of it and just laid it right down beside me on the stretcher. When they got me up there at that aid station, I was laying around there waiting for treatment. You know those magazines are spring loaded. I flipped those rounds out of that thing. I just had seventeen rounds in there. I don't know what I shot at and I don't know what I hit but I fired off three rounds."

I said, "Okay, Top, after forty years, I'll apologize."

It was forty years after the damn war was over but it had just bugged him and bugged him and bugged him.

Virgil Smith

So they put me under arrest of quarters until they could decide what they were going to do with me. Someone told me, "There's been a guy been coming in here hunting you all the time for several days."

I said, "Who was it?"

They said, "I don't know. He's a lieutenant. He said he knew you real well."

Well, Virgil Smith did not make the Normandy jump. He came over as a replacement. So I was sitting out there on the back of my Quonset hut under arrest of quarters, drinking lemonade and beer. I looked up and saw this guy on a "put-put" [motor scooter] coming up the company street.

I thought, "There's ole Virgil." So I hollered, "Hey, Muscle Head!" He like to tore that street up trying to get that thing stopped.

This little ole Shorty Mihlan said, "You really goofed up there. That is a lieutenant."

I said, "That's a muscle head from Ponca City. I've wrassled with him and played football with him for years."

Ole Virgil jumped off and shook my hand. He said, "How long have you been gone? I've been coming over here for a week."

I said, "I just got back here yesterday."

He asked, "You want to go hunting? I've got a jeep. I imagine you've got plenty of ammunition and guns."

I said, "Oh yeah."

"Well," he said, "I'm running this jump school over here. We're getting in all these volunteers."

He said, "I'll tell you what. If you want to go hunting in the morning, I'll come by and pick you up. We'll then run back out to the base and pick up a couple loads of these volunteers and jump them. Then we'll go hunting."

I said, "Okay."

Well, he had orders to jump those guys one jump a day for five days to qualify them as paratroopers. If the weather was too bad to jump one day he would jump them twice the next. He was supposed to qualify every man who came through there in five days. So we went back over to the base and jumped these two loads of paratroopers. At about noon he said, "Let's go in and eat."

I said, "Okay."

So we went right into the officers' mess. Most of those officers did not know one or the other. If someone did not have rank showing, the others would not know what he was. Smitty was right ahead of me in line. This was on Sunday and everybody was in their pinkies[57] with their girlfriends. The officer-of-the-day came up and said, "You'll have to get out of those fatigues and get in your pinks and greens to eat in here."

Smitty said, "We're on work detail. We are not going to spend two or three hours changing clothes."

This officer looked over at me. There I was, a buck private, AWOL, and under arrest of quarters. I said, "That's right. We're not changing."

We just went right on through the line. Well, Virgil and I became separated. It was a new mess hall to me. I did not know the seating order of rank. When I saw a chair open, I just walked up and plopped down in it. I was right at the head of the table sitting with the majors and colonels. Virgil was down at the other end with the lieutenants. He knew that if it came down to a show, he was the guy they were going to sling a hammer at. So we ate and got out of there and then Smitty said, "McNiece, what the hell are you doing, trying to get us both put in Leavenworth?"

[Virgil Smith related his own version of the story:]

I heard Jake was back. He was in a Quonset Hut over there. I rode a little 'put-put' motor scooter over there. When I walked in somebody hollered attention. Jake said, "Aw hell fellas, don't pay any attention to him." They had their hands behind their backs. They had stolen the officers' beer. Jake was taking up initiation dues from these new people and he would then give them a picture of Eleanor Powell. I do not know what he was charging them. He had a roll of bills.

That first time I took him to the officers mess, Jake sat down where the higher ranks were. I was just a second lieutenant at that time and I introduced him as Major McNiece from the 506th. He just started visiting with the officers

> *before we were eating there at the table. You would have thought he was a general. Nothing bothered him at all. Jake got to where he liked eating over at the officers mess because it had better food than the enlisted had. I planned on spotting him just one time but he wanted to keep coming back. It was a wonder we did not get in trouble but nobody questioned it. We were getting a lot of replacement people in.*[58]

Well, we went ahead and had a good hunt that afternoon. Over in England, all the livestock or anything that is undomesticated on a lord's property belongs to him. They will not let anyone hunt or fish except the lords and ladies. So we just went out all over that country. We killed a whole jeep full of pheasants and rabbits, and those Bobbies on bicycles were trying to block us off but we never did stop for them.[59]

REPLACEMENTS

After Normandy, I just had the four of the original thirteen left: Jack Agnew, Joe Oleskiewicz, Chuck Plauda, and Jack Womer. George Baran had complications from his wound. Max Majewski was assigned to staff. I made Oleskiewicz corporal in charge of Peepnuts's squad. So we needed eight more to make up a battalion's demolition section. I got in eight more boys as replacements, six of whom came over as new recruits: a kid named Manny Freedman, William Coad, Clarence Furtaw, A. J. Bini, Richard "Dick the Raper" Graham, and Paul Zemedia. John Dewey and John "Dinty" Mohr[60] had been with us in the demolitions platoon before Normandy. Dewey was kind of an oddball. They put all the oddballs in my outfit. The others were in the unit for such a short time that I hardly got to know them.[61]

Virgil Smith claims that I charged admission to join the Filthy 13 which was not true. I did not say they had to come into it. There was not anything I could do about it. They just came in. I was always the financial advisor. I handled the money and bought the booze. We spent the rest of our time getting ready for the next jump.

4

SURVIVING HOLLAND

OPERATION MARKET GARDEN

General Miles Dempsey was the three-star general in command of the British Second Army. His army had been driving north up the major highway that ran through Eindhoven, Holland. He was stopped short along with the Americans after they ran out of supplies. When supplies became available Dempsey and General Frederick A. M. Browning decided on a plan to jump the 101st Airborne into Eindhoven to take all waterways and crossings and highways and the city itself, then pursue northward to the next fairly large-sized city, which was Veghel. The 82nd would jump in north of Veghel and take the bridges at Nijmegen. The British Red Devils would jump in the farthest north at Arnhem and take control of the bridge over the Rhine. Dempsey gave these units six days to accomplish their missions so his army could cross the Rhine River into Germany.

The reason that Operation Market Garden had even come into consideration was that "Sonny Boy" Browning, who was the head of all English airborne forces, was a little ashamed because the British airborne had accomplished nothing and gained neither fame nor recognition from Normandy. In the first place, he used a very light contingent of his paratroopers and they jumped in areas that were not even defended by Germans. Afterwards he wanted to gain the glory like that achieved by the 101st and 82nd. So he came up with this wild scheme of dropping an airborne carpet all the way to the Rhine.[1]

At that time we had complete control of the air. We had sent reconnaissance planes all over Holland. They took photographs of everything within the area of where we were going to attack.

A British major [Major Brian Urquhart] in charge of their intelligence section, I do not remember his name, told them, "Hey, this thing won't work. They've got a thousand tanks in there and no telling how many divisions." He had aerial photographs of them. He took them in and showed them to Sonny Boy Browning and Eisenhower and anybody else who had a say in it. He told them this thing was impossible but they refused to believe him.

Browning claimed they were all fake tanks. The Americans had done the same thing. They had set up plywood and plastic tanks, trucks, and armored cars and this and that all around the beach opposite Calais to trick the Germans into thinking that we would attack right across from the white cliffs of Dover. Browning maintained that that was what the Germans were doing over there. They kept talking about it and kept talking about it but Sonny Boy Browning wanted to go ahead. So he held his ground and went ahead with the plan. When we jumped in, why those German tanks were the real McCoys, Tigers and all that.

WHITE BREAD TROOPS

When we got ready for the invasion of Normandy they told us, "This is going to be a pushover. You are going to jump in against 'white bread troops.'"

Someone then asked, "What're white bread troops?"

They answered, "Well that's old men who are so old that they have lost their teeth. Having lost their teeth they can't eat anything but white bread. They are so decrepit that they are practically invalids. They are just about nearly dead. About all we are going to have to do is cover them up."

The briefers then went into the situation and said, "The success of an airborne invasion is the quickness and stealth of it. Jump in quickly and quietly. When you get on the ground kill all the Krauts with your knife, then seize and hold the high ground." This became our standing order.

When we jumped into Normandy, it turned out we had landed right in the middle of the German 6th Parachute Regiment. I believe we were outnumbered. We fought those bastards until we nearly went blind. When we came out of that deal and got ready to jump into Holland, this ole boy named Tech-5 David Marcus in the S-2 gave us our orientation. He said, "We'll be jumping into white bread troops. This is going to be a pushover. You won't even know you are in a war."

One of the replacements asked, "What are white bread troops?"

I said, "It's the 6th Parachute Regiment of the German Army! They are the meanest sons-of-bitches that you ever saw." I told them, "We have heard this time and time again. I bet you a fifth of whiskey against a pound note that we will be in contact with the 6th Parachute Regiment."

Marcus said, "Oh no, it's not going to be like that. Be sure and do it quietly."

I said, "You better have a grenade in each hand when you go through that door. Just throw it in any direction you can get loose from it."

That is the way it worked out. We never did come out of a door that we were not shooting or throwing grenades. In Holland we ran into the 6th Parachute Regiment up around Veghel. We would later run into them again at Bastogne. Everywhere we went they were there!

HOLLAND JUMP[2]
September 17, 1944

Depending upon the type of mission a paratroop unit had, one would select his weapon. Whatever we asked for, most of the time they would give it right to us. For Holland, I asked for a Thompson submachine gun because it would be a daylight jump and our first objective was taking Eindhoven. I anticipated street fighting nearly all the way through it. We would have to fight from room to room, house to house. It was a good-sized city. So I knew I was going to be slugging it out through there for five to ten miles. I would have much more firepower with a Thompson than an M1.[3]

The Holland jump was on a Sunday afternoon, about 3:00 on September 17. Unlike Normandy, we could see what we were doing. In Holland anyone could have assembled a stick of men in under a minute and a half. They could have assembled a company in probably ten minutes. So we were fighting in groups, which was pretty comforting when one is in behind the lines like that. Plauda, however, had trouble with his chute and did not jump in with us. He rode the plane back to England and I never saw him again during the war.[4]

The 101st landed at Son, Holland, which is about eight or ten miles north of Eindhoven. We landed in a square-mile area and man, there were tanks thirty yards in any direction we looked. In fact they were so stinking thick in there that they really could not maneuver. They were fully armed and went to work on us. We immediately went to work on them. It took us probably two hours to clean out that whole area. It was pretty rough. We lost a lot of people to those tanks but we got organized after we knocked all of them out. That is where Lefty McGee[5] was shot in the head. The 101st was really very, very lucky to come out of that fight.

Our regiment fought its way down to the bridge area. The demolition platoon fought as infantry in front of the Regimental CP which followed the lead battalion. The houses came right to the edge of the sidewalk. The sidewalks were maybe three feet wide and then there was a gutter. We fought our way down the street lying on our bellies working from building to building. As we were fighting down those streets, every door we passed would crack open and the Dutch would slide us out a big ole chunk of cheese, a chunk of black bread, or a glass of gin. From every door we passed they would feed us. Later that night the citizens of Eindhoven fed us a big meal just like a smorgasbord.[6]

There were three small bridges on the Eindhoven Canal about a block apart on the northern outskirts of Eindhoven. We captured them, then attacked right down the gut of Eindhoven and saved the main bridge that went over the Wilhelmina Canal. The Wilhelmina Canal ran right along the outskirts of Eindhoven.

We took that main bridge intact and everything around it. We found and dismantled the charges on the bridges. The bridges had been wired for demolition but fortunately they had not been manned. We took the city of Eindhoven within thirty-six hours. We had her, boy, locked down knuckles and bolts and were working on clearing the highway.

We then waited there for the British Second Army to move on up. It was probably down the road another fifteen or twenty miles. They opened a corridor and came on up. They reached Eindhoven on the second day and entered on the third. I had never seen anything like it. The British had trucks, called lorries, loaded with ammunition and gasoline and everything just bumper-to-bumper up and down those roads. That same day Kraut planes flew in there and hit one of them, which caused a chain reaction of explosions.

After the British reached Eindhoven, they turned the 101st loose and sent it right on up along the highways to push the Krauts back and establish a stronghold. Our division was supposed to clear the highway up to Veghel for a width of about two and a half miles on both sides, depending upon the terrain. Meanwhile they left my demolition platoon in Eindhoven to guard the three bridges. Lieutenant Edward Haley had been assigned to my section to replace Lieutenant Mellen but he was pulled away the first day to fill in for other officers who were killed. I never had an officer over my section after that. Neither did I see much of my platoon leader, Shrabel Williams, throughout Holland. He was also needed elsewhere.

Regimental Headquarters Company had a heavy weapons platoon that we could draw from depending on the mission assigned. In Holland, they gave me one bazooka team to hold the bridge with. The company also gave Myers and Davidson a bazooka team each and all three of us were issued thirty-caliber machine guns.

So I was left in Eindhoven along with the two other demolition-saboteur sticks to guard three bridges. Eight or ten German tanks were off about a hundred and fifty yards north of us in a heavily wooded area where we could see them but they would not fire at us. We had knocked out so many tanks that they were pretty well depleted in that area. They just waited for the opportunity to come on in. We just sat there watching them. The rest of the division had moved further on up the highway to secure the small bridges and root out the Krauts that were close enough to threaten the road from either side. As the British end moved on up, why they would just occupy all the space the paratroopers had taken. We stayed on the bridges for two more days.

APPLES AND PEARS

We had very little Allied bombing accompanying our jump. We had some P-38s fly escort but none of the livestock was killed like in Normandy. We were pretty poorly supplied with food. I had not taken any K rations in on this jump either. I still thought I would find some food in there.

Our three bridges were out in the country and all we had to eat was what we could get off of the orchards. They had a lot of apples and pears but they were not ripe. Every time we would pass a tree we would pick us a piece of fruit, eat it and see if it was any different than what we had been living off for the last two or three days. It got to where every time someone handed us a pear or an apple to eat we could identify which tree it came off of because we had tried it a dozen times.

GERMAN BOMBING

8:45 P.M., September 19, 1944

Well, we got beat up pretty bad down there. Our platoon had a lieutenant named Eugene Dance. He and I were sitting there talking when here came four Messerschmitts right up the canal.

He said, "Look, that plane's on fire." He could see parachute flares coming out of it. Of course they looked like little balls of fire.

I said, "He isn't on fire. He's going to give us a light up job here. He's going to light this place up like Christmas. Them three tailing him will bomb these bridges." So I said, "Let's get out of here." I had Paul Zemedia and "Ink" Ellefson with a bazooka up on the second floor. I hollered at the guys and told them to come on out of those houses.

This lieutenant said, "Everybody stay where you are! We've got orders to guard these bridges against those tanks."

I said, "Lieutenant, you don't believe for a minute those tanks are going to come in under their own bombs!"

He said, "We've got orders to hold these bridges. That's what we are going to do."

I again hollered back at the boys, "You better get out of there, if you want out! They are going to bomb us here in about a minute."

He said, "I'll court-martial any man in the morning who leaves his position."

I kind of grinned, "You won't be here in the morning if you stay on these bridges." So I yelled, "All you guys who want out of there come on out now! I'm leaving. We'll get out of here about a block from this place and find cover." So we did.

The lieutenant went on down to the second bridge where Myers's section was. Davidson also came over. Bill Myers and Jim Davidson were trying to get him to quit and withdraw to some shelter. Dance was sticking to his ground. Those bombs that came in blew up Myers's bridge and killed both of those sergeants.[7]

It also busted up a lot of other guys. Tom Young and Steve Kovacs had been standing there at the same time. Tom Young was thrown up against a building. He was later evacuated back to the United States.[8]

Steve later told me, "Jake, do you remember how they always told you to take care of your rifle? Don't get separated from your instrument. Keep it within reach. Eat with it. Sleep with it."

I said, "Yeah."

He said, "Jake, when that bomb dropped down there, it picked me up and blew me across the street through a plate glass window and over to the wall. It rattled me. I kind of lost consciousness, but when I came to my senses, I guess thirty to forty-five seconds later, I still had that M1 in my hand!"

I said, "No kidding."

He said, "Jake, I swear it is the truth. I held onto that thing all the time the bomb blew me across the street through the plate glass window and up against the wall!"

The other bridges remained standing. Dance was only with us one day on that bridge before they needed him somewhere else. I later asked Top Kick Miller where that lieutenant came from. He told me,

"He transferred in from the Rangers."

I said, "You'd better send him back there before he gets more of our men killed."[9]

DEAD MAN'S COFFEE

Sergeant Jim Davidson was a real character. He had been a coal miner and an alcoholic before he came in the army. He and his wife had a lot of problems. They had two or three children and lived in the same town that her mother and dad did. When Jim would go out on those big drunks, she would get mad, pack up the clothes and kids and go home. They had been going through this for quite a while and then Jim tried to quit drinking. He worked for three or four hours overtime there one day. Well, he came home and she was gone. He guessed she evidently thought that he was out on another big binge.

He became infuriated to think that she had run off and taken the kids with her so he started going all through the house. All her dress clothes were all hanging in the closet. He ran into the room, got his knife and cut and slashed everything that was hanging there. Then he remembered that there was a quart of buttermilk in the ice box. He thought, "I might have missed something that she could salvage." He went back in and got that quart of buttermilk and poured it all over them. Then he started cleaning and dressing up to go out and party. When he stepped out, there was a note on the front door that read, "Jim, I'm going to shop a little bit and do this and that and I'll be back at such and such a time."

He said, "It took me nearly a year to replace her clothes."

Well, I liked coffee very much and so did Jim Davidson. In a day's K rations they had these little bitty packets of instant coffee for breakfast. For lunch the rations had a pack of instant lemonade and some more crap. Then for supper, it had cocoa mix. So it amounted that a person only received one cup of coffee a day.

They came in white tin foil that was flat and square. One could carry them real easily in the top of his boot along the side of the calf of the leg and ankle. It would keep them dry and that way they would always be easy to get to even if wounded.

After a pretty hot firefight when we could move around, Davidson and I would start looking for dead paratroopers. We would grab our trench knives and rip their bootlaces open to get at their coffee. If a guy was not yet dead but it was very obvious he was dying, we would take his coffee, too. So Jim and I had coffee all the time. This one cup a day stuff was ridiculous. We had plenty of coffee and some to spare.

We would sit down to make us a cup of coffee and everybody would be trying to drink that cocoa or lemonade but could not swallow it. We would jokingly ask, "Would you like a cup of coffee?"

They would answer, "We don't want any of that damn coffee." They knew where we were getting it.

Ole Jim did not know how hot a canteen cup could get. That cup would burn his tongue. We would be sitting around there drinking that coffee with everybody watching us and he would give a blow on that coffee and then say, "Lordy, Lordy! This is good coffee."

Years later, one of the guys asked me what was the most disappointing thing that ever happened to me or affected me the most during the war.

I said, "I guess it was that stinking bombing there at Eindhoven."

He asked, "You weren't even touched, were you?"

I said, "No, I wasn't, not by the bomb. It was when we went to help the guys who had been hit. There was Sergeant Davidson out there without any arms and legs, just elbows and so forth. I ran over to him to get his coffee but I never could find his legs. They had been blown out of the area. I imagine that was the most disappointing thing that ever happened to me. I'll bet he had two hundred of those instant coffee packets in his boots."

AMBUSH ON THE WAY TO VEGHEL[10]

September 22, 1944

After guarding the bridges for about five days, our division sent orders for us to move on up and join our original outfit since the British had secured the city. They told us to come on up and we did.

We had been very successful with our mission. Although we had only lost two men killed, we had a lot busted up. I was the only section sergeant left out of the three sections. Davidson and Myers had both been killed by the same bomb. Many of those wounded were corporals. The new platoon sergeant, Earl Boegerhausen, had survived only to be wounded later. We really did not have much sergeant material left. The division farmed the rest of the platoon out through Regimental Headquarters Company. They told me to requisition a truck to bring the platoon on up, so I picked out a German truck that had been left behind. Lieutenant Haley had been left in charge of a rear detail and also left with us.[11]

About 9:00 in the morning we loaded up and drove on up the highway. We anticipated that we would probably contact the division at Veghel, which was about twenty-five or thirty miles to the north. This was winter, the latter part of September. It was an open truck and cold as ever.[12]

The national drink in Holland is gin. Every Dutch man in Eindhoven was so happy to be liberated that he would give a paratrooper any amount of gin he wanted and they also had schnapps and cognac. Every door we came to someone would hand us a bottle. We were all drinking and in various stages of getting drunk. We were just happy and singing and drinking and living it up. We passed British troops all along the road. We just continued driving along with no fear of enemy resistance or attack.

The 101st had taken Veghel and secured it. Then they got orders to push on up the road to join the 82nd. The 82nd was supposed to have jumped in right close to Veghel and clear the road on up to Nijmegen where they would take the bridges and waterways and then continue north toward the city of Arnhem. This they did.

When the 101st moved up, the British took over what they left but all the British did was drink tea! They sat there making tea all day long and would not fight. Unknown to us, those Germans had come back in from the north and pushed the English out and retook Veghel. The British line ended only a few miles short of the town and Veghel was a pretty good-sized town. The main thoroughfare was about four or five blocks long.

I guess those Krauts did not mind letting a German truck come up that highway but they finally figured out it was a truck load of drunk paratroopers. They let us drive right up into the middle of that town, then they opened up on us from every direction. Boy, they fired at us from every window and door.[13]

There was one boy in our platoon named Winsor "Ink" Ellefson, who did not drink or gamble. He was a sightseer. He would go visit libraries and monuments and all that. He was not drinking but was in a sock-type sleeping bag that zipped clear up to his chin. I do not know where he stole it because it was not issued to paratroopers. Anyway, he was sitting right beside me. We had the side seats running the full length of the bed with a banister on it.

When the Krauts fired into us why, I grabbed the side rail and threw myself over into the gutter. Boy, we bailed out of that truck. We were right downtown. I then thought the safest place in the world was right in that building with them. I just raked the building in front of me with my Thompson submachine gun then picked out a door that I thought I could crash through to get in with the Germans. By the time I made one arc with that Tommy gun, Ink Ellefson was down in that gutter with me, still in that sack, and he was tearing it apart, boy, just trying to get out it.

The sidewalks were not very wide and the Krauts were firing out of every window and door along there. I thought all I could do was rake that wall and go through the first opening I could find. After I raked it one time and backed them off from the window, I jumped right in there with them. From then on we just fought from house to house, building to building. We just pushed and pushed and fought right up that street.

In door-to-door street fighting we would usually just throw in a hand grenade, then whip in there and kill everything as quickly as we could. We had to crawl in there on our hands and knees just spraying. Those hand grenades would stir up so much smoke and dust in those old houses, just like an Oklahoma sandstorm. We could not see. We very rarely had two men go in together like the army does today. It was usually just one guy at a time. A guy could do it pretty quick with a Thompson submachine gun. Then the next guys would move up. There were anywhere from one or two on up to six Germans in a room. The most I ran into personally were three. They were more frightened of us. They feared paratroopers. After Normandy they called us the "Big Pocket Butchers."

Every time that I would clean out a bunch, the other guys would close up on me. Another or two would hop on up ahead and we would just leap-frog on up through town. We used hand signals an awful lot. We were in close proximity to one another. We would not crowd up enough to where the Germans could ever get us with a grenade. If I was having trouble in the house I was in, then another group would sweep around me and go in it. We were attacking both sides of the street at once, moving as a group. If a bunch were killed, then one or two of our guys would go over there and fill in. We worked our way toward the edge of town.

I entered one building where furniture was made and stuff and found a hen's nest with six eggs in it. Boy, eggs were hard to come by over there. I thought, "I don't know how in the world I'll ever get out of here with these eggs intact but I'm not going to leave them. I'm going to take them with me."

I put those suckers in my thigh pockets and grabbed an old newspaper or magazine and stuffed it in for padding. Every time I had to hit the ground, I would roll over on one side. I got clear out of that town and into this coverage and only broke one of those eggs. I got out of there with five good eggs!

We wanted to escape out the north end of town to the west. When we reached the edge of town an hour and a half later, the Germans had about ten tanks on that side of town. We then started fighting these tanks and knocking them out as soon as they started working on us. TNT was ideal for blowing off tracks. A grenade would also take a tank's track off. If you get one track off, that is all you need. That is all we wanted to do was immobilize them. You got someone to set the TNT or grenade down on the track then someone else could kill the tank with a flamethrower. I guess we knocked out three or four of those tanks.[14]

Three of us had to run about forty yards to get to a defiladed area, a big drainage ditch there. There was brush out there about midway and the three of us made it to it. These tanks did not know what we were doing. When they saw three men charge out of a building still firing, they were not very anxious to go in where we might hit them with a grenade. Those German tanks were not going to come out of that town except if immediately attacked.

We got down into this little clump of bushes and I could see the ditch. It was not twenty-five yards from us. It was probably five or six feet deep and twenty feet wide. I told the other two boys, "If we come out of here firing everything in the world we've got, some of us or all of us or none of us might get to that ditch, but if we stay here we are dead ducks. So let's get with it. Get everything ready. We're going."

Stanley Spiewack and this kid, Herb Pierce, shook their heads that they were not going. I pointed my Thompson down at their bellies and said, "I'd rather kill you than let them Germans do it. If we stay here, we're dead ducks. You get going now or you're here forever."

Boy, they turned white as a sheet looking down there at that Thompson. They picked their weapons up and ran firing in every direction just spraying. All three of us made it into that ditch.

Herb asked, "Would you have killed me back there?"

I said, "I guess I would."

He said, "Well, you convinced me you would have, because if you had not, I would have stayed right there until I got killed."

Herb had fought all the way through Normandy and Holland. He was not a coward, just a kid. Our company had started with eight seventeen-year-olds back there in Georgia and by then all but Herb were dead.[15]

When I was making a run to get into that main ditch, I saw a man's trunk, just legs and half of his guts, just laying there right next to the shoulder of the road. In all those occupied countries, the German army had taken the civilians and had them dig big standing foxholes. They were about two by three feet square and six feet deep all along those main travel roads. So whenever the Germans were strafed or bombed in a convoy all the people could get out of the tanks or vehicles and crawl down in those holes. They had them all along there. Then if a guy could ever make it to the ditch, he would have it made.

Truck Horse Johnson was in one of those foxholes. Of course I had no idea which one of them that body trunk belonged to. Everybody was heading in the same general direction toward that big ditch. The biggest part of our platoon finally made it to that ditch. When I took a head count, Joe Oleskiewicz and two or three others were missing. Manny Freedman and Clarence Furtaw had been wounded in the fight.

A very good friend of mine, Joe Oleskiewicz was one of the nicest and finest young kids that I had ever met. He was one of the original Filthy 13. He was the one I was more interested in than the rest. I was really fond of Joe. I asked if anyone knew what had happened to him. They said no they did not. Nobody knew anything, or so I was told.

When we came out of Holland and returned to France, I left the outfit for the Pathfinders. I later ran into the outfit again while they were in Bastogne. I asked everybody again, "Do you know what happened to Joe? Is he carried missing in action or killed in action or POW? Have you got anything?" They always said no. So every time I was around Regimental Headquarters I would inquire about Joe. I asked Top Kick, "Are you carrying him missing in action or killed in action? What's his disposition?"

He would answer, "We've just got him listed, Jake, as missing in action."

I never learned what happened to him until the war was over.[16]

We had just gone into that ditch when I heard three rounds of mortar coming in. I hit the ground. Lieutenant Haley was standing nearby. He fell right in there beside us and hit the ground just like a pancake.

As he tried to get up, he asked, "What was that?"

I said, "It was three rounds of mortar. You better get your head down. There'll be three more coming right in on them."

Sure enough they threw three more in on us. When it was over we stood up. Haley was as skinny as a rail. I will bet he was six feet tall and did not weigh a hundred and forty pounds. He had on one of those new field jackets and I noticed his coattail was all torn to pieces.

I said, "Let me check you here, boy."

I will bet from six inches below his crotch clear on up halfway to his navel, fifty pieces of shrapnel had just shredded that uniform off of him but he was not touched. He had not bled a drop.[17]

After that, it did not take us five minutes to get together and decide what to do. Our lines were driving up the road toward the Rhine River. We followed that ditch for nearly a mile, then we took advantage of the terrain. We hugged the trees for another four to five more miles until we met up with, I think, G Company. I asked where

Regimental Headquarters Company was and they directed me to Colonel Sink or someone else [Lt. Colonel Charlie Chase]. His CP was following the main road. The regiment had halted trying to get organized. Colonel Sink was going to attack up the road in the morning. My platoon was put on perimeter defense for the night.

Push Out Of Veghel[18]

September 25, 1944

The next day our division pushed up the road. The 506th pushed up the main road with the 502nd on the left flank and the 501st on the right. We were supposed to clear out a five-mile width along the road from Veghel.

That morning when we assembled, Top Kick walked up to me and asked, "Have you got any snuff?" Top Kick dipped that gal tobacco from down in the South.

I said, "Yeah, I've got snuff."

He said, "I'm plumb out. Could I get a dip from you?"

I said, "You bet." So I handed him some Copenhagen. "I've got some more but take a dip out of this and we'll get together later in the day. It is a whole lot stouter than that gal tobacco that you've been dipping around here." I knew it was a lot stronger because I had also started out on snuff. My mother dipped snuff when I was a kid and then I started dipping Copenhagen since it was so much stouter. I told him, "Take a little pinch of it and put it in the back of your mouth, Top Kick."

He looked at me and asked, "Why, is this all you've got?"

I said, "Oh no. I've got plenty of it. I don't care what you take. I'm just telling you it is a lot different than that gal tobacco but go ahead and pack your head, boy. Load up."

So he just crammed it in and he looked just like a chipmunk running around with a coconut in his cheek. So we pushed out that afternoon. I was on the left flank as point with a demolition squad. Of course Colonel Sink, First Sergeant, and Uncle Charlie Chase were right in the middle of the company following right along behind us.

By the middle of the afternoon, we began to push in toward the center because of the defilation in the area. When I got in pretty close to ole Top Kick, well I glanced over to see if I could possibly give him another dip. He was down on his hands and knees in that ditch just puking his guts out. Others could hear him retching for ten yards from where I was. So I did not even try to give him another dip of snuff. I just moved on.

We took in fairly light fire everywhere we went. The Germans had both sides of the road. We hit two or three small concentrated fires during that day. Otherwise we were just picking up sniper and random fire all day long.

Later I saw a movement over in the weeds in a bar ditch.[19] It was a blue color, kind of like the overcoats those Krauts wore. So I signaled the column to hold up while I kept proceeding toward this ditch, right on up to the road. I just casually switched my Tommy gun to where it would be pointing to the right and I would be ready to squeeze her off. I guess I got up to within twenty feet, when I saw a great big blob of gray hair. I thought, "That's an old woman."

I kept trying to locate other bodies or soldiers in a perimeter where if any of us opened up, we would not wipe each other out. I kept walking and analyzing this thing. She was alone. Then I motioned everybody on the alert. I walked on up to this lady.

Where we were pushing these Germans back through the countryside, all the civilians that could get out would leave. They would either come on in our direction or retreat to the sides. She must have been in her eighties. She reminded me of my mother so much. She could not speak any English. I had it translated, "Have you been wounded?" I could not see any blood.

She said, "No."

I said, "Pass the word back to a medic somewhere to be sure and look this woman over as they come through." Then I just motioned the others to follow. Outside of the manual we did not have many hand signals. We made them up as situations came up rather than sit down and figure them out ahead.

We hit some pretty concentrated fire there just before it got dark. That was where we stopped. Top Kick was assigning different ones of us as outposts for the defense. So I pulled out my Copenhagen and handed it over to him. I said, "Load up there, Top."

He took a pinch of it and put it in the back of his mouth.

I said, "Go ahead, pack up. I'll get one of these cans out of my musset bag in a minute."

He said, "Yeah, you dirty rat. I saw you today laughing your ass off when your Copenhagen had me down in the ditch puking my guts out. I think I'll just take a little."

From then on he started dipping Copenhagen and he never quit. He kept it up until his dying day. I never saw Top with that stuff out of his mouth.

That evening, Colonel Sink picked out a big, two-story, rural farm house where he wanted to make his CP for the night. He told Lieutenant Sterling Horner to select two or three demolitions men to go in there and get it cleaned out of booby traps and mines so he could get a good night's sleep. They sent me and two more boys in there. We went all through and checked everything. I found six half-gallons of canned fruit and a bottle of schnapps and I picked up a few potatoes and onions. Well, when we finished all the looting, we went back to the door where Lieutenant Horner stood.

I said, "Okay, that place is as clean as a pin. You all can go in there and get you a good night's sleep."

He asked, "What is in there to eat or drink?"

I said, "Nothing," which was the truth. It was all in my jacket. I looked like I weighed three hundred pounds.

He hit me with the butt of his Tommy gun in the gut and it just rattled. He asked, "What's that? What've you got in there?"

I said, "I've got six half-gallons of canned fruit. I've got a bottle of cognac. I've got a pocket full of onions and potatoes."

He asked, "What's the Colonel going to eat if there is nothing in there?"

I said, "He had the opportunity and privilege of going in there and getting it to start with. His prerogative is now ended. This is mine. I'm going to be feeding this to my men."

He said, "Well, I want some of it."

I said, "You know where the perimeter defense of my squad is don't you?"

He answered, "Yeah."

I said, "Well, you be out there in about five minutes and you can share with us. I'm not giving you anything nor the colonel. If you want some of this, come on out and share alike. We'll be eating in about five minutes."

He said, "Okay," but he never did come out to our perimeter defense.[20]

I joined my group out there on the perimeter. I called the squad in because it was dark. I knew the Germans were not about to attack us. We were just going to be in a holding position until daybreak. So I showed them the canned fruit and other food that I had. We dug into it and started eating.

The ground was snow-covered and kind of slushy. So we were all sitting around there in a circle eating this stuff with our knees and toes on the ground and rump on our heels to stay off of that water and snow. Not twenty minutes after I had invited Horner out to eat with us, Dick Graham said, "Jake, I'm hit." The Germans were just firing at random. It was just harassment fire but they hit ole Graham in the butt.

I asked, "Pretty hard?"

He said, "Well, it's hurting."

I said, "Well, come on over here and let me look at you."

He came over there. The way he had been sitting, the left side of his body was toward the incoming fire. When that bullet hit his rump, it made an entry there and went almost clear through it. Instead of digging in it just pressed that meat down until it got over the crack of his butt. It had pressed down so much the other meat was sticking out.

I looked at it and said, "Dinty Mohr, take your trench knife and cut that out of him and put a bunch of sulfur powder on it. Give him some penicillin." Graham kind of flinched up when I told Mohr to take that trench knife and cut that bullet out of his butt.

So Mohr was looking at it. He was a big ole stout country boy. He said, "Why, I think I can punch that out with my finger."

He had that big meaty finger in there and just followed that bullet and pushed it out through the skin. It and a piece of meat just plopped down there on the snow. A big bunch of blood also came out. So they sent him back to the rear and doctored him up and gave him this and that. Graham never forgot about it.

Graham and Dinty Mohr got together at our house about fifty-two years after the war. Dinty was standing there talking with Graham and then started pointing that same finger at him. Graham said, "If you point that finger at me you lousy rat, I will break your arm clear off of you!"

The second day we held where we were and just sent out patrols. The Germans had retreated out of the area. My platoon remained on the perimeter defense around the Regimental Headquarters. We stayed in the area for a few more days.[21]

Push on to the Rhine

Our initial objective had been to take the waterways and bridges and capture Eindhoven. They gave us six days to do it and we did it in thirty-six hours. The 82nd had started dropping just fifteen miles south of Nijmegen. They had taken the highway on up to Nijmegen and secured all the waterways and about ten miles past it with a width of five miles that straddled the highway. That was their initial objective.

But each time that we turned a piece of captured territory over to the British, the Germans would come back in and kick them out. We would then have to go back in and retake it. It was just like a yo-yo all up and down there. After we cleared the road, we finally reached the Rhine. When we got on up there, General Dempsey ordered Taylor to start taking that area to the left of the 82nd.

The British Red Devils and a Polish Brigade had jumped in outside of Arnhem. The bulk of them never did get to the bridge. Only one battalion reached the bridge and they were nearly all killed or captured. The rest of the division and brigade came out of there with about two thousand men out of about eleven thousand. It was totally disastrous, a total farce. They never took nor held an inch of ground all the time they were in there. Had they dropped the 101st or 82nd in there, we would have taken those bridges. We may have lost a lot of men but we would have taken the bridges.[22]

So after they evacuated Arnhem, Dempsey just sent the 101st right on up to the Rhine next to the 82nd. Both General Taylor and General Gavin asked to be relieved after they had cleared their roads and secured the bridges. Dempsey was a three-star general and outranked every officer we had. So he kept us there and used paratroopers up there just as shock troops. We fought up there until two days after Thanksgiving.[23]

THE ISLAND[24]

October 2, 1944

Our rations were terrible. Since we were assigned to the British Second Army, they would pick up all our American rations. The Airborne did not have any logistical transportation. The British would bring our rations in and eat them, then give us the damned mutton and stuff. We could hardly even swallow it.

There was a jam factory about halfway between Nijmegen and Arnhem, about ten miles west of the highway. It was a huge, huge, huge thing. That is fruit country up in there. I think G or H Company attacked that factory which was pretty lightly defended. They took that thing. Just a squad of them would go back and forth in there to carry out all that jelly. They went in there anytime they wanted. They hauled it out of there by the trucks full and then dispersed it around to the rest of us. The Germans did not want to defend it because they did not want to tie up with a squad of paratroopers. The factory did not have any military importance.

GENERAL HIGGINS[25]

General Jerry Higgins, the assistant division commander, wanted to pass some information to Colonel Sink. Virgil Smith by then had become his aide and they drove up there in a jeep. When General Higgins went in, Virgil told the general that he wanted to wait outside. He knew I was in the area so he asked around for me. I came over and met with him. We were talking when General Higgins came out and walked up to us. Virgil said, "I would like you to meet a friend of mine." I had not bathed nor washed since the operation began. I was filthy. He shook my hand and we talked for a while.

They got in their jeep and drove back down the road. After a couple of miles General Higgins laughed and asked Virgil, "Where in the hell did you ever meet a friend like that?"

The next day my section was farmed out to C Company. Three or four days later we reached the levy which bordered the Rhine River.

[Virgil Smith described the meeting this way:[26]]

Germans had the island mined. There was this little town [probably Opheusden] and we had evacuated it. Arnhem was just on the other side of the river. The Germans had all the high ground. Jake had been out with a patrol that night on this island and the Germans had chased him all around. The next morning Jake returned to headquarters.

General Higgins went to see Colonel Sink. I told the general's driver I was going into this barn that was attached right to this house to find old Jake and if the general came out to come and get me. So I went in and woke Jake up. He had that stale cognac on his breath. He chewed that Copenhagen and it had stained his chin. He had not shaved. He was just as filthy as he could be. His hands were dirty. So he got up and we went outside. While we were standing there talking the general came out so I introduced him, "Sir, I would like for you to meet a friend of mine, Jake McNiece from Ponca City, where we grew up and played football together."

Jake had a wad of chew in his mouth. He just shifted that chew to the side of his mouth and stuck out that grimy paw. He said, "Glad to meet you, General."

We got in the jeep and went on down the road. We got about a half a mile down the road and General Higgins just started laughing. I asked, "What's the matter?"

He said, "Smitty, you sure know some characters."

A DISASTER COMPANY

In a regiment they always have one company that will be a disaster company. In mission after mission, it will be wiped out and suffer twice or three times as many casualties as the companies around it. Of course there is a reason for this. When they jump in on the first mission, why half or more of their officers and NCOs are killed. So they are replaced with green troops. So the company then has green lieutenants and green NCOs overseeing green troops that do not even know one another. The company enters their second combat in worse shape than it did the first one. They will just get killed right down again. So the losses begin to telescope. In the 506th, the disaster company was C Company. They were killed down to twenty men in Normandy.

In Holland, C Company had not been in there fifteen days until they had been killed out to twenty-six men. They had lost every officer they had except this Lieutenant Albert H. Hassenzahl. Lieuntenant Lucian H. Whitehead[27] was attached to them and he was the primary officer that I dealt with. I had maybe eight men left so they sent me up and attached me to C Company. The regiment would have done anything in the world they could to have killed my ass.[28]

I fought up there with Lieutenant Whitehead for the rest of the campaign, until they just about had to rebuild the company. It was a hard-luck outfit but Whitehead and I had developed a pretty close relationship over a period of forty-five days.

OP DUTY[29]

We did not have enough men to man a proper defense except for outposts. C Company had a strip of land from the Rhine River back to our main perimeter of defense. We positioned our outposts along that river anywhere from a hundred to a hundred and fifty yards apart. We did not have enough people to offer any resistance unless a little ole enemy squad would come by with ten or twelve men in it. If a patrol of two or three squads or platoon-size would come through, then our OPs did not even fool with them. They let them go on by and sent word back to the CP. We had a lot of telephones out there and the OPs would call Whitehead or Hassenzahl and say, "A forty-man patrol just passed us." He would then notify anyone behind us who might be concerned with the German patrol. They would gather up enough forces needed to knock their asses off. We let the Germans come and go as long as they did not directly threaten us.[30]

I believe Sergeant Campiello came in as a replacement to C Company after Normandy. I called him "Guinea" because he was an Italian. This Guinea was a small fellow, shorter than I was. He was a real soldier. Boy, he never hesitated. There were German patrols just flooding back through there all the time and Guinea never backed down from anything.

Well, Guinea would take off two trips a night and I would take two trips a night, eight-hour shifts, and check everyone of those outposts. We would go back and forth between those boys in the foxholes and find out what was happening as to what had come through, their size, and direction of movement. Then we would walk back and feed all this to the company commander in the CP.

I had this kid named Robert Reeves. He and another guy were out there in a foxhole one rainy night. Man, it was raining so hard that you could not see your hand in front of you. Reeves heard a noise. It was about the time that me or Guinea were supposed to come through and he thought we had missed his location.

There was a ditch where this noise was coming from. He crawled over to it and looked over in that ditch and there was this German lying there looking back up at him, eyeball-to-eyeball. Reeves did not even have his gun. He had left it over in his foxhole. He said that this German was not making a move, just looking at him.

Of course, Reeves thought, "I've got to get me a gun." He ran back to get his gun and came back but never did find that German again. He was the only German out there.

Lieutenant Hassenzahl was the son of a cop up there in Toledo. He was convinced the whole time that the only thing the Germans really wanted to do was attack his CP.

I had to go in there and make a report one morning about 10:00 and it was raining. I walked up and tried to open the front door but could not. Well, I turned and went around to the side of the house. Just before I got to the corner I heard someone coming. I just took a stance there and laid that Thompson on whoever it was. It was Hassenzahl. When he rounded that corner, he came to a screeching halt and asked, "Are you a demolition man?"

I said, "Yes I am."

He said, "You like to have scared me to death. I heard you at the front door and I ran out the back door. By then I was running right into you."

We checked these OPs for about ten days and then I reported in to Lieutenant Whitehead. He said that there were still British Red Devils and Polocks in homes and places being protected by Dutch people who were disgusted with the war. They had sixty of them in one spot over there on the other side of the river and Dempsey wanted to get them out if he could.[31]

Whitehead also said that we had contact with them all the time through Dutch civilians. One of them named Pete joined the paratroopers the minute we got on the ground. He was coordinating the communication between the British and the Americans and the people who were hiding them up over there. He was handling the whole show. Lieutenant Whitehead asked me to go out with him and look the situation over.

Whitehead said, "The British engineers will go over there and get them. Let's go up here on this dike and look this over." He then said, "This whole river bank is mined. What we are going to have to do is get some of you demolition boys out in there and clear a path through it. When they get ready to rescue them, you'll have to take them out through there. You will not cross over. We don't know when it will be."

The Germans had mined and booby trapped all the ground on the south side of the river. The British had a bunch of those rubber dinghies that they used with the engineers, but they were scared to go down through the minefield. The British did not know how to negotiate it.

It was pretty obvious where I wanted to make the cut. When clearing a minefield for quick passage, you want to stay pretty close to the trees because nobody enjoys digging through roots to bury a land mine. This provides some leeway where there are no mines. You just whip right through it and extend the border out to the width that you desire. I imagined those dinghies were six feet wide. From there we went back to Whitehead's CP. Whitehead assured the British engineers that he had the assets to clear the minefield.

Of course those Krauts knew where the mines were. I would watch their asses. If I saw a patrol coming past an OP quite often, I knew the mines were not in that area. Once in a while I would hear them set off a mine. We got to know that patrols were coming through one area more than any other. So Jack Agnew and I picked an area we thought had no mines.

We pulled back from the area where we wanted to clear the minefield so the Germans would not see any big troop movements. Brock was the only town in that area so it was neccessary to hold it in order to evacuate the trapped paratroopers.

C Company moved down into Brock and took up residence there, but we really never had control of it at any time. C Company only had about two squads left. I had Agnew, Marquez, Womer, Dinty Mohr, Furtaw, Bini, Dewey, Coad, and Ink Ellefson. I had picked up Nathan Sieger from somewhere. I called him "Cigar." He had not jumped with us in Holland.

We occupied Brock along with the Germans. Brock was only about a mile and a half from the Rhine River. It was the northernmost outpost we had. It would have been pretty advantageous for the Germans to have held that town but we needed it. We waited in Brock while the British coordinated the evacuation.[32]

CREAM FOR SCHNAPPS

We were up in Brock for about a week and a half or two weeks. This was late in the campaign and we were so short of men that we really could not mount an offensive. We were just holding that town to keep the Germans from taking full possession of it. There was some real high ground up there that they could have used to advantage over our cover. So we really were not trying to take this town. We were just trying to hold it and all the civilians had left.

We had occupied this little ole town just like a checkerboard. A squad of paratroopers would occupy one block where they would make their headquarters. A block or two up the street there would be a bunch of Germans, then there would be another set of paratroopers and then Germans just scattered all over. We had three CPs in there. I had one, Lieutenant Whitehead had one, and I think another sergeant had one.

It was just like checkers. The whole town of Brock was intermingled with paratroopers and Germans and each one was trying to kill the other. We would only fight at night. During the day we would listen for noises or watch for smoke or movements or anything that would give us a location of the Germans. Then we would attack them as soon as it got dark.

We would fight all night, then we would all meet back at our place just before daybreak. When we did, why, we were looting houses, potatoes, canned fruit, and canned vegetables. We would find onions once in a while. So we were eating like kings back at my place. I had even butchered a cow and a hog.

When civilians vacate a city or an area or something, they usually release their livestock so they can forage. They had turned all these cattle and hogs and everything they had loose in this little ole town of Brock. I soon had them hanging up. It was cold up there in late October and the meat stayed fresh. Everyone just cooked for themselves. If a guy wanted a steak or if he wanted a neck bone he just cut himself off a piece. Well, we were eating high on the hog.

After we fought all night, we would come in early in the morning and we would clean up and go to bed, all of us but two men. I kept two men on lookout all the time. We had found a house that had a pool table in it.

One morning, Jack Agnew was sitting there eating breakfast and he looked over at me and said, "Sergeant, you're not taking good care of your troops."

I asked, "Is that right?"

He said, "Yeah."

I said, "What's your big complaint, son?"

"Well," he said, "I bet you that those people on ration cards back in the States are eating better than we are."

I said, "Well, you think so?"

He said, "I'll bet you."

I said, "I thought you were eating pretty good. If you like pork or if you like beef, you've got it. We have all kinds of canned vegetables. We've got potatoes and onions. What is it that your little heart desires that you don't have?"

He was eating a big ole bowl of ice-cold peaches and he said, "We don't have any cream for our peaches."

I said, "Well, that's just real tough son. Do you want cream for your peaches?"

He said, "Sure, I do. I'm entitled to it. Besides we're not soldiering."

I said, "Well say, is that all? It embarrasses me to think that I don't have cream for you. I'll tell you what you do. In the morning when you get back, if you get back, bring me a cow and I'll get you enough cream to take a bath in if you want."

He asked, "How do you get cream from a cow?" He was from Philadelphia. He had probably not seen a cow until he went into the service.

I said, "Well, you idiot. You just milk that cow in a bucket and just let it set there in the cool weather until the cream rises. It is lighter. You skim it off the top and throw the rest out."

He wanted to know how to tell if the cow was giving milk. I said, "You've got four faucets right there on her belly. Just squeeze one with a downward motion and if she's giving milk, bring her in here."

The next morning they brought in three milk cows. I took the cows and started milking them. I let that cream rise up, then I would pour that cream over in another container and throw the milk out to the chickens and hogs that were loose. I had everything in the house that would hold liquids full of cream.[33]

Lieutenant Whitehead got cut off one morning and could not make it back to his command post which was about two blocks down the street from mine. He knew where we were. So he came dragging in there to our place. We were feeding him and he asked, "Where did you get this cream?"

I said, "Well, I've got three cows outside." I had every utensil in a two or three house radius that would hold liquid full of cream just sitting around all over the place.

He said, "Boy, I want some of that cream."

I said, "Well, you can have some of it." Then I asked, "Would you do some swapping?"

He asked, "Like what?"

I said, "I know stinking well, Whitehead, that you all have a barrel of schnapps up there at your place. We don't have a drop of alcohol in this whole side of town. We have looked in every house." I said, "We would like to have some schnapps and you would like to have some cream. I'll swap you cream for schnapps."

He asked, "What kind of a swap are you talking about?"

I said, "Volume for volume. If you want a quart of cream, I'll give you a quart of cream for a quart of schnapps. If you want a gallon of cream, I'll give you a gallon of cream," I paused. "For a gallon of schnapps."

He said, "Well, that wouldn't be right."

I said, "That's the only way it will work. You all ain't going to have time to drink a barrel of schnapps before we either kill them or get killed. Well, you go back and take some of that schnapps you've got and see if you think that it wouldn't be a good swap. I've got more cream here than I can use." So I said, "We'll deliver. It is supply and demand. What do you want?"

He thought and said, "Well, all right. If that's the best I can do then that's the best I can do."

I said, "Do you want some of this cream this morning and an escort back to your place? We'll do that."

He said, "Okay."

So we swapped cream for schnapps there for about another ten days. He and I worked out a real good relationship.

A JEW AND PORK

When Jewish men engage in combat where there is imminent danger of death, or the supplies are not available for them to eat according to their religion, they can eat anything that is available to sustain their strength. Well, Cigar had never been able to eat pork when he was out of a combat area. He just loved that stuff and would not eat anything but pork while with us.

This pool table was on the second floor, which provided a good vantage point to watch and observe. One could sit there all day and try to find some indication as to where the next group of Germans was. One day Cigar was on lookout while two or three of us were shooting pool. All of a sudden, he just kind of shuddered. He said, "Now, I know why the Lord won't let you eat a damn hog."

I asked, "What's the matter with you, Cigar?"

He said, "Come over here. I want to show you something."

Well the street had a lot of bodies of dead paratroopers and Germans. Hogs and cattle and chickens and dogs were just roaming the streets and there was one big ole hog out there that was eating a dead paratrooper. Hogs will eat anything.

He said, "I'll never taste another pork again!" And he never would eat any pork again.

RESCUE THE RED DEVILS
October 22–23, 1944

When the British were ready to evacuate the paratroopers, they told us.[34] I took a couple of my men out there at night to probe this minefield, map it out, then remove the mines. We just cleared out a path through there from the levy down to the Rhine River while the British waited right behind us. It was about a quarter of a mile from the levy to the bank of the river and it was covered with trees. While sweeping the minefield, I never saw any cattle in the area where the mines were. We worked on that thing for two or three nights. Then we told the British that it was cleared.

We guided the British in that next night. We led them clear to the river. Then the British engineers took those rubber dinghies out there and went across that river and rescued those sixty Red Devils. We waited until they got their people out. When the boats started coming back to the bank, we guided them out of there.[35]

After the British got their paratroopers picked up, we had no more reason to occupy Brock since the Germans were going to cross that river and fight. They had all the high ground and could hold us inside that perimeter. Neither was General Dempsey about to try and attack across that river. Our company received orders to withdraw for evacuation. We went back into OP duty and stayed there until Thanksgiving.[36]

Marquez Kills the Hog

We picked up six chickens from somewhere, and it getting close to Thanksgiving, I said, "Let's have a Thanksgiving Day dinner. We've got some real good groceries out of all these houses."

They asked, "What are we going to have?"

I said, "We'll have chicken. I have not seen any turkeys but we'll have chicken." The six chickens were so old that they had scales on their legs like alligators.

They asked, "How're you going to cook them?"

I said, "We'll boil them, fry them or anything we can do with them but we've got to have some grease."

Mike Marquez was an extra kid in my section from El Paso, a big strong kid, like a bull. I said, "I'll tell you what, Mike." We always had a bunch of stuff that we threw out. These hogs and chickens would come around there and eat. This one hog that had been hanging around had been hit by shrapnel and one leg was nearly cut off. He was just tripping along with that leg dragging. I said, "Mike, get out there and kill that hog and we'll skin him and get enough grease off of him so we can fry some of this or boil it or whatever." I said, "Don't you shoot him. Kill him with your trench knife. If you shoot him out there, we'll have forty Germans in here on us before the sun goes down. Don't make any noise—just go out there and kill him with the trench knife."

He said, "Okay."

I went around there doing something else and I heard the damnedest racket I ever heard in my life. It sounded like someone on a bulldozer was out there in the back yard. I walked over there and looked out the window. Mike had this hog around the neck and he was stabbing and cutting him with his trench knife. Of course the hog was going wild. It dragged him across that backyard a dozen times and hit everything in it.

After he finally killed it, we skinned it out. I took the fat off of his skin, just scraped it all off. So I got all the fat off of him that I could get and boiled it up. I had, I don't know, maybe half a gallon or so of grease. I tried to fry them but we could not eat those chickens. We could not even bite off a piece. It was like leather. So we threw them all in a big stew and boiled it for hours and then it turned out to be real good chicken.[37]

THANKSGIVING DINNER

We came off of OP duty two or three days after Thanksgiving and went back down and joined our company.[38] When we came out of there, Top Kick Miller asked, "Jake, what are we going to feed these people for Thanksgiving?"

I asked, "What do you want to feed them?"

He asked, "Well, can we get turkey or chicken?"

"No, you can't get turkeys or chicken. There are not enough to feed a company." I said, "If you'll give me a jeep for a little while, we can feed them beef. I know where there are some really good looking cattle that're fat."

He said, "Are you really going to go butcher something or do you just need a jeep?"

I said, "I'm going to go butcher some if you want me to."

So he gave me a jeep and two or three boys. We went out and

butchered a beef and hung her up and let it cure out for two days. A big carcass has to set for two days until the body heat leaves it, otherwise anyone who eats it will get dysentery. I took it back and gave them the beef, but I kept the liver and the heart. They can be taken right out of the belly and eaten the first day. They will not make anyone sick.

I also remembered where I had seen a garden which had cabbage and leeks. So I picked a bunch of cabbage and those leeks. Those leeks were big up there. I also knew where there were some potatoes. Everybody in Europe had potatoes but they had them hidden. I would go to a house and say I wanted some kartoffels, which meant potatoes, but of course they would tell you they did not have any kartoffels. I told them to get outside and I would look for myself. Then they would give me some potatoes.

So I brought all this stuff in. We had an ole boy up there in Headquarters Company who was a good cook. He was not a cook by trade. He was just a line man. He took that stuff and cooked it up real good.

Top Kick Miller told me about fifty years later, "Jake, I've remembered that meal a million times. That was the best meal I ever ate in my life." Of course, he had not been eating very good.

I said, "I don't imagine it would taste near as good to you right now, Top Kick. You've been eating well."

Line Repair

The communication section in Regimental Headquarters Company had lines out. They used a lot of wire. They had line men who would go out and string wire up all over the place since we were mainly on outpost perimeter defense. We were down to almost nothing. The enemy had a million of those Germans with tanks and everything. Every night those Germans would come across that river in boats with patrols of thirty or forty men. Every time they came across one of those communications lines, they would cut it. So when a bunch of those lines were cut to where we could not communicate, why we would send these line men out there to repair them. They would usually send demolitions people along for protection.

We were out there one night after Thanksgiving dinner with

Malcolm Landry, a little ole boy from down there in New Orleans. He was the line man who was repairing all these breaks while we went along to keep all those Kraut patrols from running into him. That night Herb Pierce was back at the end of the column. There were not but six of us. He was very high strung. He was talking and yakking back there and I went back and told him, "Herb, knock that off. We're out here and there are Krauts all around. We'll get these lines repaired and get out butts back out of here if we can." So I said, "Stop that. You're going to get us all killed."

I returned to the front. We walked on for a while and it was not ten minutes later before Herb was yakking again. We got to the next break where it had been cut. We had sat down to wait for Malcolm to repair the line. Herb started chattering again.

I went back there and told him, "Herb, I will tell you something boy. You can get killed if you want to but you are not going to kill all these guys. If you want to just take off on your own, get your ass on out of here. But if you make another noise until we get back to camp, I'm going to come back here and cut your head off." He turned white as a sheet. I said, "I won't talk to you any more, Herb. If you were exposing yourself that was one thing but you're exposing six other men. I will cut your head right off at your Adams apple if you make another noise." I said, "If you want to go somewhere and talk, take off."

Well, he did not want to take off and he kept his mouth shut from then on. Herb was a pretty good soldier but he was just a kid.[39]

72-Hour Pass to Mourmelon

Two days after Thanksgiving dinner we were pulled out of Holland and sent back down to Mourmelon, France, to be refitted, re-equipped, and filled up with replacements.[40]

We had been in Holland seventy-eight days without a break. I mean just straight out combat for seventy-eight days. Well after we came back, they gave each one of us a seventy-two-hour pass. Seventy-two hours was not a reward for being in Holland. Seventy-two hours was not even an hour for every day I spent up there behind the lines! I did not think it was quite fair at all—and that pass was only good for Mourmelon. The destination was written right on it.

Mourmelon was our camp. One could stand with one foot in camp and put the other foot in the city of Mourmelon and this was our reward. Mourmelon was a little town that I guess had about ten whorehouses and probably ten bars.

We had thousands of young recruits picked from all over the United States. We had lost nearly 65 percent of our men in Holland. So they had just loaded everybody as replacements who said they would be paratroopers to build our division back up to combat strength. Most of them were kids, just seventeen, eighteen, and twenty-one years old. They had never been out of the United States before. They were in that town drinking every drop of whiskey, grabbing all the prostitutes in those ten or twelve houses, and they were lined up three abreast just as far as one could see. So I looked the situation over. I could go to the back of the line and maybe get close enough to a drink of whiskey or the smell of a woman.

There was this kid with me, named Frank Kough.[41] He was a corporal and married. I said, "Well Frank, I'll see you later."

"What do you mean you'll see me later?"

I said, "Well, I'm getting out of here. I ain't going to stay here with this mess and fight this crowd. I'm going to go to Paris or Reims or somewhere."

Reims, France, was SHAEF headquarters. That is where Eisenhower and his whole staff were. I guess he had a thousand WACs in there taking care of all his paperwork. I did not know it, but the 82nd had come back a week ahead of us. Their division had given them all passes. Boy, they headed right straight to Reims. They got in there and raped and killed them WACs, tore up everything in town, killed a bunch of civilians and SHAEF finally had to send back for General Gavin to come down and take his troops out of there. Afterwards they put Reims off limits to all airborne troops. I did not know that then.

I said, "I'm getting out of here. If you stayed here for seventy-two hours you could not get close enough to get a drink of whiskey or the smell of a woman. I'm going AWOL."

"Jake," he said, "I think I'll go with you."

I said, "Kough, you're a corporal, married and they're going to bust you the minute they lay hands on you when you get in."

"Well," he said, "you always have so much fun I just wanted to go see it."

I said, "Well, come right on!"

He and I walked out on the edge of town. I stepped out on the street and started bumming trucks. The first truck that came by and stopped was a six-by with Lieutenant Whitehead and his driver in it. I had fought with him the biggest part of the time in Holland and we had become real close associates. He pulled over to the side and said, "What are you doing, Mac?"

I said, "I've got a pass."

He said, "Where's it to?"

I said, "I don't know where it is. They've got it written in French here. I don't even speak French much less read it. I don't know what the destination is."

He said, "It shows the time expiration doesn't it anyhow?"

I said, "Yes, sir."

He asked, "What does it say?"

I said, "Seventy-two hours."

He asked, "Do you think you could hitch-hike to Paris and stay drunk for two weeks and hitch-hike back in seventy-two hours?"

I said, "I don't really know. I wouldn't bet on it but I'm willing to try."

"I'll tell you something, Jake," he said. "You get rid of them wings and unblouse them boots, cut them markers off your caps, shoulders and everything else. They have brought special MP units into Reims and it is totally off limits to every airborne man in Europe. Don't you try to lay in there. You'll be safer to go on to Paris."

I said, "Okay, sounds good to me."

He hauled me clear to the outskirts of Reims and said, "I can't afford to drop you off in there." Then we took on off and got through Reims then went clear to Paris. We had a heck of a deal down there. I stayed gone for about four or five days then came back.

5

Rescue of a Division

Mourmelon, France
December 5, 1944

When I returned from AWOL, they immediately put me under arrest of quarters. Shorty Mihlan was Charge of Quarters that day. He came in and asked, "Jake, how would you like to go to England?"

I said, "Oh, is England where they are going to hang me? I don't like them French guillotines."

He said, "That's not exactly it, Jake. It's almost. They would like for you to volunteer for parachute pathfinding service."

I said, "Oh, they would, would they?"

He said, "Yeah."

So I went down to the orderly room and Browny asked me if I would volunteer for pathfinding service. It was just nearly straight suicide. Pathfinding service generally had a loss of 80 percent. They jumped ten men to a stick figuring they would lose eight of them. The two men left would operate one of two CRN-4 sets. They believed that one out of the two sets would still operate after the jump.

It was so dangerous an assignment that no one could assign anyone to it. A paratrooper had to volunteer to become a Pathfinder. It was like volunteering to kill yourself, but Browny promised that I would go out with a clean record. I did not care if I had a clean record or not. I had been in every jail from Rome to Nome and Maine to Spain.

Of course the chain of command really did not know anything about the Filthy 13 until after Holland. I did not know it but this article about the Filthy 13 dated December 4, 1944, had come out in the *Stars and Stripes* while I was AWOL. It must have caused quite a stir up at the high levels when they learned that such an outfit as that operated within the 101st Airborne. Up until that time our reputation was confined within the regiment.[1]

I got along well with my company officers. Shrable Williams was one of the best lieutenants in the whole damn army. He backed me all the way on everything. Browny and I were also very good friends but he was getting a lot of flak from higher up. So he felt convinced that he had to finally get rid of me. He was just tired of fooling with me. He must have thought, "Well, here is a real good place to get rid of McNiece."

I asked Browny, "What happened to all the guys who volunteered for this crap up in Holland?"

Browny said, "When they came back they un-volunteered."

While we were in Holland, division officers came around and asked guys if they would volunteer for pathfinding service. They wanted to have a pool to draw from when we returned from Holland. Of course a lot of those guys volunteered for it thinking they would be taken out of combat and sent back for training. When they got back to Mourmelon, division asked all these guys to get ready. Only then were they going to ship them out and train them. The guys said, "No way, we're not going into that stupid deal." So the division was really rustling around trying to find anybody for pathfinding service.

So I told Brown, "Why don't I think this over a little bit and I'll have you an answer in about an hour."

So I looked the situation over and the state the war was in and all that. I did not see any real possibility of Pathfinders being engaged in combat this near the end. We were just on the verge of achieving our principle objectives in Germany.

We had total aerial supremacy. I would see columns of B-17s. I would look at my watch when the first nine planes flew over me and then I would check my watch again when the last ones passed over and it would be forty-five minutes or an hour or an hour and a half later. This meant that the train of them was a hundred to two hundred miles long, nine-by-nine-by-nine. The German air force was nearly gone. We would go for days and days and never see a Messerschmitt. The last Messerschmitts I had encountered were back in Holland and I only saw two groups of them up there. So we had total aerial supremacy.

After I thought it all over, I figured they would never have any use for parachute pathfinders again. The purpose of pathfinding service was to jump anywhere at any time for any plausible cause. I did not figure there would be any more plausible causes. Best of all, pathfinding headquarters and the training area was at Chalgrove Air Force Base.

I thought, "My goodness, I have been eating this slop for three years. Now I would be eating that air force food. They would be responsible for our rations and quarters. No KP! And they were just eight miles from Oxford University with all the English men off to war. There would be more women and more whiskey and a better opportunity to do some postgraduate work than any place in the world." So I figured it would be a paradise. I was not being brave or anything, I just did not think anyone would ever need Pathfinders any more. Besides I kind of thought that I might enjoy that kind of warfare anyway.

So I went back and told Browny, "Yeah, I will go. I'm packing right now."

Captain Brown thanked me. He was grateful that I was getting out of there. He did not have any more responsibility for me at all. He just knew I was going to go in there and get my ass killed.

But I told him, "You've got to take me off of arrest of quarters here because I want to go around and say goodbye to a bunch of these guys and thank them for the way they served."

So he said, "Okay, you're not under arrest of quarters but you be ready to leave in the morning." He then asked, "What about Majewski? Will Majewski go with you?"

I said, "Wait a minute, Browny. I'm not encouraging Majewski or anyone else to go into pathfinding service. That's your problem. You all talk to him. I am well satisfied with the decision that I have made but I would not try to influence anyone to go into Pathfinder service."

They hated Majewski. Max looked like a big stupid idiot. His father was Polish, and I think his mother was German. He was the one who got the officers burned from Eisenhower on down.

At that time in Europe the *Stars and Stripes*, a little ole newspaper for the military, had a column in there called "Bitch Bag." They advertised to any enlisted man or officer who felt he had a legitimate bitch to mail it straight in to "B-Bag," which answered to Eisenhower himself. If it was a legitimate call he would take action.

Max had earned the combat infantryman's badge during Normandy.[2] When we returned to England he had taken off into town and picked up a dose of clap. The commander rescinded the order on his combat infantryman's badge as a punitive measure for getting a dose of clap. Well that was stupid. Why, only an idiot would resort to something like that, taking a combat award away from a man because he got a venereal disease.[3]

Well, Max wrote right straight to Eisenhower and denounced this treatment. Ole Eisenhower started right back down the chain of command, from the top man right down to the bottom man, eventually to Colonel Sink and right on down through the chain to the lowest echelon. Boy, he chewed their asses like you would not believe. They really took a lot of heat for it and this was waiting for them when we came back from Holland. Well, they really wanted to get rid of Max after that. They wanted him dead. They would put him on any special assignment where he might get killed. So about thirty minutes after I started packing up my gear, Majewski came in and asked, "Jake, what are you doing?"

I said, "I'm packing my stuff."

He said, "Why? Where are you going? I thought you were under arrest of quarters. I did not know you had privileges to travel?"

I said, "Yeah, I have. There'll be a plane here in the morning to kick me out."

He said, "Well, Captain Brown called me in and said he would like for me to go with you. What made you determine this was a good move?"

I told him what the deal was and how I had it figured and analyzed. I told him, "I don't believe they will ever be used again."

He said, "I think I'll go back down and talk to Captain Brown again. You've probably got this thing figured out right. I believe I'm going too."

I said, "Don't let me influence you. This is just what I believe. This is not firsthand knowledge. I can't give you any guarantee."

So he went down and volunteered. Then he came back and started packing. By that time the word got out to the other men that I had volunteered for this mess.

Well, Jack Agnew found out about it. He did not even talk to me but just went right straight in to Captain Browny and asked if Majewski and McNiece were going. Browny said, "Yeah."

Jack said, "I believe I'll go too." He then came in and told me, "I'm going with you!"[4]

Then a kid named William Coad came in. When he saw what was happening, he said he would go. Then John Dewey came in and volunteered. By then we had five enlisted men.

That night, Lieutenant Williams came in and talked to us. He asked, "What's the deal here? I'm losing half of my demolition platoon."

So I told him what I figured and how I had it analyzed. We shot it over, back and forth. I said, "It isn't foolproof but it's almost. I don't think a one of us will ever jump again." Well, then Williams went down and signed up.

So that night five men volunteered for this with me: Lieutenant Williams, John Dewey, Jack Agnew, Bill Coad, and Max Majewski. Every man in my platoon, to whom I had faithfully promised there could never be another mission, jumped on the first emergency pathfinder job that came along.[5]

9th Troop Carrier Command Pathfinders Chalgrove, England

When we arrived at the barracks in England, I just went straight to bed. Someone woke me and told me to report to the company commander [Captain Frank L. Brown]. So I reported in to the company commander as a staff sergeant and asked, "What's your big problem? I don't know what it is but I did not do it. I just got here last evening at five o'clock and went to bed. I don't know what your big deal is but I was not even involved."

He said, "Sergeant, I don't know you or anything about you. I know you are a goof-off or you wouldn't be here, but I need an acting first sergeant and you've been recommended."

I said, "Boy, somebody's been pulling your leg. What do you mean I've been recommended? I've been in here for nearly three years now and haven't made PFC yet. I don't care about garrison soldiering or military discipline or courtesies and that sort of thing. I'd have my arm fall off before I would salute an officer. I would not pick up a cigarette butt if you all were going to put me in chains. I don't go for any of that. I don't care any about that whole malarkey. You don't want me as the first sergeant. I'm not first sergeant material. I'm the biggest goof-off in the army."[6]

He said, "I'm here for the same reason you are. I'm a goof-off. I don't care about military discipline or saluting or cigarette butt-picking and all that. We've got four hundred goof-offs here, a hundred from the 101st, a hundred from the 82nd, a hundred from the 17th and a hundred from the foreigners. They told me that you have been through this thing since day one, Normandy and on through and made two jumps and that you could whip this deal into shape and get it right and ready quick. That's what I want."

I said, "It sounds like we might be dealing right on the table." I told him what all my demands would be for the men, for myself, and how we expected to be treated—halfway reasonable for a change. "We have never had a square meal since we went in the army three years ago. I want good food. I want good, reasonable quarters, and want these people just to have an almost permanent pass as long as they'll respect it." I said, "The first thing they're going to do is take a three-day pass to London."

He said, "That may be beyond the line of reason, McNiece. How many do you think we'd get back?"

I said, "You'll get back all of them except the ones that are in jail and just as quick as they notify us, we'll go get them. Most of these boys are fine soldiers. Everyone of these boys is like me. They're just field soldiers, combat men, not garrison. These are a good bunch of men. They have been behind enemy lines for seventy-eight days. They need to get into town and let some steam off."

He said, "Well, I'll tell you what I'll do. I'll get you a pass book and you can let everybody in here have a three day pass without destination, but you've got to stay here and get these sticks organized and a training program set up. You're going to have to pick you out a stick. You all will stay here the three days while they're gone and familiarize yourself with the whole organization and objective. When they get back then you can go."

I said, "Okay, I'll be the acting first sergeant under that kind of a deal."

He said, "We don't have any table of organization. You'll just serve in here in the same grade that you came in."

I said, "The pay doesn't mean much to me. Just let me jump in where there is money and I'll get my own pay raises." As demolition men we blew every safe we came upon.

I gave the rest three day passes to London and everybody came back except the ones we had to go pick up from jail. I would have loved to have gone with them but I stayed there and I selected the men who I had fought with for a long time. I knew them, knew what they were capable of, and how they would perform under fire. I also picked George Blain because he had been in Pathfinder service since Normandy. So I picked me a stick from what I thought was the cream of the crop, which is what I got. If a guy has got any sense at all that is what he would do. It is just common logic that he would take proven material against inexperience. We went on our three day pass after the others came back.[7]

CRN-4

When I came back from pass (on time) we began Pathfinder training. We used dummy CRN-4 sets. We practiced laying out panels in a circle like pie-shaped cuts. This would help send out the signal. The ground was covered with snow so we did not do any practice jumping.

The Pathfinders did not have any supplies there at all. We just made do with what we had in the way of clothing. I still had the same pair of boots that I had jumped into Normandy and Holland with and they had holes in them the size of quarters. I put paste board in the soles.

The CRN-4 sets belonged to the air corps. They set them up and coded them. They just had two buttons on them. We would push one every thirty seconds and it would send out a signal to a C-47 that was equipped with a G set. It had a crosshair in it that looked just like a scope and a dot showed up on there. If the dot was over to the right then the pilot would start pulling over to the left until he was on the perpendicular line and the plane would fly on that azimuth. When the dot got down to the intersection of the cross hair, then he unloaded whatever he was bringing in, supplies or men or whatever.

Our instructions were if we saw that we were going to be captured or were severely wounded then we pushed that second button. It was loaded with explosive. It would blow that CRN-4 set up and maybe us with it. Then the Germans could hardly diagnose the mechanism or its operation. Our S-3s and intelligence had not determined if the Germans had the CRN-4. That is why we had absolute orders to destroy it. The existence of the CRN-4 was a secret and the air corps wanted to keep it that way.

While in Chalgrove, we put on a demonstration for some air force officers. Max did not know anything more about this machine than to push the two buttons. Neither did I. He had been one of the best soldiers over there but he was no longer stable since his wife died. He became a hair trigger. I did not pick him for my stick. Majewski was a heck of a shrewd soldier but he was a fool sometimes.

So Max was explaining how that CRN-4 set operated: "This button here, you just press it on and off, on and off, and on and off. It will send these signals so they can pick you up with their G set."

This lieutenant-colonel said, "You mean intermittently?"

Max said sarcastically, "Let me see. On and off, on and off. Yes, colonel that would be intermittently. I think."

BASTOGNE JUMP[8]

December 23, 1944

None of us had any idea that the Battle of the Bulge was just around the corner. We had complete aerial supremacy. The Allies had photographed every move that the Germans made. So someone should have known. I am confident that Eisenhower, Marshall, Montgomery, and all of them knew that this was about to happen because they had just put two of the greenest divisions they had right in front of that area.[9] They also had the 28th "Bloody Bucket" Division establish their command post at Bastogne. They were a real seasoned combat division but they had been decimated at the Huertgen Forest.[10] There was practically nothing left of the original lot. They had been replaced with infantry people who had never heard a shot nor seen a drop of blood.

So I thought it was a conscious decision that our commanders had made. This was the exact same attack that Hitler had made clear to the coast in 1940. So this was going to be a repeat of that. They knew that Hitler was not a madman. Twenty-some German divisions can make a point, without being serious about it.

We had not been in England for ten days when I had organized the company into ten pathfinding sticks for each of these boys' four divisions. I had forty sticks set up and trained. I was walking up the company street on the morning of the twenty-second of December when Lieutenant Williams walked up to me and said, "Jake, have your stick ready to jump at one o'clock."

I said, "Willy, let's forget this jump out here in this snow." The snow was ass deep to a tall Indian. I said, "What are you thinking about to jump in these conditions when every one of them has forty, fifty, up to a hundred jumps. They don't need this. Just knock it off. You find some other way to occupy your time. You'll get legs broken, backs broken. You'll have men disqualified forever. We're not jumping, on account of the weather."

He said, "Yeah, you are. Not here. Over in Belgium. It's a combat mission."

I had not yet heard about the Bulge. I said, "What are you talking about?"

He said, "The 101st is cut off in Bastogne. We're going on a combat mission, one o'clock this afternoon."

I said, "When are we going to be briefed?

He said, "They'll brief you at the plane."

I said, "Do you know that not a man in the outfit has any combat equipment. We don't have a CRN-4 set."

He said, "They're working on it right now. They'll be at the plane."

I said, "You are really serious about this."

He said, "I am and you have not heard the worst of it. You be at the orderly room with your stick at one o'clock. We'll have jeeps to run you out to the plane."

So we ran out to the runway and they had that C-47 revved up with two air corps colonels standing there. They shook hands with me and said, "Good luck."

I asked, "What do you mean 'good luck.' Where are we going and what's the deal? When are we going to get briefed?"

He said, "Right now." He pulled out a map that looked like a state highway map with a circle about two miles in diameter and said, "See that circle?"

I said, "Yeah."

He said, "That's Bastogne. Your division is cut off in there and completely encircled. At least they were the last time we heard from them. We have not heard from them in two days. Whether they are still there or not I don't know. All indications are they still are. You are going to jump in there on a resupply mission. They are out of ammunition, medicine, and food. They have nothing left but a handful of men in there. We have to maintain and control Bastogne to prevent the blitzkrieg from succeeding."

They had sent General McAuliffe with the 101st in by truck. The entire American army was in total disarray and retreating. They told General McAuliffe, "Do not retreat an inch. Stay and fight and die to the last man."[11] Well, they were holding their position while everyone else was retreating. The Germans were following the others and pushing them back. After the 106th and the Bloody Bucket had retreated, the 101st had about a two-mile-diameter perimeter and was cut off without supplies. They had not been in Mourmelon long enough to be refitted and resupplied. Many of the boys did not have much ammunition when they went in there. It was about ten miles from the point of their advancement back to our main line of defense. In every direction there were about ten miles of Krauts.[12]

He said, "Well, good luck."

I said, "I don't need good luck, I need a miracle. This is ridiculous, absolutely ridiculous." I said, "You all couldn't find that place in three days even if you didn't have any interference at all. You are trying to hit a two-mile diameter circle flying four hundred miles to it in a C-47 that has no navigational aids or instruments."

He said, "Pretty tough deal boy, but that's the way it is."[13]

So we loaded in that plane. We took off and we flew and flew and flew. It was foggy. We could not see any ground for two miles. Then it would lighten up and we would see a spot of real estate, then we would go a little further and we were in soup and snow and rain and fog. This pilot had communications with someone on the ground and determined where he thought Bastogne was. Through his radio he finally realized that he was thirty-five miles past Bastogne. So he turned back around to Chalgrove.[14]

When we got back, I said, "Hey, let's go down to the war room where they've got some maps and so forth and see what the best plan of attack is."

They said, "Okay."

So they fed us a good meal in the air force mess, then we went in there and sat down. I suggested that on another day, if we attempted it again, that we produce two plane loads of Pathfinders. From what I could see flying over the first day, there was a possibility of losing a plane or maybe two or three. I said, "Let's take two planeloads. I'll be in the first plane."

They said, "We've got a crackerjack pilot[15] who can hit that place easily Jake."

I said (sarcastically), "I hope so. You missed it by thirty-five miles today. Everything would be a little happier if you could get a crackerjack pilot who could put me in or near Bastogne. I'll take black and orange smoke grenades. When I have visibility enough to recognize the situation, if it looks feasible that we could get in and start a resupply mission, I will throw out orange smoke grenades." Orange was a friendly military signal then. I said, "If I see we are utterly off the target, I'll throw out black smoke which means danger or disaster. If they see the orange smoke then they are to drop the next plane load right on top of me. If it's a hopeless case and they see black, why just circle. Try to relocate and drop them on the target."[16]

Before we left on the twenty-third, I did not have anything on me but orange smoke grenades. I did not take any black. I was going to look like an orange juice tank truck exploding. I thought twenty was better than ten under any circumstance when landing in the middle of five million Germans.[17]

This ole boy [Crouch] who was going to fly us in asked me when we left England, "You don't have any confidence in this do you?"

I said, "No. I got carried on a merry chase yesterday and I'm expecting the same thing today."

He said, "I can fly you in there. I'll prove it to you. Let's synchronize our watches." We synchronized our watches. "Now, at 9:15, I'll pull this thing down out of the fog and we'll be right over Lille, France."

I said, "Good."

So at the set time he pulled her down. I was right up front in the cabin with him. He pulled her down and we were right over Lille, France, right in the middle of it. I think the next place that he said he would hit was Luxembourg at such and such a time, and he did. He pulled her right down.

I said, "Well, this gives me a little more hope."

He flew us in there and just before we jumped, he gave us the red light. They were shooting us up pretty good and we stood up and hooked up and stood in the door.

Cleo Merz from C Company was just a little bitty fellow. He was the nicest and quietest guy and always had a little bit of a smile on his face. While we were flying into Bastogne he was directly behind me. We were getting a lot of antiaircraft fire and it was hitting the plane pretty good. We both flinched. I looked over at Merz and he kind of grinned and then he stuck his finger through a bullet hole where it had come right between us.

I was standing in the door watching for that green light to come on when the pilot nosed that plane down through the clouds and that snow was black with German infantry, tanks and everything else. It looked like a carpet down there and boy they went crazy when he pulled that C-47 down. They were anticipating fire and bombs. Then he pulled her right up and it was just a minute until he gave me the green light. Then out we went.[18]

Where the paratroopers had their main line of defense, it was about a hundred and fifty yards to the circumference of the German line of offense. The first thing I saw was a graveyard, a big graveyard. They had huge monuments which provided good cover from enemy fire. So I knew I was in the immediate proximity of a pretty good-sized city and Bastogne was really the only city in that area that would accommodate a graveyard like that. I began throwing out all the orange smoke that I could get a hold of so that the others would be dropped right on top of us.[19]

BASTOGNE

We landed about halfway between the two main lines of resistance. Of course when we jumped out of that plane, the paratroopers there on defense opened up on those Krauts with everything they had. That second stick came right in on top of us and we made a run into that graveyard where there was plenty of protection behind those stones. Every paratrooper that was on our line of defense opened up and gave us good cover. We got in all in one bunch. Of the nineteen men I had with me, I only lost one.

We landed not too far from C Company, 506th. The first news I heard when I was safe within their lines was, "Jake, Colonel LaP was killed in his CP last night!"

Lieutenant-Colonel James LaPrade had been the commander of the 1st Battalion and some of the guys hated him. I thought it was funny that they were more interested in telling me that than asking what my mission was.[20]

We had four CRN-4 sets and we laid out panels and infrared lights. Then we set our antennas up and started transmitting. When we jumped in there, the air corps had hundreds of C-47s loaded with combat equipment, gear and ammunition and gasoline. They had them rendezvous over France waiting to see if we could get a signal out to them.

We set up our CRN-4 sets initially on three different locations; the brick pile, a small hill, and another hill a few hundred yards from the enemy front. We had to abandon the last one because it was too close to the enemy. The Germans had the ability to pinpoint our location when we sent out our radio signal. We would send out a signal from one location for a while then send it from the other.[21]

As soon as we sent out the signals they picked them up and began to fly into Bastogne. It was not even an hour and we had a trail of C-47s. The first day, we brought in two hundred and forty-four C-47s full of supplies. The next day we brought in one hundred and sixty and then the next day, which was just a special order of gliders, we got in only forty-four. The next day came two hundred and sixty-nine C-47s and by the fifth day a hundred and twenty-nine. We brought in over six hundred planeloads of ammunition, gas, special equipment they needed and this and that.[22]

> [John "Dinty" Mohr remembered:[23]]
> *We were fighting since the 18th of December. On Christmas day we needed supplies and they couldn't get through with planes or anything. A few of our guys had gone somewhere to a special school, and on Christmas day our planes come in and dropped a lot of supplies. These fellas that went on special duty to England, I dreamed that night that one of these guys, Jake McNiece, was singing and coming through the barracks in England, and the very next day there he was.*
> *. . . That very day I seen him and 3 or 4 other guys that came to where we were in a little town where we had moved to after being in the Battle of the Bulge, Luzery near Bastogne. I thought that was something, dreaming of him and then he come.*

QUARTERS

We had run those panels and CRN-4 sets all day long that first day. When it started getting dark, we had not even looked around for some place to stay. We found a big three-story chateau near there. We walked in and there was a major in charge of it. Those guys were not even paratroopers. There were a group of people who had been cut off in their retreat through Bastogne.

So I told this major, "I've got eighteen men here with me and I've got some real special equipment here that's got to be protected from the weather and artillery. I want to stay here tonight until I have time tomorrow to locate us some quarters."

He said, "You can't stay here. We're loaded."

I said, "You're not that loaded. We can stay in the basement. You have no one in the basement. That's where we will stay."

He said, "You ain't staying here."

I did not have anything on me for rank and he asked, "Who are you?"

I said, "I am Private McNiece, 506th Regimental Headquarters Company. I have a lot of pathfinding equipment here. That's why you've been seeing all these damn planes coming in here today. I've got to protect it."[24]

He said, "Well, you can't stay here."

I said, "I'll tell you one thing. You get on that damn phone and call down and talk to McAuliffe and tell him that Private McNiece is here with the Pathfinders requesting quarters and that you don't have room for him. I'm going to stay here but I don't know what you're going to do. Me and my men are going to stay here in this house tonight, I guarantee you."

He jumped on that phone and called down to headquarters, then he told me, "Well, you can stay here. That's what they told me down at Division Headquarters."

I knew the basement was the safest place. It also had those big furnaces with heat rolling out of them. Those Germans were bombing and shelling all over the 101st area. We were not in there thirty minutes when those lousy-ass Germans came in there and hit that chateau roof with bombs. Down came the ceiling and dust. They blew the top two floors just about clear off, I mean just shredded it. It looked like the whole house was caving in on us and we were going to be buried alive. It was so scary that it made the hair stand up on my head. So we immediately scrambled to get out of there. It was so smoky and dusty that we could hardly see. There was just one little passage in which we could get out. Agnew found it and hollered. So we all assembled over there on his voice.

There was a shell casing laying about four feet in front of this opening. I looked at that thing and thought, "That damn thing could go off any minute." I said, "You guys follow me. We are going to get over that and get our asses out of here and down."

I made a run and dived over that shell casing. I will bet I slid twenty feet. Of course when I did, the others started crawling out of there.

The next day when we got to checking things out, it had never gone off. It was what the Germans called a butterfly bomb. They would load those big casings up with grenades. Those grenades would have a ring on them. They would slide them on there like a string of beads. After the bomb would eject off the airplane, it would blow those rods out and scatter them like a covey of quail. That activated them. They were anti-personnel bombs. We would only have about five seconds to get under cover. They used them a whole lot on us.

After we escaped from the basement, I told the guys, "Let's get the hell out of here. The only thing to do evidently is get just as close to that German line of perimeter defense as we can."

It was still at night, sometime after nine o'clock. We took off from there. I started hunting around the perimeter to see if I could find any place where we could get in out of that weather. We came up on a little ole house. That thing was not a hundred yards from the main line of German resistance. So we moved in there, shook it down and checked it for booby traps. We did not find a thing.[25]

Like most of those houses up there, it had a half basement. The yard had twelve chickens and a cow, a horse and an area that was walled off full of rutabagas. There was a feather mattress down there on the rutabagas. So I walked over there and got to feeling around through it for booby traps and mines. I felt this big aluminum tank about the size of a big platter and about four inches deep and it was full of water. It was a hot water box. I never had seen a metal one before. On checking it further I felt that the water in it was still warm. So I thought, "Shit, there has been someone here very recently." So I put Majewski[26] out on the edge of the building facing the lines. I also put someone else on the other end. The rest of us went in and went to bed.

We could neither come nor go from that house to our position by daylight. So we would go out early while it was still dark. Everybody was going to man those machines. Then we would come back at dark. So early the next morning, I killed three of those chickens and skinned them out and put them in a pot to cook. We found some flour and ole George Blain was a good cook. He took that flour and whatever else he could find and started making everybody hotcakes.

This old farm house was as rickety as shit. The Germans were still bombing and shelling all through there. This plaster would fall down from the ceiling into that pancake batter. George would just go ahead and fry it right up. There was not any way to prevent it. Someone was eating it and bit into one of those big chunks of plaster and asked, "What in the shit is this?"

"It's plaster."

He said, "Well, I'm not going to eat this damn stuff."

George told him, "Well, there's half a dozen guys right beside you that would be glad to get it. If you don't like it, why just pass it on."

He was cooking breakfast while I was fixing those chickens. The next thing that I knew it was time to get out of there. Then I heard ole George yakking over at the door. He spoke good French and Belgian. The two languages are just about alike. If you can converse in one, you can converse in the other. When I heard all this yak, yak, yak going on I walked over. There were two women and a boy about fourteen standing there. George was talking to them.

I asked, "Who are they?"

He said, "They own this house."

I asked, "What do they want?"

He said, "They want to come in."

I said, "Ask them where they were last night."

They had a friend about two hundred yards from us who had a big deep wine cellar. They would go in there at night to get out of this shelling and bombing.

I said, "George, you tell them women that they can come in here if they want to. You tell them this. We have three of their chickens cooking. We will share and share alike on that. We will not kill any more of their chickens." Chickens were a very valuable piece of property in war. I said, "Tell them that they won't be molested. They will be treated like ladies and we will not kill the boy. But tell them if they step a foot in this room they're here to stay for the duration. They can't leave tonight and go back up to this other cellar."

George said, "Aw hell, Jake. Do you think I'm going to tell them that?"

I asked, "Why not? It's the truth."

He said, "You're just being too damn good to them. You're going to let them eat some of their chickens. You ain't going to rape them.

You ain't going to kill the kid and they are your prisoners. They can't leave once they come in here."

I said, "George, give it a little bit of thought. Do you want them to come in here with us all day and then tonight take off and go up there two hundred yards and tell them Krauts that all the pathfinders of this outfit that are bringing in all these supplies were in that farmhouse down there? Why, shit. Those Krauts would sacrifice two thousand men just to get rid of the nineteen of us. If we were Germans, them gals would be fucked before they could get through that front door and that kid would be killed. You know that is what the Germans did. They killed them kids. They won't feed them. I'm giving them the very best deal I can."

George said, "Well, I guess you are, Jake. It does not sound like it's very flattering."

I said, "It's the only right deal. I think."

So he told them and they said they would love to. They came right in there and lived with us for another five or six days until the armor started coming in.[27]

The civilians had evacuated the whole town. Of course they could not take their food and stuff with them. So every one of these units had canned food, a few potatoes, a few onions, and this and that.

I had told those women that we would not kill any more of their chickens and that I would have meat there that night. That second day, I was just running through apartments picking up jellies and fruits and vegetables. I found a hog in one of those apartments uptown. They were three-story apartments, two above ground and one below. That hog must have weighed three hundred pounds. I shot him. Then I hung him up on the stairwell, gutted him and skinned him out, cut his head off and just kicked it all down the stairs. I saved the heart and the liver to eat that day. I put that heart and liver in a pillow slipper. I wrapped the hog up in a sheet and had another guy carry it back just as quick as it got dark.

When I went in our house, the first thing I smelled was chicken cooking. I said, "Okay, who killed the chickens? All of you know what we agreed to this morning. Who killed the chickens?"

They said, "Nobody."

I said, "Somebody killed chickens because I can smell them cooking."

They said, "Well, we did not kill any chickens. Them girls took them bones and beat them up. They've made a soup."

I said, "That's something I'm going to have to see to believe."

I counted my chickens and still had nine left. Sure enough they had cooked up the bones. They put some potatoes and some green vegetables in the soup. I do not know whether they had them in the house or what. That snow was waist deep to an Indian. They had chopped up some of those rutabagas. That turned out to be the best soup that I ever tasted in my life. I learned that the marrow would cook out and that gristle would dissolve. I told my wife about it shortly after we were married and we have never thrown out the carcass of a turkey since. It was the best soup that I have ever eaten.

We had borrowed a fifty-caliber machine gun from somewhere. I do not know how we got ahold of it but we used it for our defense. Max was on guard one night with that fifty caliber not a hundred yards from the German lines. All I wanted him to do was kill any Germans who moved forward. He was not on air raid patrol. The Germans still bombed us every night. Well, he opened up on those planes with his fifty caliber and shot up ten belts. He had gotten to be an impulsive guy.

ATTACK ON THE FIELD HOSPITAL

2200 Hours, December 19, 1944

The rest of my demolition platoon fought out on the line. They had been there since the eighteenth. The Germans had a complete perimeter defense around the town of Bastogne. My division got so low on people and ammunition, they would just take up a defensive position anywhere out there. If the Germans hit heavy in one spot and a paratrooper lost his weapon, then he would just go find another and take up another position out there on that defensive line.

After I had gone into the Pathfinder service they had promoted Keith Carpenter from corporal to sergeant of my section. They were up there on the front lines one day and Keith told Trigger Gann to do something. Trigger refused to do it. Keith told him, "Yeah, you're going to do it. That's our assignment and we've got to take care of it. If you don't take care of your end of it, you may get thirty more people killed."

Trigger said, "Well I'm not going to do it."

Keith said, "Well, you will do it. I am the sergeant in charge of you and oversee your activities. I replaced McNiece and that's the way McNiece would have done it."

Well, about that time Trigger got up there in that hole and the Germans dropped artillery within two feet of the edge of it. Well, he just went ape. There were a lot of boys that were going ape during the fighting at Bastogne. All anyone could do was send them down to the hospital and give them some pills and rest. The medics would take their guns away and confine the guys as hostile. Well as soon as the medics could get them back on their feet they would give them their guns and of course send them back to their officers. So Keith sent Trigger down there. He was not down there thirty minutes I suppose until the whole thing was machine-gunned.

The Germans had seven divisions attacking the 101st at Bastogne. They had three regular infantry divisions, the 5th Parachute Division, and three armored divisions. They drove right straight in to the hospital before anyone could stop them. They went in there and machine-gunned the whole thing. They loaded the prisoners up like cord wood in their trucks and hauled them out of there. Doc Yeary[28] happened to be in the hospital at that time. The Germans took him clear up into Russia. He remained a prisoner of war clear through to the end of the war.

After the end of the war, Captain Browny came in and said, "Jake, I am getting a lot of letters from Trigger Gann. He said he survived that mess there in Bastogne as a prisoner of war. He's got a terrible complex about this whole thing. Would you mind writing him a letter. You were about as close to Trigger as anyone. Would you mind writing him a letter? I'll get it through. I'll do the censoring."

I said, "Okay." So I wrote Trigger a nice letter. I told him he did not need to have a guilt complex about it. Some people were out there under so much strain and stress that they will break, no matter how big, how tough or how rough they are. It will finally break your mind. Well, I tried to console him and then I received a letter right back.

He wrote, "Jake, I guess that I got shell-shocked. I thought I was shell-shocked there when Carpenter was putting me in position. It looked like sure death. It really touched me off. I just went crazy. Then I got in the hospital. They took my guns away from me and my knives. They put me in there and kind of talked to me and gave me some medication. I was ready to go back to the unit. I told them, 'I just flipped. I'm okay now. Can I have my guns and stuff?' Right then the Germans attacked me in that hospital."

He said, "They came in and machine-gunned everything in that hospital. Then they loaded us on those trucks just like cord wood—just body after body after body. If you were laying there with your head in a pool of blood or in somebody's guts and you tried to raise up, they would just get you with a gun butt and knock you right back in it. As we pulled out of course it had snowed chin deep to a gnome. We all ended up there in zero degree weather. As we rolled along, if a guy was dead or it was pretty apparent that he was dying, we just rolled him on through the stack and threw him out as we drove along.

Boy, I had just thought I was shell-shocked. The shell-shock really hit me then. I had just reached the breaking point up there at the front lines but I've come out of it pretty good."

BARANOWSKI'S DOG

Somebody gave Lieutenant Peter Baranowski a dog back in England. He went down to the riggers and had them make a parachute harness for him. He taught that dog to jump and it liked it. It would race him out the door. It jumped into Normandy and Holland. Everywhere someone saw Baranowski, that dog was with him. It followed at his heels. After they had been in Bastogne for two or three days it went nuts and they had to shoot it. That dog had survived two combat jumps but could not take it in Bastogne. That showed how bad it was up there.

In the paratroops if a man began to hesitate or became unreliable in combat to where he gained a reputation, we would not fool with him any more. We would just send him back to the Repo Depot [Replacement Depot]. I do not think we had anybody who we had to send back but a couple came close.

THE FIGHT FOR FOY

We got together down on Tom Young's ranch about fifty years after the war. One of the girls told Browny, "Browny, get rid of that garbage," and was sort of rough about it.

He said, "I will not. Give that to Private McNiece. Let him take care of it."

She said, "You get that garbage and you get it out of here."

He said, "Oh no, get McNiece or one of his boys to take care of it."

I told her, "He is the most bull-headed man that ever stepped on the range. He was shot four times over there. The last time he was shot, they took a 30.06 bullet out of him and he still wouldn't transfer."

A 30.06 was an American bullet but I do not imagine anyone wanted to kill him. Everyone liked him. He was in a firefight and either took a ricochet or somebody mistook him for a German.

It happened when he led the attack on that little village of Foy, right there on the outskirts of Bastogne. It was really a pretty important town with a lot of high ground. The Americans wanted it for an observation post. From there we could look right down in the Germans' shirt pocket. The Krauts knew it was important too. Brown had been given command of a line company. After Brown rooted them out, in about an hour the Krauts came back in and kicked their asses out. His company would go back in there and take it, then they would drive him out, then he would go in and take it, then they would drive him out again.[29]

At some point someone decided that they would establish a command post there. So they had a bunch of my demolition boys clear all the booby traps, mines, and stuff out of this one building. One of them found a dead Kraut in the snow. I guess when he was hit he reached out for the ground to break his fall. He just landed in that position and froze stiff as a board with his arm reaching out.

So someone picked him up and stood him up against the doorway of that building with this outstretched hand up against the door jam. Then this guy hung the German's rifle over the crook of his arm. Someone else found a silk hat and put it on him. They just left him standing there. After regiment set up this command post, a chaplain came in and boy he began to raise Cain like you never saw in your life. He started talking about respect for the dead and what the Geneva Convention said. Of course he never did find out who did it.

Brown took that town four times but never gained full control of it. The fourth time the Germans took it, they held it. But during the last time they took that town someone shot Browny with an M1.

He was evacuated to a hospital back in England where they were going to operate to take that bullet out. The division, however, came across a safe over there that they thought might have a lot of important German army documents that they wanted to get out. Of course, nearly anyone in the demolition platoon could have blown it open. We had been blowing safes open ever since D-Day. Everytime we found a safe, that was the first thing we attacked. But Browny was awful good at demolitions. We would have just blown up that safe and everything in it. So someone called the hospital over in England and said, "Release Captain Brown. We have need of him."[30]

The hospital said, "You don't have need of this man and you're not going to get him. He is in need of attention. He is not fit for combat duty."

So they jumped it right on up through channels and so forth clear up to Maxwell Taylor who was commanding general of the whole corps. He verified the absolute need for having that officer. He sent them orders to release Browny immediately and he would have him back to the hospital for surgery upon completion of the assignment. They flew him back from England just to blow up a safe for them and then they flew him right back. I do not think they found anything of importance, because Browny laughed about it. He joked mostly about what was not in there. Brown was a good man.

VICK UTZ'S WATCH

Vick Utz was one of the finest men I ever met in my life. He had been All-American out of Rutgers. He was full-blood German and spoke the language just like a native. Because of the language he worked in intelligence.

In Bastogne his arm was shot off right at his shoulder. He just had enough of a stub left that he could grab in order to cut off the bleeding. The aid station was only about a hundred and fifty yards from him. He walked in and there were men in every stage of dying. So Vick just waited his turn. One of the aid men put a tourniquet on his arm and then he waited until they could dress it.

He was engaged to a little ole girl named Dotty whom he would marry and raise four children. Vick asked Chaplain Maloney, "Captain will you do me a favor?"

He said, "Sure."

Vick said, "My fiancée sent me a beautiful gold watch. She sent that to me for Christmas and it means a lot to me. It's on my arm. I couldn't manage to get it and hold this stub. My arm's laying up there in the snow bank, right in the corner of this field."

Maloney said, "Sure, I'll go get it."

So he made a mad dash up there and came back very shortly and said, "Vick, your arm is laying there right where you told me but there was no watch on it."

Well, I knew they had shot his arm off but I was not aware his watch was missing. After the war, the first time that I had gotten all the guys together in Nashville, Chaplain Maloney and Gene Brown and his wife invited Martha and me out for dinner.

Chaplain Maloney said, "I had a problem with Vick."

I asked, "You did. When?"

He said, "There at Bastogne."

I said, "That kind of amazes me. Vick was not the kind of guy you would hardly have a problem with. I just would not believe that he would be the creator of a problem."

He said, "Well, it was not that, Jake." Then he told me about being in that first-aid station when Vick asked him to go up and get his watch. He said, "I went up there and the arm was laying there with no watch. Some paratrooper had stolen his watch."

I said, "Let me inject just a little bit of reason and logic into this thing. You know how everyone from corporal up was issued a watch?"

He said, "Yeah."

I said, "They were very valuable to coordinate attacks or withdrawls or strikes. They were very essential to a good operation. If my rifle blinked out or I ran out of ammunition, the first thing I did was grab ammunition or a gun off of a guy who had been killed. If I had found that arm there with a gold watch on it, I would not have cared if it was gold or brass or tin foil. I would have taken it to use as an instrument of war. If I had a thousand dollars in my pocket, I would not mind throwing it on a bunk and leaving it and going on about my business. If I was going to be gone two or three days, it would not have been bothered. I never saw a paratrooper steal one thing off of another paratrooper, unless it was food, whiskey, or women. Paratroopers did not steal from one another. Let's put you in the boots of the guy who found the arm with a beautiful watch. What are you going to do with it? Are you going to grab this arm and start running around all through the area asking, 'Whose arm have I got? Here, you left your watch on it.'"

Ole Captain Brown was sitting there and he kind of grinned and said, "Hell, Maloney. If I'd have found it I would have taken it."

Maloney then said, "Well, that makes me feel better. I really had not thought of it in that fashion."

I said, "Boy, a watch was a valuable instrument of war over there. When you are few and far between like you often were in paratroop units, you establish times and places where you will strike and where you are going to meet. They are very valuable. No one was stealing his watch. They did not know who in the hell's arm it was."

HERB PIERCE

By the time we got out of Holland, we only had one of those eight teenage kids left. All the rest of them had been killed. Kid Pierce was the only one still alive. Ole Top Kick Miller was a great man. He loved his troops. Boy, he really did. Top Kick told me about when they got ready to load on those trucks to go to Bastogne, "I just could not take that last kid in, Jake. I had eight of them kids and already got seven of them killed. So I just assigned Herb to rear echelon detail. He was so mad at me, he could have killed me." So Herb never did go to Bastogne.

All around Bastogne were pretty tall pine trees and firs. The Germans would try to kill us with those trees. They did not have good artillery air bursts. They did not have time detonation that would go off in so many seconds at such and such altitude. Theirs were not that sophisticated. So what they did was fire into those trees with point detonation. It was just like standing in a rainstorm of shrapnel and grenades. So they completely obliterated a number of growths of timber around Bastogne.

They had a big ceremony over there about fifty years after the war. Herb was over there. When the veterans all gathered in there, the citizens of Bastogne took their names and forged brass plates with the name of every paratrooper and his rank on them. They took these saplings and replanted this forest, then they put the nameplates on the individual trees. So when they came to Herb, he said he would not let them put his name on a tree out there because he had not been involved in the battle. They said they would like to anyway but he said, "No, I was not here. I am not going to name one of those trees."

A lady was there from Son, Holland, where the 506th had landed. She was kind of impressed with his act. She asked if Herb and his wife, Elaine, would come and spend a week with them. So they returned by Holland and greeted her. When they arrived in Holland, the lady had placed a twenty-foot tree out there with his nameplate on it. They had three bands out there and the mayor just for Herb, him alone.[31]

WAITING

Our division stayed in there about seven days until Patton pulled through with the 4th Armored.[32] Of course the Germans had about all they could take. They were out of gasoline and nearly everything else. They could not do anything further without having taken Bastogne with its communication and road and railroad networks. So that is why Bastogne was considered very important for their operation. The 101st then helped push the Germans back out of the Bulge.

They moved my two Pathfinder sticks back down to France near an air base. We were supposed to fly back to England the next morning and we were all packed up waiting in this Quonset hut. We just had our war gear. Some air force person came in and said, "The flight's off. We're weathered in."

So we took our gun belts off and hung them on the bed posts. We laid there all day and piddled around. The next morning at eight o'clock someone stepped in there and said, "The flight's off, boys."

Jake McNiece in Ponca City, Oklahoma, in late fall 1942, having finished basic training at Camp Toccoa, Georgia, and jump school at Fort Benning, Georgia. He was home on leave before going on to extensive training and maneuvers as a demolition saboteur in Regiment Headquarter Company, 506th Parachute Infantry Regiment, 101st Airborne. The 506th PIR was the first regiment that trained as a regiment for parachute duty.

Left to right: Jack Agnew (served in 101st Airborne and Pathfinders), John Dewey (served in 101st Airborne and Pathfinders), Charles "Trigger" Gann (captured as POW in Bastogne).

Littlecote Manor House, the home of Sir Ernest Wills. This photo was taken by Jack Agnew during a trip back for the 35th or 40th anniversary of D-Day. The 506th was stationed on the estate in 1943-44.

Regimental Headquarters Company Demolition Platoon at Littlecote Manor in England:
Standing: *Hayford, Bogerhausen, Armando Marquez, Tom Young, Burl Prickett, Frank Kough*
Kneeling: *Steve Kovacs, John Mohr, Mike Marquez, Milo Kane, Stacey Kingsley*
Laying: *John Klack*

Some of the Filthy Thirteen and other members of the Regimental Headquarters Company gang are shown on this and the next three pages.

Back row (l to r): *Andrew E. "Rasputin" Rasmussen (wounded in Normandy)*
Jake McNiece
Joe Oleskiewicz (died in Holland)
George Baran (wounded in Normandy)

Front row (l to r): *Jack Agnew*
Charles "Trigger" Gann (captured in Bastogne)
Chuck Plauda

Back row (l to r):	*William "Piccadilly Willy" Green (died over Normandy)* *Joe Oleskiewicz (died in Holland)* *Jake McNiece* *George Baran (wounded in Normandy)*
Front row (l to r):	*George "Googoo" Radeka (died in Normandy)* *Thomas E. "Old Man" Lonegran* *John F. "Peepnuts" Hale (died in Normandy)*

Back row (l to r): *Frank Kough, Clarence Ware (wounded in Normandy), Mike Marquez, Thomas Lonegran, Tom Young (wounded in Holland), Jim Davidson (died in Holland).*

Front row (l to r): *Joe Oleskiewicz (died in Holland), Herb Pierce, Frank "Shorty" Mihlan, Steve Kovacs (wounded in Holland).*

Roland R. Baribeau (died in Normandy)

Back row (l to r):
George "Googoo" Redeka
John "Dinty" Mohr
Leach

Kneeling (left):
Andrew E. "Rasputin" Rasmussen

Sitting (middle):
Thomas E. Lonegran

Hayford, John F. "Peepnuts" Hale, and William "Piccadilly Willy" Green

*Probably taken at Chalgrove Airforce Base outside Oxford, England, in February 1945, this photo is of men at the Pathfinder school at Chalgrove. Those men whose names are marked below with * were in the first plane, and those marked ** were in the second plane of Pathfinders that flew into Bastogne.*

Note the three hash marks above the cuffs of most of the men. The 506th sailed for England in September 1943, and each hash represents six months service overseas.

Back row, from left to right
*Lt. Shrable Williams **
? White
*John (Jack) Agnew **
*Lockland Tillman ***
*Charles Parlow ***
James Benson

Front row, from left to right
Richard Wright
*Irving Shumaker ***
*James (Jake) McNiece **
*George Blain **

A glider approaching a drop zone marked by the Pathfinders at Bastogne between December 23–26, 1944.

This picture shows the field where the Pathfinders landed on December 23; 1944, with the cemetery, church building, and Bastogne in the background. (Photo was taken in 1990s.)

The famous brick pile at Bastogne. Pathfinders are seen operating their CRN-4 set. Jack Agnew is on top of the brick pile.

Supply drop at Bastogne, December 1944.

This was the group that made the practice jump at Zell-am Zee on July 4, 1945, trying out the new quick-release parachute harness. The landing in the middle of Zell-am-Zee was a very cold one!

Back row from left to right:
Lt. Robert Haley
Lt. Ed MacMahan
Lt. Sterling Horner
Lt. Leo Monoghan
Lt. John Stegeman

Kneeling, from left to right:
Jake McNiece (Pathfinder)
Harold Anderson
Leonard Cardwell
Ed Borey
Stacey Kingsley
John Dewey (Pathfinder)

Raymond H. McNiece, captain in U.S. Army Air Corps, and James E. (Jake) McNiece, Pvt. in U.S. Army Paratroopers. Photo was taken in Ponca City in December 1943 while both men were on leave.

Note the Third Army patch on Jake's shoulder. After Jake returned from this leave the 506th Parachute Infantry Regiment was attached to the 101st Airborne Division. Jake was proud of the fact that he never rose above the rank of private.

Raymond ended up in the China/Burma/India Pacific theater flying supplies, etc. He made many trips over the "Hump," flying supplies to China for Allied bases in southern and southwestern China until those bases were taken by the Japanese. Raymond attained the rank of lieutenant colonel before discharge after the war.

Well, we were again all ready to go back to England. On the third day when they canceled it, ole Whitey reached down and grabbed his forty-five, jacked one in it and jammed it against his helmet. I was real close to him. As I was reaching for him, he pulled that trigger and it knocked a hole as big as a half dollar through that tin roof just above his head.

I slapped that gun out of his hand and asked, "What in the world are you doing? You idiot!"

He said, "I wasn't trying to blow my head off, Jake. I was just disgusted but I knew my pistol was empty."

I asked, "How did you know it was empty?"

He said, "Because when we got back here and had no more fighting, I took the clip out of it and threw it away."

Agnew was standing there and grinned. "Whitey, I was walking up the aisle there the other day and I noticed you had lost your clip. So I had some extra and I just put one in it."

Whitey said, "I don't know what in the world happened. I was not about to shoot myself. I would rather a German do that, but just before I squeezed the trigger, something said, 'Get it away from your head.' Then I just flexed my wrist."

MORE PATHFINDER MISSIONS

REWARD

So we finally flew back to Chalgrove and waited until needed again. Some officer recommended that all the men on the operation receive the silver star because of the danger. It had not been any different from anything else I had ever done. Colonel Sink said, "Aw hell, that's just normal activities for paratroopers. Give them another bronze star."

So we all received the bronze star for that action in addition to one for the inserted entry. In total we earned two bronze stars at Bastogne. Colonel Sink also found out that none of us had been killed. That is why he had sent us into the Pathfinders to begin with. So he sent a cablegram over to our company commander: "You send those six men out of Regimental Headquarters Company back to me. Evidently, I can kill them quicker than you can!" He actually did this. He was a rough old coot. He did not mind laying it out on the line.

That Pathfinder company commander sent him a letter back: "You can have five of them but you can't have McNiece. I've got the highest priority there is in Europe and he is essential to this operation." I was the guy they were wanting to get rid of all the time. So he sent the others back. I stayed with Pathfinders another two months and made one more jump.

We conducted regular infantry training along with our Pathfinder training. We studied patterns of panels and various levels of infrared lights so that the Germans could not see them from the ground. We had unlimited passes. The guys would go into London anytime they liked. I just told the guys to show up for training. We had a ball.

Prume Jump

February 13, 1945

The Americans were just getting ready to cross at the Remagen bridgehead and penetrate German soil. So they figured that they might need some Pathfinders. They took nine of my 101st sticks and strategically placed them behind objectives where they thought they might need pathfinding services. There were three of us in my ten-man section—Lockland Tillman, George Blain, and myself—who had three combat jumps. One and a half was the average life expectancy of a combat paratrooper. So in order to do us a favor, they held us in reserve and did not station us at any one of the strategic points.

We were standing there watching the others load up. Lockland said, "I feel sorry for them poor bastards."

I asked, "Why?"

He said, "Well, you know they are going to use some of them. You cannot have this big of an operation without any pathfinding service."

I said, "Yeah, I realize that Lockland, but I will tell you what. I bet you a good bottle of whiskey that you and I jump before they do." I really did not know. I was just trying to shake his confidence.

He said, "Oh no, Jake. They're holding us in reserve because we've already got three combat jumps."

I said, "Okay, let's sit down and just kind of figure this deal out logically as to what's going to happen. Now they're telling generals and commanders where these guys are. You've got a general up there and he's got two hundred thousand men under his command and divisions and artillery and this and that. He's a pretty busy boy. He knows that Chalgrove Air Force Base in England is the headquarters of Pathfinders. If he needs one quick, that's where he is going to go. He is not going to go to all these emergency spots. Every general in Europe knows where Chalgrove Air Force Base is and that there is immediate help there for anything. That's what is going to happen. They're going to get their tail in a crack and they are going to call right here and say, 'Get a stick in the air right now.'"

He said, "Oh no, I don't think so Jake."

I said, "Well, I do. Bet you a whiskey."

He said, "Naw." I had already planted the seed of doubt in his mind. I had drawn down his great sense of humor. "Naw, I won't bet you, Jake."

Well it was just three days later when the 90th Division got cut off in there at Prume, Germany. Earl Robins was in one of those cavalry units of the 90th Division. They would rush through areas and if they just intercepted small-arms fire, light resistance, they did not even fool with it. They just kept going, kept going, and kept going. Then of course the column followed them. The Germans let them run clear through St. Vith and up into the middle of the Siegfried Line before they opened up on the 90th from every direction and really started eating them up. The 90th had been in such a rush and covered so much distance in a short time that they were out of everything. We loaded up and jumped into that Siegfried Line. That was our fourth combat jump for the three of us. The date was Friday, February 13.

The jump was uneventful. We could reach up and grab two risers on one side and pull them down. That would let that air shoot through the panels so we could control the direction of our descent. There was a hedgerow with tall slender poplar trees. So we started slipping and that wind caught us and blew us right over that hedge of trees on the other side of a pillbox. We landed about a hundred yards from it. After that we began to maneuver on down to our objective. Of the ten men I took in, I think I only lost one. I reversed the percentages of Pathfinder casualties. They had been losing eight out of every ten and I got in there with nine out of ten men.

As I was running across the field I saw one lung lying there in that snow. It was bleached out as white as paper. There was not a drop of blood anywhere around it. There were not any animal tracks. I could not see signs where people had been engaged in any fighting. I was trying to figure out what was going on. I could only figure that a plane had been blown apart over that area. That thing just fell down there.

The 90th Infantry Division gave us quarters on the third floor of a building right close to the CP. We had one kid named Malcolm. He whistled and hummed all the damn time. This building we were in was shot up pretty bad. The rails were busted off the stairway. He walked out there to the wrong side of it. When he stepped out, there was nothing there. He plunged down three floors and hit his chin on the edge of one of those stairways. It drove his front teeth clear up into his gums and lips.

So I sent him down to the aid station and they patched him up. When he came back, he could hardly talk. He did not have any diction. George Blain said, "Well, you son-of-a-bitch, you won't be whistling all day around here anymore."

When we came back from Prume, all opportunity for airborne operations on a mass scale was just out of sight. That is when they returned me to my demolition platoon.

RETURN THROUGH ST. VITH

I do not remember exactly why but they gave me a two-and-a-half-ton truck to take my stick of Pathfinders back to Luxembourg. They had a big air base there where these shot-up C-47s and B-24s would limp back to set down for repairs before they were sent back to their assigned bases in England. So we left for Luxembourg where we would request passage back to England.

We drove through this little old town of St. Vith and did not see anything. It did not have a brick over a foot high anywhere throughout. I mean it was just flat. Not a house had been left standing. They blanket bombed it starting west of town in the middle of the cemetery and the craters overlapped one another clear through.

I looked at it and thought, "I don't see any military importance or essence to this town." There was not high ground or any elevated area, but I did see where a few tanks had been knocked out. We drove through that town with great difficulty because of all the rubble. I just wondered why they would have that kind of melee there.

After the war, Earl Robins worked for the bank in Ponca City and had taken some tours back over to Europe with his 90th Division. I asked him one time, "Say Earl, tell me something. Did you fight through St. Vith?"

He said, "I just drove through it Jake, we did not meet any resistance in it."

I asked, "What's the story with it? Do you know? That place was blanket bombed."

He said, "Jake, there is kind of a funny story about that. I'll show you a picture of it from when I was over there on this tour. What had happened was that the German high command had contacted Patton and told him that the little old city of St. Vith had great sentimental value for various reasons to the German people. They would appreciate it very much if he would just bypass it, just go through it and not destroy it. They told him there would be no resistance there and all that cock and bull. So Patton did. His people went through, the light infantry and the cavalry and all that. Then when they got into it with a column of heavy tanks, the Germans opened up on them from every side. Boy they killed them by the hundreds, knocking out tanks, trucks, and armor.

"Patton told the air force, 'I want that thing blanket bombed, east to west, north to south.' And so they did it."

Earl then showed me the picture. It showed a pedestal in the middle of that town with a statue of Jesus Christ standing on it and across the base it said, "THOU SHALL NOT LIE!"

THE TRUTH COMES OUT

We were sitting around at a "get together" one day and this guy asked, 'Where did you get four bronze stars on your wings? What jumps did you make?"

I said, "Well, I jumped into Normandy. That was an arrowhead deal. I made the invasion of Holland. That was considered an invasion, an arrowhead jump. After that I volunteered for pathfinder parachute duty."

Captain Brown was sitting there and said, "What do you mean you volunteered for it? I shanghaied you into that."

I said, "I have been waiting years for you to tell the truth about this and it finally came out. You dirty rat. You shanghaied me into pathfinding service to get me killed, and in seven days you all were burning the wires up, begging and pleading for them to send McNiece in there to save the DIVISION!"

He then said, "Well, that's not true. I did not shanghai you in there. All I had to do was tell you something was going to be exciting and pretty tough and you would say, 'I'll try that.' That's what happened. I did not shanghai you."

I said, "You already said you did, Browny. So don't hem-haw around." He laughed.

I said, "I made a jump into Bastogne after Normandy and Holland. After I got back out of Bastogne, it was just a little while before Patton had his 90th Division cut off and encircled in the middle of the Siegfried Line at Prume, Germany. I jumped in there on Friday, February the thirteenth. So I've got four.[33]

He asked, "And you're still a private?"

I laughed, "Yes, still a private. I would almost be ashamed to be anything but a buck private. I would not even want to be a PFC because people start classifying you with that group." We all laughed.

6

END OF THE WAR

LEACH'S PATROL[1]

Hitler had engaged twenty of his divisions during the Battle of the Bulge for his last thrust of the war. After that failed, the Germans had little else to fight with. By then it was all but over. The Allies just used the 101st as shock troops driving down through southern Germany and Austria.

While I was still in the Pathfinders, the division had moved into Haguenau, France. They still had some pretty heavy fighting. Across the Rhine lay Germany. They could hardly get across that river in rubber boats because the Germans would just eat them up. It was pretty tough in there at first but the Germans kept pulling out. Eventually it got to where the paratroopers would cross the river of an evening and find no Germans. Once in a while they might encounter some light resistance, but as long as it was light they would just keep rowing. If they ran into any concentrated fire, they would drift with the stream down to our own lines. It finally got to where the men who went over at night would get drunk. They would be over there with these *frauleins*[2] drinking all night instead of fighting.

Leach had not been in the S-2 very long before Colonel Sink

moved him up to the S-3 and promoted him to major. He was supposed to issue orders and keep track of all troop movements so that if anything drifted in front of our men, shortly after the time a patrol went out, then it was considered friendly. Any other time, they should shoot it out of the water.

Around about the time they were closing the Ruhr pocket, Leach decided he would finally lead a patrol. I guess he wanted to earn some medals. He took with him Frank Pellechia, Alfred Tucker, and three other guys. Tucker was also in the S-2 section.[3]

Well, Dog Company had relieved G Company that night. So their outposts had changed. For some reason, the word did not get down to Dog Company that there would be a crossing attempted at such and such an hour. The patrol ran into just light resistance but Leach said, "Let's go down the river."

When they drifted out in front of a boy with a BAR,[4] he just ate them up. He killed four or five including Leach.[5] I think Tucker was the only one who survived. He had been a very pleasant and quiet fellow but the war really got to him. He went home and became a total alcoholic. He would later call Top Kick Miller and talk as long as two hours, drunker than nine hundred dollars. He would not tell him where he was.

Top said, "I don't know how he was doing it. He may have been wiring a line of his own because I would try to trace the call and couldn't."

Leach's dad had money galore and contacts, too. He wrote some of the highest ranking officers in the United States and asked them to recommend his son for the Medal of Honor. They wrote back, "No dice."

For the Pathfinders nothing much happened after the Rhineland jump. On March 7, 1945, the Americans had established a bridgehead across the Rhine River at Remagen. As the Allies started pushing out from the bridgehead and through the Siegfried Line, the Germans began to pull back. That just eliminated any further need for Pathfinders so they returned us to our outfits.

I asked a lot of different guys after the war, "What unit were you in?"

One would say, "I was in the 45th to begin with." He may be able to name one or two officers in the 45th. "But I left there and went over to the 2nd Armored. I stayed there so long, then I got shot and they sent me to a Repo Depot, then I joined the 90th Division or something." They were in anywhere from two to three different units and they really never learned the names of their officers. They would have a first sergeant for a month or so, then he would be transferred, then they had a new first sergeant.[6]

I had gone into Regimental Headquarters Company, Demolition-Saboteur Platoon in September 1942. I had the same first sergeant clear through the war and never moved out of the Demolition-Saboteur Platoon except to go into Pathfinders. We had a lot of lieutenants killed and so forth, some of whom I have forgotten. We had five or six different company commanders in that period of time. I knew all of them by name and just about where and when they were killed.

In April, the army gave us transportation back to our units. I had the hundred Pathfinders from the 101st with me. I went back and rejoined the 506th Regimental Headquarters. I met up with my regiment just before they reached Lansburg. After we reported in, the regiment returned us to our original companies. My company put me right back in charge of my old section. I think Keith Carpenter returned to his old section. There were hardly any of the original men left but those who were were glad to see me because they knew they would be fed good. By that time there was very little fighting going on.

The 506th had pushed down into the Austrian Alps. Herman Goering had a castle as his headquarters over on the Koenig Sea. His place presented a tactical problem because of its location. His castle was back in the end of a canyon which opened onto eight miles of lake. That attack was where I rejoined my regiment. We borrowed Goering's boats to storm the castle and capture him. It was a little tough. Those SS and blackshirt boys defended him. I did not approach the castle, but set up right at the dam in case it became necessary to blow it and drain his lake. But our boys took his headquarters pretty easily.

We then went down to the Eagle's Nest in Berchtesgaden. It was Hitler's headquarters down there in the Alps. We also took that pretty easily. The SS had two-story barracks up there in Berchtesgaden. The living quarters for two soldiers was as big as the living room of a house. Between every third barracks they had an ammunition storage box filled with arms and ammunition. It was there for them to use whenever they wanted. We had fun with it instead.

We hauled out of both Goering's castle and the Eagle's Nest two-and-a-half-ton truckloads of the best whiskey, cognac, and wine that you ever saw. Goering was also a great lover of horse flesh. I will bet he had two hundred racehorses he had stolen from all those countries Germany invaded.

From the time the division headed south it met light resistance all along the way unless we ran into a concentration camp or something run by the SS boys. We would then go in there and kill their asses. The German army did not have any fuel left. Nearly all of their transportation was horsedrawn. When we tied in with a group of them, the first thing we did was kill their horses so they could not maneuver or move equipment around.

By that time we fought little ole kids, twelve and thirteen years old, and old men of seventy-five to eighty. So we picked out their SS officers and noncommissioned officers and killed them. It was very easy to observe who was an SS man, because those old men and kids were not doing any fighting. They were trying to find the biggest and deepest hole they could get into. The kids would be crying and the old men would be in shock. We just took those old men and little kids and stripped them of their knives and grenades and guns and ammunition. We laid their rifles on a curb, then ran back and forth over them with a truck to bust them up. Then we just told them to go on home. We did not have any transportation to handle POWs.

ZELL-AM-SEE

That was about all the action we saw in April and May. We finally ended up as occupational troops in the city of Zell-am-See, one of the biggest resort towns in Austria. It had nice big, plush hotels and a lovely lake. Colonel Sink pulled Jack Agnew off to be his boat man.[7] We began living high on the hog.

VE Day came on the 8th of May 1945, but we did not hear about it until the tenth. Everybody was thrilled to death, especially the officers. We immediately went GI just like back in training. We set up separate messes for the three grades: officers, noncoms and privates. I usually ate with my guys instead of with the NCOs.

One day I came into the mess hall and someone said, "I guess you'll not be eating with us."

I asked, "Why?"

He said, "They have hot bread and butter in the sergeants' mess."

I said, "I think I'll go in there and get me some of that." So I went in there with all those sergeants sitting around. I reached down and picked me up some of that hot bread and butter and started eating it.

This one sergeant asked, "Soldier, do you see anything else on this table that you want?" He knew I never ate with them.

I said, "The army pays the same amount a day for rations for all soldiers. Every soldier has the same right to this food. If I want any of it, I'll help myself to it."

He started to push back his chair to get up when Top Kick said, "You keep your ass glued to that chair. If McNiece wants it, you can believe he'll take it."

MOPEY

Zell-am-See was full of Northern Pike. We took all the boats and recreation vehicles in town. I made a fish run every day. I still had plenty of demolitions. I would rig a three-pound block with a three-second time fuse and drop it in the lake. The explosion would give the fish a concussion. We would then gather up into the boat all the fish that floated to the surface. We traded them for whiskey and cognac and other necessities that were hard for us to come by.

Troy Decker of the communications platoon had a little dog named Mopey. He called it Mopey because it just moped around. He had been shot up in Normandy and had not recovered enough to jump with us into Holland. He and Top Kick had been watching us load the planes when this English woman who was also watching asked Troy if he wanted a puppy. Her cocker spaniel had just had a litter. Well, she gave him the runt of the litter. When he and Top Kick were brought into Holland, he had that two to three-week-old puppy in his musset bag. He kept it with him all through the war and it grew up to be a beautiful cocker spaniel.

It always went with Troy and me when we went fishing with explosives. It had fun. We would throw Mopey out in the lake and he would swim back and shake that water off on us. That dog always stood right beside me and watched my every move. It had the routine down. After the explosion it would stand on that gunwale and as soon as it saw fish it started yipping.

One day Troy wanted to get a great big fish. He believed there had to be some big ones down in that deep water. We had always fished in the shallow water. So I rigged a ten-pound charge with a thirty-second fuse. I thought that might give it enough time to reach the bottom. It would have been better if I had used a forty- or fifty-second fuse. When it blew, it raised a bubble as big as one's living room and just as high. Those boards on that boat started flapping. Mopey was standing right there on the front of that boat as usual and it scared him.

Right after that ten-pound charge went off, we did not see any fish float to the top. Then we saw something white under the boat. I reached down with an oar and pulled it up. It was a four-foot-long grass pike. It was four inches wide from the head back to the tail. We cut the tail off and kept it for ourselves, then traded the rest.

From that day forth when I dropped in a charge, Mopey would run and hide under the cowling. The minute he heard the explosion then he came out and stood on that gunwale. We did not fish that way too much longer for we found a trap up there and started getting our fish out that way.

We discovered the Austrians had cheese houses back up in those mountains. They had cakes of cheese probably two feet in diameter and six to eight inches thick, just like a disc. The oldest cheese was the best. It had a crust of black mold an inch thick. Of course, we had plenty of it so we did not care how much we ate or wasted. We just trimmed all that black off of it and it was the best cheese that I ever ate. We also had opportunities to butcher all the meat we wanted. Once again we ate well.

Reroute River

They had a heck of a rain up there one day. The river that ran around the town had flooded and the water ran right down through the middle of the town. The burgermeister called regimental headquarters to ask if there was anything the military could do. Willy asked me what we could do about it.

I said, "We have some Composition C-2 and some TNT. Let's go down and see what the situation is."

We saw that the river had steep embankments and had flooded into a gully at a fork. It formed into two rivers, one that went into town and another that went around it. If we could collapse enough of one embankment then we could redirect the river around the town. This was up in the mountains and the embankment was all rock.

Willy asked, "How much explosive do you think we should use?"

I said, "Let's use all we've got, except some of the TNT in case we need to blow the other embankment."

We dug into the embankment about two or three feet, set our charges and blew that thing. It closed that gully off and the river shot around that town like a bullet. I saw that if I collapsed the other embankment it would seal it off real tight. Well about that time the mayor of the town came running up there and asked what we were going to do. I told him we were going to blow the other embankment with the rest of the TNT.

He said, "Nein, nein! You've broken every window in the village. We will be better off with the flood."

Acting First Sergeant

They started shipping guys home on the point system. A man received so many points for a medal and so many for a period of time overseas and so many for being wounded. They figured it out that when the war ended, they would go through all the records and pick out the guys who were going to come home early.

Top Kick Miller was the only first sergeant I ever had. I served with him for three and a half years. Top Kick had enough points from medals and wounds so he got an early release to go home right after VE Day. He shipped out and went back to the States in June. I had more points than he did, but the army was showing preference to the regular army people. When they shipped him out, Captain Brown called me in and made me the acting first sergeant of Regimental Headquarters Company. He gave no explanation why. Browny and I always got along well together. It was funny that he would not promote me to PFC but he made me the acting first sergeant.[8]

FOURTH OF JULY[9]

As the first sergeant, I just kept records and handled company food and quarters. I later received a message to secure rations and quarters for 125 athletes. The division was going to hold a big Fourth of July celebration at Zell-am-See. We had a baseball game with about four or five teams. They also had a track and field competition. I had requisitioned hotels and resorts for quarters.

I was going to participate in a water jump demonstration. About ten of us went down to Salzburg, Germany, to get a C-47 to fly across the Alps where we planned to bail out into that lake. Zell-am-See was fed by mountain streams. Of course we were drunk and so was the pilot. He liked to never have found the lake. He finally located it and we jumped.

By the end of the war the army had come out with a new quick-release parachute harness. When we got within ten or fifteen feet of the water each of us turned our little ole buckles, slipped out of the harnesses and plunged into the icy water. There were supposed to be other paratroopers in boats waiting to pick us up. Well, these guys in the boats were all drunk and not paying any attention. We nearly froze, but after a while they finally found us.

Goering was a collector of fine horse flesh and we had borrowed his horses so our guys could have a rodeo and horse races. Most of them were city boys from New York, Chicago, and Philadelphia. They did not know anything about horses. They ran those horses until they got to lathering, then they ran them out into that ice-cold water to cool them off. The horses just dropped dead as soon as they hit the water. I will bet those guys killed about ten million dollars worth of racehorses that day.

Hotel Fire

I was going with a pretty little ole Austrian girl named Media Feistower. Her father had been the commander of the Hitler Youth movement and she had been in the Hitler Youth all along. He owned a big four-storied hotel. They had turned it into a hospital for the German soldiers wounded in Italy and Germany.

One day Media asked me for some kerosene. I thought she wanted gasoline, so I filled up a glass gallon jug full of gasoline. I had been drinking when I carried it in. I went through and bumped the door with that glass jug and it spilled all over the place. Well, Media's apartment was on the second floor. There was a stairwell that went right up to it. I told the little ole slave laborer, "Clean that up."

I went up and walked into Media's apartment and told her, "Media, I spilled that gasoline and I'm going to go help that girl clean that mess up."

When I opened the door, here came a wall of flames. It sounded like a tornado going up that stairwell. So I ran over to jump out of that second story window. This was directly across the street from our mess hall where the guys were eating. The officers came pouring out of the mess hall. The army was pretty tough on fraternization with civilians. When I looked out there and saw those idiots, the patients were jumping out of those second, third, and fourth story windows. I stuck my head out and yelled, "Come on in here you cowardly SOBs and help me save these poor people." Then I began to find ways that I could get out of that building.

Media's older sister tried every way in the world to stick me with a war crimes atrocity so our government would pay for the building. She claimed that I had done this on purpose. The army had moved in the Allied Military Government (AMG) to occupy countries and protect the civilians. It was made up of civilians and some army people. We had one right there in Zell-am-See. They generally accepted an officer's recommendation. The officers were real good about protecting a soldier who they thought was halfway honest. So they hushed it right up. They never did prefer charges.

JOE OLESKIEWICZ

Sergeant Johnson and I were sitting there drinking one day. We were getting drunk and he said, "Jake, I'm going to tell you something you've wanted to know for a long time."

I said, "What is that, Johnnie?"

He said, "Naw, I'm not going to tell you. You'll be mad."

I said, "No, I won't be mad." I thought it was something he had reported or ratted on and got me into trouble. Back when I blew up the barracks, he was the guy who suggested they include "acting NCOs."

We were sitting there getting drunker and he would get a little looser and say, "I'm going to tell you something you've been wanting to know a long time." His tongue was as thick as the sole of a shoe and about as flexible.

I said, "Johnnie come on. What are you talking about?"

He said, "No, you'll get mad."

I said, "Johnnie, I don't care what happened. Just let it alone."

"So, Jake," he said, "I'm going to tell you now. You know how you had hunted and hunted and sought to find information about Joe Oleskiewicz.

I said, "Yeah. Have you all heard anything?"

He said, "Well, I'm going to tell you what happened to Joe."

I said, "Okay, tell me."

He said, "When we got into Veghel, you know, we did not know what the situation was. So we got through the town in pretty good shape and then we ran into those tanks and their supporting infantry. Me, Oleskiewicz, and Speedwack [Stanley Spiewack] were fighting that tank there and he was firing directly at us with the eighty-eight. It got pretty rough on us. We made a run to get down inside one of those foxholes. That foxhole had been run over two or three times by the tracks of those tanks. It had caved in filling up a lot of it. There was only room for two of us to get in and three of us were running shoulder to shoulder for it. Me and Speedwack got down in it but Joe did not make it. So he stood up to run for the ditch. Them tanks were ten or twelve yards from him. One lowered that barrel down and hit him with an eighty-eight right in the guts."

I said, "Well, I ran right past the same spot and I saw the trunk and legs laying there but I did not have any idea which one of the boys it was."

He said, "I never have told anyone because at D-Day I had a little difficulty and got mixed up in things. I've always felt badly about it. I've always had a complex and I did not have guts enough to tell you what happened to Joe, afraid you'd figure I had ushered him out of the way and beat him to the foxhole."

I said, "No way. I just appreciate knowing what happened to the kid."

I still have a lot of nightmares about seeing his body there.

When we had jumped into Normandy we had a company commander named Captain Edward Peters. He and a stick of demolition men had got into some heavy machine-gun fire. So Captain Peters took these paratroopers and attacked those machine-gun nests. Tom Young, Sergeant Bill Myers, and a couple of other guys with Captain Peters charged in on one machine-gun nest. They threw a grenade in and put it out of commission. Peters turned around and held up three fingers to show he had killed three of them and knocked the gun out. He no more than got them up than a Kraut shot him right in the temple and just near tore his head off.

When they had charged in, Truck Horse Johnson kind of slowed down. He really did not charge in like he should have. For a moment or two he lost his composure. Had he not, he might have saved the captain's life. No one can ever tell. At least he would have done something. All the guys who went in on the charge had witnessed that Truck Horse kind of chickened out. When a guy exhibits that characteristic, people never feel real confident with him. Everybody else learned about it and it gave him a complex. Nonetheless, he turned out to be a good soldier. I never did see him waver after that. But he always had a little bit of a complex about it through the rest of the war.

Writing the Families

At the end of the war, Captain Browny said, "Jake, I have been getting letter after letter from the families of all those boys killed in the Filthy 13. I really don't know what to tell them."

I said, "You know about as much about it as I do. You were as close to them as anybody."

He said, "If you would write each one of the families a letter I will censor and mail them. When you get them written just bring them down and you and I will review them."

He knew that I was kind of the platoon lawyer. I represented the men and helped them through their problems. I had written letters for this guy and that guy over problems they had back home. So I wrote each one of the families. Anyway, a peculiar thing happened.

Just before we went overseas, Loulip had come up and said, "Jake, we're going to ship out pretty quick and I have a fiancé at home that I would kind of like to bust it up with. I would like to send her a 'Dear John' letter. Could you compose me a letter to this young lady and make her feel real good?"

I said, "Sure I can."

So I composed a nice letter to this young lady telling her that he loved her so much, that it would be absolutely unfair for him to keep her on a string for six months or two years when there was only one chance in a million of him even returning. He could not bear to think that she was going to wait there and be faithful to him for that long. As much as he loved her he could not do it. So she should not let any opportunities go by. He considered the relationship as over. So Loulip copied this letter and sent it to her. She accepted it very graciously. She even wrote him back saying she still loved him very much but she would defer to his decision.

Lou later asked me, "Jake, do you care if I keep this copy? I might want to do this two or three more times."

I said, "No, go ahead and keep it. If the situation changes, I'll come over and borrow it from you."

After I wrote a letter to his folks, I immediately got a letter back from his sister. She said, "Jake, we got Lou's personal effects box after Normandy." Before paratroopers jump into combat, they leave a personal effects box with stuff going to whomever they so desire. It had Lou's knife, wings, and other things.

She said, "In it was a letter that had been composed by you. It was identical to the letter Lou had sent to his young lady. We had no idea before who had composed the letter. After we got your letter, I recognized the handwriting the minute I saw it."

Well, I have a kind of a peculiar handwriting. It is not necessarily pretty but it is real different. I kind of write backhanded and print letters instead of writing them. When it comes to dotting something I just make a circle.

Well, she said, "So you are the one who wrote the letter for Lou. Now I would like to ask you to do me one more favor. Would you mind writing that young lady a letter and give her the details of Lou's death? She is still as bereaved as she was the day it happened."

I dropped his sister a line and told her I'd be happy to. So I wrote the letter. It was a crazy war.

Schroeder

Around August, Browny shipped back to the States and Bruno Schroeder was made a captain and acting company commander of Regimental Headquarters Company. We served together from that day on and he hated me. He was a rat, a total rat.

Little Shorty Mihlan asked him one time, "Schroeder, would you recommend me for a Good Conduct Medal?"

Well of course, Shorty had been busted. He was an alcoholic but had soldiered all the way from Normandy clear through that war. So it was not going to break the government to give him a Good Conduct Medal.[10]

Schroeder said, "I would not recommend you for getting it. You're a scum bum."

Little ole Shorty looked up at him and said, "I'll tell you one thing you son-of-a-bitch, I would hate to be one of your kids."

That was the end of the conversation. Schroeder went back home to Austin, Texas, after the war where he refereed the Texas-OU football games and the Cotton Bowl games. He had three children, two boys and a girl. His fifteen-year-old boy committed suicide. About a year and a half later the other boy committed suicide. About four or five years later, Schroeder also committed suicide. I will bet that when the boys started committing suicide, Schroeder remembered many times what that little ole drunken bum had told him.

Schroeder's wife was one of the sweetest ladies you would ever meet so we invited them to our get togethers after the war. He had always attended but no one really made friends with him. One day he was drinking and said, "Say, McNiece, let me ask you a question."

I said, "Go ahead."

He asked, "Why did you represent the enlisted men? How did you know what the men had in their minds?"

As the platoon lawyer I always spoke up for the men. If a man had a problem he usually came to me. Browny answered for me, "That's easy. Whatever they had in their minds, McNiece probably put it there."

BLACK MARKET

I had promised my mother and dad that I would take them on a tour of the United States when I returned. I would need a lot of money to do that. A person could sell a carton of cigarettes for two hundred dollars. One could sell an overcoat for two or three hundred. Those Austrian people had money but they did not have any produce to buy except from the American GI. I made enough money to last me about a year after I got out.

Nearly every place I went I had boots on. I always kept that money in my boots but did not flash it around. Paratroopers did not steal valuables from other paratroopers. I could leave a roll of hundred dollar bills on my bunk for a week and it would still be there when I came back. Now if it was something useful for combat it disappeared the minute I turned my back. I had no trouble getting that money back home.

FINAL DAYS IN SERVICE

PARIS ONE MORE TIME

It must have been August when we moved from Zell-am-See, Austria over to Auxerre, France. I did not know it at first but they were getting ready to disband our division. Well, I probably had more points than anyone in the company but I could not leave early. As the acting first sergeant I had to clean up the records and get the company organized so they could ship out. We were the next bunch to go. We were going to leave on September 12 and go down to either Chesterfield, Camel, or one of those other cigarette camps.

So I gave all of the guys who were going to be shipping out the next day a midnight pass to Paris to let them do the town one more time. I furnished them a truck and driver and they took off. I had just a little bit of book work left to do. I was finishing that stinking paperwork because the next morning we were going to the disembarkation area. I finished my work up to snuff or as good as it could be arranged by about 3:00. So I got out and hitchhiked into Paris. I knew everyone of those guys would go right straight to Pig Alley.[11] I just figured I would run into one or two of them there and have me a ball one more time before I came home. I got in there and started drinking and carousing around.

Pig Alley had sidewalk cafes all along there. It was one of the world's largest black market areas. I saw a boy from the Third Army who was by himself arguing with some Frenchmen. Well, two GIs can whip a whole street full of those Frogs. So I moved over near him. When he saw me move in, boy he grabbed that Frog he was messing with and busted him down and stomped and kicked him around. I just walked around the fight slowly and if anyone stepped out I would drop them. That Frog got up and the other boy hit him and knocked him back up into this wall of people that circled us. That soldier stepped up in there, grabbed the Frog and yanked him back out of that circle. When he did, one of them hit him with a bottle of wine and dropped him right then and there. I grabbed the guy who hit him with a wine bottle and busted him down, just started stomping him and kicking him around. When I did they came at me from all sides.

That Third Army GI got out of there someway fast. He left me fighting that whole street full of them. Of course I could not keep all of them off. They cut my head across the temple and back down my neck and ear. I was losing a lot of blood but they still did not have me down. Three of those Free French soldiers came along and saw what was happening. They jumped in with me and boy we went to work on those Frenchmen, sure enough. Then the MPs came along. They gathered me up and took me back down to an American aid station.

They had aid stations set up all over Pig Alley. They had "blood buckets" driving those streets picking up bodies all day long. So they moved me down to an aid station and worked on me for a while and then they found an ambulance that could take me over to a general hospital right there in Paris. I went in there first thing the next morning. Of course I missed my ship. So my company carried me as AWOL. I eventually went through three hospitals in France.

Scar tissue will rise above the surface and those holes down in the ear drum are not that big. My ear was cut up so bad that after they got through packing and bandaging it, it had grown back together. So I finally told them, "Well, ship me back to the United States. I've got a quarter-inch drill and I can do a better job than you all."

BACK IN THE STATES

Well, they shipped me back on a hospital ship. We arrived at Camp Kilmer, New Jersey, on the twentieth of December. The transportation corps people, who wore a big steering gear patch on their shoulders, loaded us onto hospital trains bound for different destinations. They had hospitals set up to accommodate different types of wounds and injuries and sickness. I needed some plastic surgery on my ear so they loaded me on a train that was heading down to Camp Chaffee, Arkansas.

We took off and headed north. The first thing I knew we were in Canada. Then they cut back west and headed south again to Chicago. We were a low priority. Every time another train would be on the same track as us, they would park us to the side and let the civilians pass. So I was not in too good of a mood. We were on that train for four days and nights going from Camp Kilmer to Camp Chaffee.

My mother had died the previous January. After I had seen what the point system was, I had called Dad from France and told him, "Dad I'll spend Christmas with you." I intended to keep my promise. We were scheduled to arrive at Camp Chaffee on Christmas Eve. Most of the officers, of course, would be on leave. I figured my records would be all goofed up. I did not know at that time that they did not even have records on me. I thought, "You'll get in there and you will not even see daylight." I decided that I would bail off of that train and hitchhike home.

The hospital train was an old type of train. It had an observation platform between each car. I had moved my duffel bag out on this platform and had my musset bag on. The area had had a terrible storm the night before and snow was hip deep to a tall Indian all along the right of way. I was kind of standing there looking for a drift that was big enough to break my fall. This "Wagon Wheel" captain and his sergeant came along. They counted me one-twenty-three or something.

I asked, "What are you doing?"

He said, "We are counting heads so we will know how many people we are responsible for when we get to Chaffee."

I said, "You better subtract one off of your total because I won't be there."

He said, "Yeah, you will."

I repeated, "I won't be there."

He said, "We're only about twenty miles from Chaffee. We don't stop between here and Chaffee."

I said, "You watch this."

I kicked my duffel bag and away it went with me right after it rolling and tumbling in that snow. That captain watched the whole time.

I got up and started walking. I had whiskey and different things in that big duffel bag. It was tough to carry but there was a little old country store right there close to where I jumped off. I walked in there and they asked, "Can we do something for you?"

I said, "Yeah, you sure can. I've got my world's possessions in this duffel bag. There is a Swastika flag that will cover any wall you've got in here and it is in good condition. I'm trying to hitchhike to Ponca City, Oklahoma, and I don't want to fool with this. If you will store this here for me, I will pay you whatever the charges are when I come back and pick it up. If I don't make it back to pick it up, it is yours stock free."

They said, "We can store it under here for you. We will hold it for a long, long time. It is not any trouble."

So they stored my duffel bag there. I got out and all I had was my musset bag. I hitchhiked and got home the evening of December the twenty-fourth. I stayed for about ten days.

My brother and father decided they would just drive me over to Camp Chaffee. That way we could get in a little more visiting. When we arrived at Camp Chaffee we stopped right there at the main gate and I told this MP, "I'm reporting in."

He asked, "Who are you?"

I said, "I'm James McNiece, 18131236."

He read the list and said, "We don't have a record of you."

I said, "I jumped off a hospital train about ten days ago. I've been AWOL ever since. I think I'll report back in."

He said, "Well, we don't even have any record of you. Let me call up ahead."

He called somewhere and they did not know anything about me either. They told him to put me in some transportation and bring me up to such and such section of the hospital.

When he turned me loose, I reported to a lieutenant. I told her what had happened. She also said, "We do not even have a record of you anyway."

I said, "I should have stayed home is what I should have done."

I needed plastic surgery on my head and ear and neck. The nearest plastic surgery center was Springfield, Missouri, and boy, it was really crowded. There were guys they had been working on for a little over a year. They just took people by necessity. I waited at Chaffee until a bed opened up at Springfield. So I hung around there for about another ten days.

I went in and asked for a midnight pass into Fort Smith just as quick as I could get straightened out there and learn the ropes.

This little ole nurse said, "Okay, fine and dandy."

There was really nothing physically wrong with me. She gave me a seventy-two-hour pass and I went back and started getting ready to do the town up right. I had really not been in an American city except Ponca City since the war. Just in a little while she called me up to the phone. My brother Jack was up in Philadelphia. He was a major in the air corps who had flown the Hump in the China-Burma-India theater.

Jack said, "Sidney is home in Ponca City this weekend and he does not have much time." Sid was my other brother who had been an underwater demolitions man with the Seabees down in the South Pacific. He was getting ready to enroll in college. Jack said, "If you want, I'll pull in there in the morning about nine o'clock. I've got a C-47 at my command. How about I pick you up in the morning and let's fly over to Ponca City and the three of us get together and shoot the breeze." We had not seen one another in years.

I said, "Okay, fine and dandy."

He asked, "You can go can't you?"

I said, "Oh yeah, I can go. No problem."

I talked to the nurse, "Now listen. I have two brothers whom I have not seen in two and a half or three years. One would like to pick me up in the morning at nine o'clock. We'll fly to Ponca City and spend a day or two and then he'll bring me right back."

She said, "That'll be all right. You can go if you're back here tonight at midnight."

I said, "I'll be back."

I went into town and got all drunked up. A couple of MPs told me to get out of town. I do not remember any of this. I just remember what they said at the court martial. Evidently, I whipped those two MPs in this bar and told them, "You all go get you some reinforcements. That's what your problem is. There's not enough of you. I'll be right here."

Well, they came back with a captain, a sergeant, and another private. The captain said, "When we entered the bar, paratrooper McNiece was sitting at the bar like he said. When he looked around and saw us enter, he charged us and started putting the ugly all over us."

They filed charges against me. I went in and was listening to all this. If I had been the captain, I would have never said this. I would have thought up another charge of some kind but he said, "He called me a draft-dodging, slacking, noncombatant son-of-a-bitch. Boy, and it went to the dirt. We finally controlled him and took him back and put him in the stockade."

This MP officer asked me, "If you held a certain opinion of someone or something, you might be quiet about it. But if you got drunk, you would likely be able to make that remark."

I said, "Oh yeah. Let me tell you something. I would not have to be drunk to tell you that. In the soberest moment of my life my evaluation of you would be the same."

He asked, "Do you remember calling me that?"

I said, "I don't remember it but I'm not denying it. I don't know if it would do me much good to deny it when you have four witnesses plus your own story."

He said, "This is a real peculiar thing. You've got about twenty decorations issued in combat. There is no record of you ever having problems with officers, but with an attitude like yours, we don't know how you got through with this kind of a service record."

I said, "Why, it's very simple. I can give you an answer real quick. The officers that we had in airborne units were some of the finest soldiers that ever lived. They took every chance that we did. They were as susceptible to that enemy fire as we were and they stood there and looked it right in the eye. We had good officers. I did not have any problems with them. It's just people like you that I have problems with."

He said, "Well, we've reviewed your record. You've been in the stockade half the time that you've been in but you've never been court-martialed. We can't understand it really. Nonetheless, we're going to court-martial you. Then you had better watch your step. We have found out that they are going to ship you up to O'Reilly because of plastic surgery. If you ever set foot in this town again, it is the first step towards Leavenworth."[12]

I said, "Well, I want to tell you something. I'm going to do a little leveling with you. If I come back here to Chaffee, there will be a piece of paper that will declare me a civilian. Buddy, you had better give me a big wide berth. Because I will be out from under your jurisdiction and I'm going to beat you to death."

He said, "Okay."

They court-martialed me right there. I did not get to see my brothers as planned. I then went up to O'Reilly and had the plastic surgery. The medical people were very good. It was just like clockwork to them. They made a hole down in my ear. It is not shaped like the other but it's straight in and I have lost very little hearing in that ear.

They shipped me back to Camp Chaffee. There was a captain who interviewed us as we were being separated. He tried to figure out our Military Occupational Skill (MOS) from talking with us. We were supposed to have some preference for employment if that field came open. This guy was talking to me and I said, "The main thing I am in here for is that separation money. Let's see some green laying up out there on this table."

He said, "McNiece, I'm not sure but that you owe us some

money. It looks like you've got as much bad time as you've got good time."

I said, "That depends upon the definition that you're using. Everything that you all thought was bad time, to me it was good time and what you all thought was good time to me was bad time."

He was real nice about it. They separated me from the service on February 26, 1946, as a staff sergeant. I had been in the army for three years, five months, and twenty-six days. I enjoyed every minute of it. I never had so much fun in any three and a half years of my life. I had a lot of hard times and a lot of bad times but it was a great experience. Some say that I may have led a charmed life. Someone asked me after the war why I thought I survived four combat jumps.

I said, "I think I know why I lived through them. I wasn't any more skilled than anyone else but at that time the Lord had only two places he was putting people—in heaven and in hell. I don't think he had a place for me. I don't think he wanted me to goof either place up."

7

GET-TOGETHER

A PROMISE

My mother and dad had worked like dogs to raise ten kids along with Dad's two younger half-brothers. They had never traveled a whole lot. They could not afford to. So I had told Mom and Dad that when the war was over I would show them the whole United States, just make a tour of it. My mother died while I was overseas so when I returned home after the war, I picked up Dad and we toured the whole eastern part of the country. We drove by car right straight through to the Carolinas, up to Washington, D.C. and Philadelphia, to Buffalo, New York, and Niagara Falls, and crossed over into Canada. We then started retracing our route but veered off and came back through the Allegheny Mountains and down through the midwest, where there were not a lot of tourist sites. We were gone about three weeks or so on that leg of the journey.

I then told Dad when we got back home, "Now you get rested up and we'll take off and go to the west coast." A short time later, we headed out to California. We traveled clear up Highway 101 then came back down through the Redwood National Forest and saw the big dams. We just had a great time. That jaunt lasted about another three weeks.

After that I asked Dad, "Is there any place in this country that you would like to see?" Boy, I was really loaded. I had loot like you would not believe. I had enough to last me a year and we had not spent a lot of money.

Dad had been an orphan kid down in Arkansas since he was three years old. He said that he would love to go back down to Newport, Arkansas, and visit the children of some of the families that had taken care of him. He had just moved from one farmer's house to another. He lived with them for either six months, a year, or two years, and then they would let another farmer have him. The people were very good to Dad. They did not mistreat him at all. He worked hard but so did the other children. The families treated him like one of their own and Dad loved them.

He remembered several children his same age so we spent two weeks down there just visiting from one house to another. Those people welcomed him just like he was their brother. There still was a lot of admiration and respect between them.

TULARE, CALIFORNIA

When we returned from Arkansas, I took off for California. I knew I could make pretty good money out there. That was the first place where they began to use parachute firefighters. They would pay those firefighters good money to parachute into the wildfires. I think they were paying them two hundred and eighty dollars a month. I went out there and tried to sign up with them.

They asked me, "How old are you?"

I said, "I'm twenty-eight."

They said, "That exceeds the limit. We cannot employ people that old."

I asked, "You can't employ people that old?"

They said, "Yeah."

I said, "I was not too old a year ago in Europe to be kicked out of every airplane that got off of the ground just to kill Germans for twenty dollars a month. It seems to me like you have a sudden increase in qualifications."

Of course I was irritated because I felt that I was just as good as them since I had been in the paratroops. But they would not hire me because of my age. I instead went to work for the Southern Pacific Railroad.

I was an alcoholic when I went in the army and when I came out. I pursued it for several years. I was in a brawl nearly every night somewhere. I really was not belligerent. I think a lot of people got the idea that if they could whip an ex-paratrooper, that would put them high up on the stick. A lot of my fighting was due to circumstances that I did not create, but then I did not take "boo" from anybody. When drunk, a person is going to place himself in a position where it will be more convenient to fight than explain.

I had lots of problems. I was in jail a whole lot but I always had a good paying job. I was just saving money to build me a nest egg. But just as soon as I got some money, I would go out and get drunk. While I was in Los Angeles, I owned a twelve-cylinder Lincoln Zepher. I was driving up the street one morning stone cold drunk and passed out. When I woke up I was driving through an underpass. I just missed the concrete pillar by a coat of paint. I could have been killed. I thought for the first time, "I've got to change."

I worked as a fireman on the railroad for about nine months. They had great packing sheds where farmers brought their harvested crops in to freight. We had a big stop at Bakersfield where men would lash down those reefers after they were loaded. Then we would take off from Bakersfield about midnight and would pull a trainload of empty reefers up to Tulare. We would arrive at six o'clock in the morning. There was a hotel and a cafe right beside the depot. We would just pile off of that train, go in and clean up, eat breakfast then go to bed. Of course, we would sleep all day while others were loading those reefers. They would have that done by six o'clock that evening. Then the same train crew—engineer, brakeman, and fireman—would report in, mount that engine and haul those back down to Bakersfield where they would ice them down.

So we pulled into Tulare one morning. We went up and the rooms were not clean. So we went to breakfast and I started drinking. I got so drunk I could not hit the floor with my hat in thirty throws. All of the others had gone on up to bed. I kept drinking and kept drinking and kept drinking until I just passed out at the bar. I was not bothering anyone or disturbing anything. The first thing that I knew some rat had my wrist twisted up between my shoulder blades and was shoving and yanking me around.

If a guy had walked up to me and said, "Jake, I'll take you and get you a drink." Why, I would have followed him through hell or high water. But the way this guy was abusing me why, I yanked him around in front of me and busted him right in the chin. At that time nearly all railroad men wore those heavy wool checkered shirts. I had on one of those. He had my arm twisted up so tight that it tore my shirt sleeve off. He just sailed through that big plate glass window with my shirt sleeve. I jumped right out there on him and started kicking and stomping him around. His buddy came up and hit me with a sap.[1] He hit me with it so hard it knocked my shoe off.

I backed up and he had a hog leg [pistol] in one hand and that sap in the other. Those two turned out to be police officers. That fellow on the sidewalk got up and was standing right over my shoe. He said, "Put your shoe on!"

I said, "I would be happy to. Take a couple of steps back."

He said, "I told you to put your shoe on!"

I said, "I want to tell you something, buster. I don't believe that two of you can whip my ass and there are too many people here watching this for you to shoot me. I'm not going to walk over there and let you work me over with that sap. Back off of that shoe and I'll put it on. I just don't go for your attitude. I won't give you any trouble. I didn't know who I was hitting. If you all would have walked up here and approached me any other way, I would have walked right to the jail with you."

So he backed off and I put my shoe on. They loaded me in the car and put me in the jug. Right outside of Tulare they had the Tulare Industrial Road Gang which operated just like a chain gang. When the police arrested someone and shook him down they found out how much money he had and the judge would fine him a greater amount. Then they put him on this chain gang and he would work off his fine along the way. They built roads and canals, various things like that for public use. They paid each prisoner fifty cents a day credit on his fine.

Well, they took me in real quick and fined me about seventy-five dollars. I did not have it on me. I had about twenty-five, which meant I was going to spend a hundred days on the chain gang. Every day that they worked us on a state or county project the city received five dollars paid for each of our services. So they took me up to the chain gang.

I had hotel rooms at both ends of the rail line. I had one in Bakersfield, one in Fresno, and one in Los Angeles. I would be in one of those three places every day. Well, the people I had a room with up in Fresno found out what had happened by talking with the other railroad people. After about ten days, the guy who owned the hotel came down and bailed me out. Of course, the people who ran the railroad immediately fired me on Rule Z—use of intoxicants on or off the job.

Peepnuts's Dog

After the railroad fired me I decided that I would go to Alaska. In 1947 there was big money to be made up there. I stopped by Seattle, Washington. Peepnuts's mother and dad and sister lived right across the harbor on Bremerton Island. After I had written the families of the boys killed, most of the parents wrote back, "When you get back to the States we would love to visit with you if possible."

I called and Peepnuts's mother answered it and I told her that I was passing through and wanted to pay my respects to his parents for the great service that he had done for his country. I wanted to tell them that I had enjoyed knowing their son very much and that they could be proud of him. She asked, "Well, where are you at?"

I said, "I'm just here in Seattle."

She said, "You are going to come out here and visit with us, James. We need to talk to you."

I had to catch a ferry across the harbor. She was fixing dinner and as I approached the house there was a big collie out in the yard. It was real friendly. I walked on up and Peepnuts's mother came to the door and invited me in. She and I had a long talk and began to reminisce. She said, "You know that dog out there, Jake?"

I said, "Yeah."

She said, "That was Peepnuts's dog. Peepnuts rode the school bus to school and back. Every morning at eight thirty that dog would go up to that gate there with Peepnuts. Every afternoon at three thirty he waited at that gate. How he figured the time out, I don't know. That went on for years while he was going to school and after he joined the army. On June the sixth, that dog quit going to that gate."

I said, "No kidding."

She said, "That's right. I told his dad, something bad has happened to Peepnuts because it has affected this dog so that he does not keep up this pattern that he has followed for years. About ten days after that, we were notified that he had been killed in action. That dog never went back to that gate again."

BACK TO CALIFORNIA

After the visit, a feeling told me that there was something wrong down in Los Angeles. I had bought my dad a new Plymouth and he loved to drive. He would advertise in the Daily Oklahoman down there, "Car leaving for Los Angeles on such and such day." This was quite common. He would get a whole load of people and they would pay him so much per head. He was commuting back and forth at his leisure. He decided that since three of his daughters lived out there, he wanted to live closer to them. He went to work in some little old club as a night security man. I had bought a house on the GI Bill of Rights out in Whittier and gave it to my dad. He also remarried while living in California.

So I called Dad. He said, "I did not know how to get a hold of you. I've been calling Bakersfield and they could not locate you. The VA is about to repossess this house because you are not occupying it."

I said, "I'm not exactly following you, Dad."

He said, "They said that if they don't come to some satisfaction within another month then they are going to revoke your contract."

I said, "I'll be home in a couple of days."

So I went back down to Los Angeles and visited this real estate office which was handling my case. I asked, "What's wrong with you people?"

They said, "You bought a house on the GI Bill of Rights that you don't occupy. You've offered it to your stepmother and dad."

I said, "Well, that isn't true. That is my home. That is my permanent residence. I don't use it very often for the simple reason that I'm a railroad man. I am never in the same spot for two nights. That is a place where I can rest up when I'm back down in this area, which isn't that frequent. It would benefit me to have my dad and stepmother occupy and safeguard it against burglary or stuff like that."

I talked with him for quite a while and he said, "Well, since it has reached this stage, we'll have to have a new credit rating."

I was no longer employed but I said, "Well okay. Send one up there and get it. You've got my employee file." I knew it would take them at least a week to wrap this all up. I knew by the end of one week I would have a good paying job. So I moved back into the house with my Dad.

I told one of my brothers-in-law about my situation and he said, "Say, Jake. Out there on one of those construction projects, a mason is looking for a helper. It wouldn't pay you anything like what you need." I needed about a hundred and seventy-five dollars income to have the proper credit rating.

I said "I'll go out and talk to him in the morning."

The next day I went out and got a hold of Dave, one of the owners of the partnership. I told him, "Dave, I need to go to work."

He asked, "What can you do? Can you plaster?"

I said, "I'm not a plasterer, don't know which side of a trowel that you'd use. My brother-in-law said you were looking for a helper."

He said, "Yep, I am."

I said, "I like that job but there is one stipulation that I have to make. I am going to need a hundred and seventy-five dollars a week to establish credit. I know you don't pay that kind of money but I will tell you what I will do. If you'll give me a check, once a week for a hundred and seventy-five dollars, I'll endorse it and hand it right back to you. I'll work for nothing if I get the credit rating."

He asked, "What's the deal?" And I told him. He said, "Do you mean that they're pulling that on you?"

I said, "I sure do. If you'll just issue me a credit rating when they call, I'll work for nothing."

He said, "Well, I wouldn't do that. I'll issue you a credit rating on that order and I'll pay you eight dollars a day. Now Jake, I want to talk to you here a little bit. We're out here to build houses. If you come out here and have a fight with that hod carrier,[2] you'll be gone. I can't have that out here."

I said, "Don't worry. He'll show me everything involved with this job. In two or three weeks, I'll be the hod carrier."

Well that other guy was lazy. So while he was showing me around, I was watching and learning everything. In about three weeks they ran that other guy off and I became the head hod carrier for that whole mess.

MAX AND SHORTY

That was when California was in a construction boom. I worked on construction projects out there where they took bulldozers and carryalls to plow down a square mile of orange grove, just tear her up and haul it off. The companies had five house plans and they would just start selling those lots off. Those lots were side-by-side, but each house was different from the house adjacent to it. They hired enough craftsmen of every kind to keep up with that flood of construction.

While I was living in Whittier, I got a call from Max Majewski. He found my number in the phone book. Well, Majewski and I began to keep in touch. Max was real smart. He picked him up some licenses and went into the construction business. He became very wealthy. It got to where he was invited to those political dinners and fundraisers at five hundred dollars a ticket. Max had been married five times and several of the women had met unexplained deaths. One of them was shot, one of them died from an overdose, and two were killed in accidents.[3] By the time he called me, he was living alone. He even asked me to come out and work for him but I was doing very well where I was at.

Eventually, he made so much money that he decided to leave this country and go to Greece. He sold his business and netted around ten million dollars. He then went down and applied for a passport. About halfway through the interview, the official told him, "We can not give you a passport or a visa at all."

Max asked, "Why not?"

The other guy said, "Oh, you're not an American citizen."

Max said, "What do you mean that I'm not an American citizen? I grew up in this country. I went to all your colleges and schools. I've married half the women in southern California. I've paid the government millions of dollars in taxes. I fought all through World War II for you. Now what do you mean that I'm not an American citizen?"

He said, "Well, you aren't. The records show that your daddy and mother were in this country without full visas." Max's dad was an engineer. He had an opportunity to go down and work in Mexico in those mines for a while. The official pointed out, "You were born in Mexico. Your mother came back and your father returned to Poland or wherever he was from." Max's father had a bad disease and that was why they deported him. He died over there. The official finished, "You have never taken any steps toward receiving citizenship, nor has your mother. You're not a citizen. You're a citizen of Mexico!"

Max hit the ceiling. "Well send me to Mexico then, anything to get out of this filthy mess!" He had fought that whole war, paid millions of dollars in taxes, married half the women in southern California, which should have counted toward something, and he was not even considered an American citizen.

Well, they shipped him down to Mexico. He was only down there a few years before the Mexicans beat him out of every penny he had. He married a young lady doctor. They came to the States and the customs agents picked him up for being an alien. Max and his wife eventually divorced.

One day in 1948, my phone rang while I was in Whittier. I answered, "McNiece speaking."

A woman asked, "Do you know who this is?"

I said, "No, I don't know who you are."

She asked, "Did you ever know a Buzzy?"

I said, "I never knew a Buzzy. I had a friend in the service who carried a picture of a young lady with him. Her name was Buzzy. Of course, I never had the opportunity to meet her except he showed us a photo of her in her panties. She was very proud of us. Are you this Buzzy?"

She said, "Sure."

I said, "Where in the world are you and why are you calling?"

She said, "Well, Shorty and I are out here throwing some parties."

I said, "That's great. What bar are you all in?" She told me and I said, "I'll be right down." So I went down there.

They were so drunk they could not hit the floor with their hat in thirty throws and just as happy as could be. Shorty told me that he had gone to work for the Baltimore and Ohio Railroad after he came back. He had been a fireman on a goat. He was involved in an accident which derailed the engine, tore it up, and many other things. As much as I knew about railroads and from his description, I believed that he had caused the accident when they were yanking the trains in the yards. He was drunk all the time. Anyway, he sued them and won about a sixty thousand dollar settlement out of it, which was big, big money back then.

We talked and laughed and reviewed. He asked, "Where is Majewski?" I told him. He told me, "I'm going to see Majewski tomorrow." When Max came home from work his house was so full of flowers that he could hardly walk through it. Shorty and Buzzy stayed with him for a while. After that we never heard from Shorty again.

SETTLING DOWN

After three years in California, I had a chance to go to work in Lake Charles, Louisiana, with the City Service of Continental Refinery as an A operator. So I quit my construction job and went out there. When I arrived they did not have the refinery completed to where they needed operators so I came back to Ponca City just to fool around.

I had a blind date one Saturday night with Rosita Vitale. I enjoyed the evening very much and I told her that I was going to marry her.

She answered, "I'm a young widow woman out here. If you're so hot to marry, why hasn't it happened quicker?"

I told her, "I've just never met anybody that I wanted that bad."

She said, "Jake, I've got a daughter that is thirteen years old. I have the responsibility of running a dress shop up town. I own my home. There is just too much at stake here. I really have enjoyed the evening with you. You are really interesting. But I could not do anything like that." Then she asked, "What are you doing tomorrow?"

I said, "Nothing in particular."

She asked, "Will you have lunch with me?"

I said, "You bet."

The next day I had lunch with her and said, "Rosita, you've got to make up your mind, Baby, because I'm leaving town in the morning."

She asked, "Where are you going?"

I said, "I'm going down to Texas to open up a beer joint and barbecue stand for my brother. I'll be down there seven days."

She asked, "Where are you going after that?"

I answered, "I haven't any idea. I'm just freelancing here and there. But that is where I'll be for the next seven days."

She said, "Jake, you're so interesting but I went out dancing with you just one time and an awful lot of people saw it. It seems like you know everybody in Ponca City or they know you. I have heard more bad things about you today than all the other men in Ponca City put together. You fascinate me in a way but then I'm scared to death of you."

I said, "Well, I'm leaving here tomorrow."

She asked me to give her my phone number and address and I did. She called me every day. Finally she asked, "Are you still leaving there?"

I said, "Yeah, I'm leaving."

She said, "Well, come on back home. We'll get married. We'll have to wait six weeks because I'm Catholic. On Catholic marriages you have to announce it six weeks in advance."

So I came back and married Rosita on July 6, 1949. I decided to change my lifestyle. I told her, "I'm not a social drinker. If I take a drink, I'll get drunk. It's time I knocked it off." I gave up drinking except for the times I got together with the other guys from Regimental Headquarters Company.

I then went to work for the Ponca City flour mill. They had about two thousand pounds of flour that had gotten bugs and worms in it and they needed to process that flour for export to foreign lands. All we had to do was dump it in a great big hopper exposed to extremely high heat which killed those bugs. I worked down there on a temporary basis for about a month and a half.

Afterwards my brother-in-law told me, "Jake, they need a coke knocker down at City Service.[4] Would you go to work as a coke knocker?"

I said, "Yeah, I will."

He said, "It is real tough, hard and dangerous work."

I asked, "They've got other people doing that?"

He said, "Yeah, but it is really tough, Jake."

I said, "Well, I'll go down and check it out and see."

He said, "Nobody in the plant wants it."

So I went down and talked to the head man, Fred Walker. "I would be very interested in it. I am sure that I am physically capable of doing it."

He asked, "Where did you work here in Ponca City?" And I told him. He then said, "You come back here in the morning."

When I came back the following day he said, "Jake, I would like to hire you but I am a little scared. You don't have too rosy a reputation. You've been in and out of that jail a hundred times for fighting and brawling. You would be working under some of the roughest and meanest men in the company. They have a regular knock-down and drag-out affair once a week somewhere. They work under conditions with the heat and danger. Four men on a scaffold one foot wide swinging them picks, jerking coke that is glowing red hot. Of course it will get in someone's boot or shirt and the battle is on."

I told him, "Fred, do me a favor. Before you say no, call Kenneth Long. He is the fire chief over here. I have worked longer with Kenny than any other place that I've been. Ask Kenny if I have ever had any problems on the job with any other person. I get along good with people. I have been in and out of jail because about all we had to do around here for recreation was get drunk and fight. I have never had any problem anywhere that I worked."

So he said, "Come on back the next day." I did and he said, "Jake, I get a bit of a different story from Kenneth Long than I have heard everywhere else. I kind of believe that you are telling the truth. I am going to put you to work down here. But the first time that you get out there and start a brawl, you're out the gate."

So I went to work as a coke knocker and worked down there for about six months until they had a company-wide layoff. Well, I was the newest man in the refinery. They laid off by seniority and importance of job. I was the first guy out of the gate.

This was late in November or December and the Christmas mail was beginning to pick up at the post office. They always hired forty or fifty extra people during the month of December. I went up and applied for this temporary employment. They put me to work. In January when they were getting ready to let all of us go, the postal department decided that they would issue a civil service examination to hire new full-time postal employees. They needed eight people in Ponca City. The post office had not hired anybody since the war. Of the hundred and twenty-five who took the examination down at the American Legion building, I made the eighth highest score. So I saw that and thought, "Boy, this sure will be no sweat."

They finally called me down to the office. The postal inspector asked, "Is everything you've got on this application true?"

I said, "Yeah, sure is."

He said, "You've listed a lot of places where you have been arrested. I have been checking and it all turns out to be good but it seems like you forgot one of them."

I thought that I had listed everything on it except that deal out in Tulare, California, at which I felt that I had not violated any law other than just getting drunk. But the police report had listed it and this postal inspector had found out about it. I said, "I don't feel guilty about the affair in Tulare. I was not raising hell or anything. I was just drunk."

He said, "I'll tell you what we are going to do. We are going to put you on probation for six months while we check everything out."

I said, "That's fine and dandy with me."

So I went to work for the post office in the early part of 1950 and worked twenty-seven and a half years until I retired. I had three years and five months military service which also counted toward any civil service retirement. So I walked out of there when I was fifty-eight years old.

I was married to Rosita for three years until she died of cancer. I then met Martha Louise Beam-Wonders near the end of 1952. Her husband had also died within a week of Rosita. We married on September 4, 1953. She had a fifteen-month-old son. I raised him and Rosita's daughter. Martha and I had two children of our own; Rebecca, born in 1956, and Hugh, born in 1959.

After I married Rosita, I became a very serious Christian. Because of the way that I had lived, it has made me appreciate very much my relationship with God and the kind of guy that He is. When the Lord forgives something, He remembers it no more.

KEEPING IN TOUCH

After settling down, there were a few of the guys I wanted to get in touch with. Rosita's family was from Brooklyn, New York. When we went up to visit them I looked up Vick Utz, who had lost his arm at Bastogne. Someone had told me he worked for Johnson and Johnson. I called the company and they gave me his address and phone number. We visited and began to keep in touch.

I remembered where many of the others had lived before the war. I knew the Marquez brothers lived in El Paso. I also got in touch with Jack Agnew and Herb Pierce. In spite of having threatened to kill each other, Herb and I became good friends.

Herb was the only one of those young kids to make it. When he came home he got messed up with the military in some way and got shipped out to Korea during the war. He told me, "Jake, you don't know how lucky we were in airborne units. Boy, those American soldiers don't have any idea what a war is. I never saw so much disorganization in my life." He was wounded pretty bad in a village and they sent him back to the hospital where they operated on him. When they took the bullet out of him, it was a forty-five slug. He was hit by his own men.

Tom Young was one guy I really wanted to meet. His brother had been killed with the 82nd in Normandy. He and I were so much alike in many respects that Tom took to me as his brother. I went through Austin, Texas, a dozen times after the war but could not find him. In 1954 he and his wife were driving north and passed through Ponca City. They stopped for gas and he said, "Jake lives here. I'll look him up and call him." Martha answered the phone. He told her who he was. She told him I was out fishing and would be back soon so he should come on over to visit. I did not get back for three hours and there he was after all my searching, sitting with Martha at my table.

We have kept in close touch ever since. Tom became a rancher. He picked up a spread down in the hill country that lacked thirty acres of containing four square miles. All of his children became professional people.

I remembered Bobby Reeves lived in Cleveland, Ohio. He had served on outpost duty with me up in Holland. In 1955 Martha and I passed through one night. Fortunately there were only two Reeves in the phone book. Bob had become an upper manager in a chocolate factory.

Trigger Gann became a total alcoholic for a number of years after he was released from the prison camp. He must have called me half a dozen times. He would be somewhere and needed some money for him or his family or something. I had sent him money three different times and would always get another call. I thought, "This is not helping him. It is hurting him." So I told him, "Trigger, I wouldn't give you a penny, son, not a dollar. But I'll tell you what I'll do. If you would come here to Ponca City, I will get you employed and give you all the help I can, but you have to give up that stump juice."

I never gave him any more money and lost all track of the trooper. One of the boys came to a "get-together" many years later and told me Trigger went back into the airborne. During the 1950s the army froze all promotions for NCOs. Trigger was the only one that received a promotion to command sergeant major during that four-year period. He also received all kinds of awards for good discipline. He came out of the army smelling like a rose.

In the late seventies, Keith Carpenter sent me a Christmas card. I then started corresponding with him. I visited his home two or three times and he always had some little company that sold things like janitorial supplies. He had made a lot of money. Anyway, he asked me if I knew Steve Kovacs lived in Oklahoma City. Steve had been wounded during that bombing in Eindhoven. I said, "No." So I went down and started visiting with him. Steve was surprised to see me. He told me he thought that I was killed up in Holland when those Messerschmitts bombed us.

CLOSURE

One day I received a call from a woman asking if I was the Jake McNiece who served with Frenchy Baribeau. I asked, "How did you locate me?" She said, "My grandmother, Frenchy's wife, died about three months ago and we were going through his personal effects. He had a cigar box. It had his cap and insignia, 'Screaming Eagle' patch,[5] the folded flag, and little ole things like that. In there was a newspaper clipping dated December 4, 1944. It had a caption on it, 'The Story of the Filthy 13 Can Now Be Released.' It was not a very complete description but it named about eight other men and their hometowns." She said, "We have been calling all those towns trying to locate those people who had served with him. We haven't found anybody. So I said, 'We'll try Jake McNiece of Ponca City.'"

I said, "There's not much need of you wasting all your money on this information. All those guys are dead. There's not a lot of them left." Baribeau may have been on the bottom of the stack of paratroopers we buried over there in Normandy. But his family talked with me and we had a real good visit.

I got inquiries like this quite often. I received a letter from a lady [Laura Erikson] up in McLean, Virginia. She wrote, "Dear Mister McNiece, If you are the McNiece that was in a demolition platoon in Europe, I am curious to know if you have ever known a Lieutenant Mellen? Call me collect if you are the one. I know that there was a Jake McNiece with the company."

I called back. She had a recorder on and I told her, "I am the Jake McNiece who fought with Lt. Mellen." I gave her my phone number and told her to return my call. Boy it was not two hours until she was on that phone. She said that her uncle was about twenty years older than she. They knew that he was killed in action there at Normandy but they did not know any of the details.

I told her, "He was killed that night. He never saw the sun come up. He went out of the front of the plane and I took out the last section. I never saw him after I got out of the plane. Other boys saw him. He was hit at least two or three times and kept going. I did not know anything personal about him other than he was just my lieutenant. He was a good officer. I'll give you the name of six or seven officers who are still alive and if you'll contact them they will give you all the information you could possibly want."

I helped resolve questions in their mind. The families were always very curious about the details.

TOP KICK

One Sunday evening back in 1979 I had been having problems with my back. The phone rang and Martha answered it. She said, "Jake, you've got a long distance call."

I said, "Let me go back and get me a cigarette."

She said, "It's long distance."

I said, "That does not have anything to do with it. Whoever is calling long distance, if they do not have enough money for me to have a cigarette, they shouldn't be calling long distance." I asked, "Who is it?"

She said, "I don't know."

I lit me a cigarette and picked up the phone, "McNiece speaking."

A voice asked, "Did you blow up any barracks today?"

I said, "No."

He asked, "Did you steal a freight train and bring it back to camp?"

His voice was familiar but I could not recognize it. I said, "No I didn't." I asked, "Who is this speaking?" I knew it had to be someone who had been in the outfit pretty early on to know of these incidents.

He said, "This is A. H. Miller."

I asked, "Do you mean this is Top Kick Albert Miller?"

He said, "Yeah."

I said, "Well, you idiot. What do you mean calling me? Albert, I had no idea that you were still alive." I had not heard from him since the war.

He said, "Jake, I've thought of you a million times since the war. I have often wanted to contact you but I was afraid that I might find out a whole bunch of stuff that I did not want to know. You wasn't a very promising prospect to be revitalized back into society."

It was June 5, the anniversary of our jump into Normandy. He said, "Today has been D-Day all day to me. I have thought of you a hundred times today. I finally told my wife awhile ago that I'm going to call you and talk to you."

Miller was a deputy sheriff in Atlanta, Georgia. He said, "The county sheriff had a couple of prisoners here from Kay County. They were wanted back in Oklahoma and the sheriff department sent a couple of deputies over here from Kay County. I got to talking with them and so forth. I finally asked them if they knew you. They said, 'Oh yeah, we know Jake.' Then I asked, 'And how's he doing?' They said, 'He's one of the outstanding citizens in Ponca City. He's a church member and he is the nicest guy. He has no problem with anybody. He's killed a dog or two that were running loose and dangerous to the neighborhood children and things like that. But he faces no criminal charges for that or anything else.' I talked to them for a while and I thought, 'Well I'm going to call him.'"

Top Kick had been hit the moment he got on the ground so he knew very little about what happened to my guys. He wanted to know all about them and this and that. He kept asking questions and I answered them. Finally Martha came into the bedroom and pointed at her watch.

I said, "Top Kick, we've been talking for about forty-five minutes. I'll tell you what. I don't have all the answers right in mind to answer you on a bunch of this stuff. I need to think some of it over. We've been talking for over forty-five minutes and it will cost you a river bottom farm down there to pay for this call." So I told him, "I'll hang up. Then I'll put this down in a written form and send it to you."

He said, "Don't you hang up. I want to ask you a question."

I said, "All right."

He asked, "Jake, how long were you in the army?"

I said, "I was in there three years, five months and twenty-six days, seven hours, fifteen minutes and four seconds."

He said, "That's what I thought." Then he asked, "Did you ever make PFC?"

I said, "Top, that's really a tough yes or no answer. I had all the confirmations and recommendations and parlevouzed with a bunch of officers, but no I never did make PFC."

He said, "Now that is what I thought. Now let me tell you something. Did you know that I was first sergeant when you came in down there?"

I said, "Yeah."

He asked, "Did you know that I was a first sergeant when you left?"

I said, "Yeah."

He said, "I stayed in for a full career to retire and I was still a first sergeant. Now here is the way you've got to deduce this pretty quick. I had you outranked when you came in and I had you outranked when you left and I've got you outranked now. When you get ready to hang up, I'll tell you!" We talked forty-five more minutes!

The 101st Airborne Division Association was having a national reunion over in Hot Springs, Arkansas, that year. I asked, "Are you going to go to that, Albert?"

He said, "Yeah, I believe I will."

I told him, "I never have been to one. I really don't think I would enjoy them but if you're going to be there, I'll tell you what I'll do. I'll be down on Lake Texoma that week and I'll call Tom Young and Marge down in Texas. They can come up to Lake Texoma and meet Martha and I and we'll come over and visit with you."

He said, "Okay, that would be the best gift I have had in my life."

So Tom and Marge drove up from Texas and we took off for Hot Springs. After we arrived, Tom and I went in. We got to looking around there and they were holding some kind of memorial service. Those national reunions always have a memorial service, then an award service. They are scheduled and regulated just like the damned army. We walked around looking at those boys until we finally saw Top Kick way back in the back sitting by himself. He had a table there with his cane laying across his leg. So Tom and I just marched right back to his table. When we got near, Top Kick looked up and saw us coming. Boy, he jumped up, grabbed that cane and was pushing himself up from the table. Top Kick was a big man. Tom and him grabbed one another and hugged. Tears were running down their cheeks and we were having a real good "get-together." Suddenly Palys, who was also in the room, saw that commotion and recognized the three of us. He came over. So did Sergeant Smith. When they got in the huddle with us, I said, "Hey, we're causing a pretty big disturbance here. Let's get out of here and I'll buy you some dinner. Then we can talk and visit as long as we want to."

So we went out and ate a big meal and talked. It was just like seeing a long lost brother. After we came home, I started thinking about it. I told Martha, "I think I'm going to get these guys together, just the survivors of the original Regimental Headquarters Company." I had probably ten or fifteen addresses that I knew were good.

Martha said, "It won't work, Jake. You can't get those people together after thirty years."

I said, "Yeah, these are a different breed of cats. All I've got to do is get the word out to them."

She said, "Well, I'll type any communication you want but it won't work."

I sent everyone of the guys I knew an invitation to attend a Regimental Headquarters Company reunion in conjunction with the annual 101st Airborne Reunion at Nashville, Tennessee, that next year. I sent them a roster of everyone I had already notified. I sent them a form and asked them if they knew someone whom they could contact or else have them call me. Before this thing was over that phone started ringing off the hook.

Epilogue

The Moral of the Story

Jake McNiece had picked the 1980 101st Airborne Division Reunion in Nashville, Tennessee, for the first reunion of Regimental Headquarters Company. Using the 506th Regiment's membership roster, Jake wrote all the veterans on the west half of the United States while Jack Agnew wrote those on the east. In their letters they asked the recipients to forward an invitation to anyone not on the list. Most of the men had kept in touch with a war buddy and in this manner Jake and Jack contacted just about everyone.

When Gene Brown received his invitation, he turned to his wife and said that they were going. Although he had never had interest in attending any of the previous 101st reunions or any other veterans organization, he said if Jake was behind the planning of this, it would have to be a party. He would never miss another company reunion while he was alive.

Jake was amazed at the number of Regimental Headquarters Company veterans to turn up. Men who had not seen each other since the war embraced each other like long-lost brothers. He was even more amazed at how many veterans whom he did not know sported little name tags with "The Filthy 13" on them.

Jack Agnew had not seen Jake since the war. After checking into the hotel he went down to the crowded foyer. He tried to enter but a bald-headed old man with his back to him blocked his way. Jack tried to scan the lobby for his dear old friend, but every time he tried to move, the bald man also moved, not letting Jack pass. After three attempts to pass, the old paratrooper became irritated and turned his attention to the man blocking his path, only to recognize the ears on that bald head. Jake McNiece turned around with that familiar grin.

Different companies rented out rooms for their separate bars. Jake performed his old role as the provider of the company booze. He opened a hospitality room with a bar. Brown arrived first and met with Jake. He asked who was paying for the whiskey and insisted on paying himself. Jake said it was taken care of until Brown pulled out three one hundred dollar bills. Gene said he had a whole wallet full of them. Gene had done real well for himself after the war, so Jake let him help out with the tab. The bar was open all night.

Tom and Marge brought up a crockpot full of beans and chili. Jake hired someone to cook cornbread. That first day the guests feasted in their rooms. The three-day reunion consisted mostly of eating, drinking, and socializing from room to room.

The reunion was like a fountain of youth for the old paratroopers. They consumed life with a renewed passion. Most were up to their old tricks. Jake, Jack Agnew, and Tom Young heard someone had a bar full of bourbon on the tenth floor so they proceeded up there immediately. It was not long before Jake was "feeling no pain." The paratrooper looked out over the balcony and said, "Jack, I think we can make it down with a couple of bed sheets." Tom told them he would take the stairs and meet them on the ground. He left while the other two regained their senses.

The wives had discovered a whole new side to their husbands. Food and alcohol had been an integral part of their husbands' lives during the war and it became so again. The men bought steaks which they cooked by the pool on a big grill provided by the hotel. One wife commented that she had never before seen her husband eat so much food. Martha told her that these men were no longer in their fifties but in their twenties. From then on, whenever the men gathered together they became those young men in Toccoa again. Not having seen each other for as long as thirty years, these men shared a love greater than that of brothers. They swapped stories about the war while the wives listened. For the first time many of the wives learned about a part of their husbands' lives that they had kept guarded. Most had never discussed the war. When they returned home, many were finally able to share that experience.

As the first reunion came to a close, Jack Agnew reminded Jake to be sure to have Top Kick up in his room at a certain time. They wanted to make a presentation. Jake felt a little left out since he had not been asked to contribute. When he offered to pay, Jack told him he had already done enough with the reunion. When everyone arrived, Jack, the master of ceremonies, called Albert Miller up in front of the others. He proceeded to laud all the things that Top Kick had done for them and how the men revered him. As a token of their respect and esteem they had all pitched in and bought him a lifetime membership to the 101st Airborne Division Association. Jake still felt disappointed that he had not contributed to the gift.

After Miller thanked everyone, Jack then stood and called Jake up front. He began reading off a military statement of charges signed by George Koskimaki, the 101st Association secretary. It listed the cost of a stolen train, the repair cost of a barracks that had been blown up, and finally the cost that the officers had paid for the deer killed on Sir Ernest Wells's manor. It looked like the army was finally going to get restitution for all the damage Jake had caused. After a good laugh, Jack explained that the company had decided to forgive Jake's debt and instead presented him too with a lifetime membership to the 101st Association.

From then on the "get-togethers" became annual events which started a new chapter in their lives. Most of the men in this story were regulars and never missed a reunion. Their wives even became the best of friends. The veterans told and retold stories of their wartime experiences and the reunions provided fuel for new ones. Most had heard the stories enough to know them by heart. Each one had his favorite. Most stories were introduced by someone saying, "Tell us about the time when . . ." Then everyone would stop what they were doing to listen. The stories became an integral part of their lore, much like stories of coup among Indian warrior societies.

The next year, they met at Tom Young's ranch in Texas and the guests bunked in his hunting lodge. They gathered at a little stone church built from donations dedicated to the memory of Tom Young's brother, Kaiser Young. Kaiser had been killed while fighting with the 82nd Airborne on D-Day. There they witnessed firsthand Jake's gift as a lay preacher. Jake dedicated the first memorial service to Kaiser Young, and all those paratroopers who had not returned from the war. He found twelve biblical scriptures about eagles, with which he alluded to the Screaming Eagles of the 101st Airborne Division. He summarized his sermon by describing the strength of the bonds of brotherhood, leaving not a dry eye in the church. As everyone left, each touched the funeral flag of Kaiser at the entrance of the chapel.

From then on, different members of the company took their turn hosting the reunions in their hometowns. Tom hosted three more. Jake hosted two in Ponca City, and even Brown held one at his lodge in Oregon. They usually closed their get-togethers with everyone clasping hands in a circle for a prayer. As the years passed, their numbers grew smaller. Health prevented more and more from attending. Jake commented that in the early days each man would show up with two suitcases, one for clothes and the other for alcohol. They usually rented one room just for the bar. Yet he pointed out that as they got older, they would show up with one suitcase full of clothes and the other full of prescription pills.

This story began with just one man and finished with a handful of survivors. The legend of the Filthy 13 grew during World War II by accident, or perhaps by providence. They surfaced in the public spotlight only for a brief moment at the height of the war and then quickly disappeared. Jake McNiece was minding his own business on the eve of the invasion of Normandy, as usual coming up with some spur of the moment hi-jinks. Unknown to him, a cameraman happened to be around when he shaved a scalp-lock on his head and put on war paint. When the other members of the Filthy 13 followed Jake's lead, the cameraman immortalized the moment. This incident was no different than any other to Jake. A few hours later, the war-painted, scalp-locked demolition-saboteur section jumped into Normandy. But that brief moment of preparation preserved by the cameraman excited the imagination of the public. All the American public had left was a collection of photographs of some of their best fighting men on the eve of battle, and a name that signified adventure.

To feed the public appetite, war correspondents sought out the story of this colorful unit. The name itself added to the mystique—"The Filthy 13." Only a few elite units during the war earned the privilege to attain a recognizable name. War correspondents for the *Stars and Stripes* made sure that the Filthy 13 secured its place in history. Unfortunately, the unit was in combat when the interest was first aroused. War correspondent Tom Hoge had to piece together their accounts from a trail of rumors. His version claimed that these full-blooded Indians had sworn not to bathe until the invasion and that only their white lieutenant could command their respect by besting them in fights. This June 1944 *Stars and Stripes* article was picked up nationwide. The more accurate account in the *Stars and Stripes* came from a follow-up article where the author evidently interviewed the members after their return from Normandy. It was not released until early December and was also picked up by other newspapers. Hoge's story was too good to leave alone to such few facts. The best embellishment came from *True Magazine*'s war correspondent, Arch Whitehouse. Where it comes to sensationalism, he was truly a gifted writer. His story would provide the inspiration for the later movie. Tom Hoge provided the ingredients that Whitehouse turned into a story.

Jake's brother, Jack, continued to fly after the war. On one occasion in the 1950s, he flew several movie executives down to Mexico. While they were sitting around drinking, Jack told them some stories about his brother and the Filthy 13 during World War II. They became interested. George Koskimaki, a veteran of the 506th PIR and historian of the 101st Airborne during World War II, was also approached by an author, probably E. M. Nathanson, during the 1950s for the story of the Filthy 13. He referred them to Jake McNiece. Nathanson probably did not follow up on this advice for he introduced his book, *The Dirty Dozen*, published in 1965 with "This story is fiction. I have heard a legend that there might have been men like them, but nowhere in the archives of the United States government, or in its military history did I find it recorded."

When approached with the prospect of making a movie about his unit, Jake turned them down. He said it was too soon after the war and the memory of his lost comrades was still fresh. At that time Jake was not in contact with but a handful of the survivors of his company. He did not want to make any "blood money" off the memory of the dead. They told him that they had "The Filthy Thirteen" article written by Arch Whitehouse for *True Magazine*. If he would not tell them the story, they would use what they had.

In it, a lieutenant was assigned to a section of twelve undisciplined and rebellious Indians who resented any semblance of authority and had sworn an oath not to bathe until they jumped into Normandy. Each day the lieutenant returned and beat them in a fight until they finally accepted him as their leader. Whipping out a knife they made him a blood brother. As the thirteenth man to join the unit they became known as the Filthy 13.

The story was mostly a sensationalized work of fiction and Jake knew it. He told them that they could make the movie but could not use the name, the Filthy 13. In 1967, MGM released its version of the story with an all-star cast headed by Lee Marvin. The men were portrayed as condemned criminals given a chance at freedom if they volunteered to train as commandos for a suicide mission on D-Day. The screenwriter borrowed the name, "The Dirty Dozen," from Whitehouse's name for the original twelve Indian paratroopers. The storyline reflected little of the real unit's experiences. Only two events in the movie could be based on fact: the capture of the command post during training maneuvers and the pre-invasion party. The real veterans resented being portrayed as criminals and forever after would have to begin their war stories with, "We were troublemakers but not criminals!" From that time on the survivors of the Filthy 13 had to defend their reputation.

The only member who did come close to possessing that reputation, however, was Jake McNiece. Jake was well-liked in the company but many believed that his wild ways would lead to his ruin. Everyone was pleased to learn the worst had not happened. Once he gave up his vices, Jake became a born-again Christian and actively involved in the Church of Christ. He applied the same energy to his spiritual life and helping widows as he had to raising hell. This was one area that he would not boast of. Others willingly did that for him. When it came to things he did for other people, he lived by the scripture that one hand should not know what the other was doing. In this way blessings are stored up in heaven. He has been instrumental in starting programs to provide food and transportation for widows. He even became a lay preacher for the Church of Christ in the little town of Kaw. Otherwise, if he was not fishing, he and Martha could be found studying the Scriptures.

Many believed that Jake changed, but those who have known him best believe not. He is now the same man he always was. He just had three vices—drinking, fighting, and chasing loose women—and he indulged them. After he gave those up, he was the same man but without such distractions. It was his good traits that people admired while his former vices simply made him all the more interesting.

Most of the other veterans also came home from the war to lead productive lives. Frank Palys, Max Majewski, Shorty Mihlan, Maw Darnell, Jack Agnew, Jack Womer, George Baran, and Chuck Plauda were the original surviving members of the unit prior to the Normandy jump. Palys returned to Chicago and went to work in the steel mills. Majewski became a millionaire during the construction boom in California. Mihlan collected a small fortune in a settlement after a railroad accident. He was never heard from again. Agnew went to college to study law enforcement but ended up working thirty-five years for Western Electric and retired in Pennsylvania. Jack Womer returned to work in the steel mills in the Baltimore area where he retired. The fact that a mortar round landed right next to Jack and did not wound him left a lasting impression on him. He saved the singed left sleeve of his jump jacket and had it framed. Maw Darnell, like many of the paratroopers who were captured during the war, suffered severely from the trauma. He dealt with it through alcohol, like Trigger Gann and so many others. Gann, however, straightened himself out and made a successful career in the army. Plauda also stayed in the army and fought in Korea. He died in a motorcycle accident in Japan.

Of the replacements, Richard Graham stayed in the army and retired as a command sergeant major. John "Dinty" Mohr returned to farm corn in Iowa.

Mike Marquez, who ended up fighting with the Filthy 13 in Normandy and Holland, returned to El Paso, Texas. In 1948 he visited Vienna, Austria, and picked up a job with the U.S. Forces Austria as an illustrator. He returned to the United States where he illustrated farm machinery for Guinness Printing Company in Blair, Nebraska. He finally settled back down in his hometown of El Paso as a freelance illustrator until his vision deteriorated.

Tom Young, who was also associated closely with the Filthy 13, returned to his family's ranch in Texas. When his parents died, the one surviving brother, who had a metal plate in his head from a wound during the war, and his two sisters did not have any interest in ranching so Tom offered to buy their shares. At that time a number of large businesses were buying up ranches and converting them to resorts for their executives. They wanted to restore them to their rustic images complete with split rail fences. Tom knew how to build them so he won the contracts and hired some work crews. Those contracts enabled him to pay off the ranch.

Andy Rasmussen, another associate member of the Filthy 13, returned home to become a union carpenter. He spent forty years in construction, most of it in supervision. He worked on such projects as the atomic research buildings at MIT and Harvard, the New York Thruway, and the Massachussets and Connecticut Turnpikes.

Herb Pierce also stayed in the army. He became an NCO in the under-strength and undertrained 3rd Infantry Division. The state of discipline in the army had deteriorated. His company commander reprimanded him for tipping a recruit out of his bunk who had refused on numerous times to get up and do his morning chores. The commander was more worried about the kid writing his congressman than instilling discipline. When the Korean War broke out, Herb only had three months left on his enlistment. All enlistments were extended and he deployed with the division to Japan in September 1950, and then to the X Corps sector in Korea in November. The Far East Command considered the 3rd Division "worthless" for combat and placed it in reserve.

When the Chinese attacked at the end of the month, Herb's unit fell apart. It resembled nothing he had seen with the airborne in World War II. The officers did not stay with their men on the line. As one of the few combat veterans, Herb was abandoned several times on OP duty with only three or four other men while the rest of the company retreated. During the retreat to Hungnam, a Chinese soldier shot Herb in the stomach with a captured Thompson submachine gun. Herb spent nine months recovering in the Valley Forge Army Hospital and was then discharged from the army. He returned to Pennsylvania and worked for NARCO Avionics for twenty-six years and then the Malox Company. After a year or two he had a heart attack and finally retired.

Robert Cone worked at plumbing for a while but his arm never fully recovered from its wound. He went to work for the post office and retired after twenty-fours years. Although he heard about some 101st reunions, he never attended any. He did not want to think about the war. He did keep in touch with a few men of the 505th Regiment who were prisoners with him. For that reason, no one in the 506th knew he was alive. Not surprisingly, Jake was the only member of his orginal company he could not forget. On June 5, 2002, at the urging of his son, he called Jake.

First Sergeant Albert Miller retired from the army and became a deputy sheriff in Atlanta, Georgia. He had no better luck on the streets than he did in combat. He was gut-shot in a shoot-out and had to retire from law enforcement.

Hank Hannah spent about a year in military hospitals recovering from his shoulder wound. The doctors decided to let the bones fuse together instead of inserting an artificial joint. The fused joint resulted in only limited disability and he led an active life. He picked up right where he had left off, returning to teach Agricultural Law at the University of Illinois. He also served as the director of a division of Special Services for War Veterans at the university in the first two years immediately after the war. The division was a degree-granting entity which would accept veterans with a variety of academic backgrounds and help them achieve degrees. This was a time when a multitude of veterans attended college thanks to the GI Bill. Hannah played a key role in helping veterans advance their education.

Gene Brown returned to his home in Oregon right when Americans began to mine uranium for atomic energy. He moved in on the ground floor and was elected as a representative to the state legislature. While there he helped write most of the state's mining laws and became an expert on the subject. It did not take him long to realize that he could do better financially out on his own. He became the head of a law firm that employed twelve attorneys.

Shrable D. Williams stayed in the army. He fought in the Korean War and then joined up with Special Forces where he donned the green beret. While in Special Forces he was involved in the training of soldiers in Laos just prior to the war in Vietnam. After he retired as a lieutenant-colonel from the army in 1963, he found his real passion. He became a car enthusiast. He restored a Ford Falcon, with which he entered and won numerous contests. Eventually he restored as many as twenty-two vehicles, including the first Coleman Dairy delivery truck. His enthusiasm led him to become a founding member of the Falcon Club.

Far from being the criminals depicted in the movie, nearly all the men returned home to lead productive lives, and the wild exuberance of their airborne days had just been an adventure to last a lifetime.

Nearly thirty men passed through the ranks of the demolition section known as the Filthy 13. While Colonel Sink did his best to instill some form of discipline in the regiment, physical fitness seemed to be the top priority for combat readiness. Of the nearly six thousand men to volunteer, the physical training at Camp Toccoa weeded the 506th Parachute Infantry down to two thousand. Those who could measure up or even set the standards were valuable commodities for the tasks that would be assigned to them in combat. The regiment expected 50 percent casualties and in many units Normandy validated that prediction. For this reason, Sink and other officers cast a blind eye to the transgressions of some of their paratroopers.

Probably no one man deserves more credit for seeing the worth in Jake and his accomplices than First Sergeant Albert Miller. No one soldier was more revered than that old regular army man. No other man was more tempered to measure another's worth, and this regular army NCO's opinion was held in high regard by officers of all ranks. In everyone's opinion there was no better first sergeant for Regimental Headquarters Company. The combination of Top Kick's ability to measure the value of a man and the wisdom and fairness of their first company commander, Hank Hannah, probably saved these men for combat. The Filthy 13's lack of discipline was not a failing but had become a source of pride.

Gene Brown had grown close to his men and even closer during the get-togethers. He ranks among the officers who Jake greatly respected. Someone once asked Gene what it took to be a successful company commander. He replied, "Get yourself a good first sergeant, then get rid of all the rats but one. Keep the best rat because he will keep the others in line and get things you need." He had the best first sergeant with Albert Miller and there was no better rat than Jake McNiece.

Finally this story returns to one man. Jake, like the others, enlisted to fight a war. Life during the Great Depression forced him to mature at an early age. Regardless of his claim of not being well educated, he had a sharp mind with quick wit. He was blessed with incredible common sense that was critical in combat. He always found a solution to a problem no matter how unconventional. While many claimed that Jake was the toughest man in the outfit, there was too much chance involved in who would live and who would die in combat. Jake believed that there were many men killed who were better soldiers than he. He therefore concluded that he had survived because he took advantage of every opportunity that came his way. To be more specific, Jake acted without hesitation. No matter how overwhelming the odds, he kept his focus on staying alive and killing as many of the enemy as he could. By surrounding himself with men who would similarly follow without hesitation he increased his prospects of survival. This was the source of Jake's success as a combat paratrooper.

Leaders of soldiers have debated for ages over the definition of discipline in the military. Many feel that it is a soldier's willingness to follow orders. Some officers adhere so strictly to this philosophy that they will even issue orders that make no sense simply to test discipline. Such discipline, as measured in military drill, parades, and formations, tends to relate to the molding of individuals into a cohesive and collective body. This idea was born in a time when men marched into battle shoulder-to-shoulder, each man locked into place with the men next to him. But warfare has changed.

The other school of thought believes that discipline is the measure of doing what one knows to be right, in spite of the odds or the absence of supervision. In the confusion following a combat jump, officers were not always around to give orders. In addition, a rifle squad in World War II had more firepower and covered the same front as an infantry company during the Civil War. Sergeants then supervised the same amount of battlefield as once commanded by captains and lieutenants. Jake ascribed to this philosophy. Surprisingly, many of his men often expressed their reasoning when instructing someone else on a problem by saying, "Because that's the way Jake would have done it."

To him, standing formation and picking up cigarette butts contributed little to one's ability to kill the enemy. Fighting, on the other hand, did! Neither did shining boots nor shaving improve ones fighting ability. One shined and shaved to impress the girls so this was only necessary to go into town. Why should they clean up every day when the whole purpose of training was to get dirty? A bath once a week was enough to maintain a healthy hygiene. If it worked for cowboys, why not for paratroopers? In combat, most men would go weeks or even months without a bath. All agreed that saluting was a sign of respect. Jake, like many paratroopers, felt that respect was something a man had to earn. Whether they saluted an officer or not did not make them respect him any more. Nor did a commission inspire the men to follow a man in combat. Performance did. Surprisingly, most of the regular army men, with the exception of First Sergeant Miller, did not fit well in the paratroops. They were too inflexible. Citizen soldiers instead became the NCOs in the company. Jake's appointment to first sergeant at the end of the war validated his beliefs.

The story of the Filthy 13 is the story of Jake McNiece and twelve accomplices. For Jake, the company of men of his own nature brought out the best and worst in him. And in the army, he had the time of his life. He acted instinctively. Gene Brown summed it up best: "If there was a woman, a bottle of whiskey and a jeep sitting unguarded, while everyone else was figuring out how to get away with them, Jake would have already stolen the jeep, drank the bottle and had his way with the woman."

While Jake was the leader, he surrounded himself with men who, by his unique standards, he considered the best. Jack Agnew was probably the best all-around qualified soldier. He had a multitude of skills that a small, resourceful unit might need in combat. He was a leader in his own right but had such an admiration for Jake that he preferred to follow him anywhere. Jack Womer, although limited in his demolition experience, was another highly qualified soldier. Jake recognized that from the start. Ragsman Cone was a hulk of a man whose biceps stretched out the fabric on his baggy jump jacket. Jake felt that had he gotten through Normandy, he would have accounted for himself very well. Frenchy Baribeau, with his toughness and fluency in French, would also have been a tremendous asset had he lived.

The number one trait that Jake looked for was a man's tendency not to hesitate. Fights were won by superior firepower and teamwork. When charging in on the enemy, a paratrooper should not need to worry about whether his buddy was with him. On the occasions when men of the Filthy 13 and their associates were killed, all died attacking the enemy. Even Herb Pierce, the youngest surviving member of the company, fought through the thick of it and stayed by Jake's side, even when confronted with tanks. It broke his heart when Top Kick assigned him to rear detail when the division moved to Bastogne. This was no fault of Herb's. All the other seventeen-year-olds who had enlisted in the company were dead and Top Kick could not bear to lose another.

Combat proved Top Kick's prediction about Jake correct. In spite of the odds in Normandy, Jake was determined to get to his bridges. His men were scattered eight miles across the Cotentin Peninsula. He no longer had the men nor the demolitions to accomplish his mission. Nonetheless, he set out for his objective. He would collect enough men and explosives along the way. Similarly, Jack Agnew and Jack Womer began to round up men. Agnew linked up with Jake and Womer fell in with the 501st Regiment's defense at Hell's Corner.

In a time of crisis the average soldier will gravitate to anyone willing to assume responsibility. Officers are no exception. When a superior gives an order, an officer is bound to state his case, but more often than not is grateful for someone else to place him in a subordinate position. The responsibility for success or failure then rests upon the shoulders of somebody else. During the chaos of the missed drops in Normandy, there were plenty of examples of men rising to accept the challenge. Even though Colonel Johnson countermanned Sink's orders, Jake continued to his original destination, even to the surprise of his men. They reached their bridges and wired them for demolition. Of all the men to reach the bridge, Jake probably had the farthest to walk.

In Eindhoven, they completed their mission according to the plan. There was little room for heroics. The next action was a different story. On their way through Veghel they ran into a German penetration. The last they heard, their Regimental Headquarters Company was up ahead in Uden. Meanwhile the bulk of their regiment was still in Veghel and the Germans controlled the road between the two elements. Most of Jake's men still fought their way up to their company when they had every reason to wait it out until Colonel Sink organized an advance to reopen the road. The rest of the campaign on the "Island" was an effort to survive as comfortably as one could. With all the other demolition sergeants killed or wounded, it fell to Jake's section to clear a path through the minefield on the banks of the Rhine for the rescue of the British paratroopers. Jake's role was a minor part ignored by history. The bulk of the responsibility fell to E Company and the engineers.

While their actions in Normandy were the best testament to their determination, probably the single most significant act performed by the survivors of the original Filthy 13 happened in Bastogne. The irony of it all was that their superiors thought they were ridding themselves of troublemakers and Jake had believed he was going to sit out the war on easy street. By circumstance, the 101st Airborne Division became encircled and in a desperate struggle for survival. The mission for accurate drops regardless of the weather required Pathfinders. The superb navigational and flying skills of the transport pilots delivered them into the target, and pure luck kept the Pathfinders from losing more than one man. Ignored by most historians and even the official accounts by the air corps, the role of the Pathfinders in Bastogne saved the 101st Division. It required no heroics on the part of any one man. Each did his job the way he had been trained. Pushing the odds, Jake repeated this performance in another jump into Germany.

In two campaigns, this section lost more than 75 percent of its ranks. Of the thirteen members of the Filthy 13 to jump into Normandy only Jake, Womer, and Agnew finished out the war in the same section. Other members of the section from the Toccoa days, like Majewski, Mihlan, and Palys, served out the war on Regimental staff. Mike Marquez, by circumstance, fought with the Filthy 13 in its first two battles.

So what is the lesson of the Filthy 13? Like a fairy tale, every war story has to have a moral. The story of the Filthy 13 is the story of the kind of men who won World War II. These men were tough and their leader the toughest. Jake provides the example of the kind of man others gravitate to in combat. The qualities that he looked for in others were those that would get the job done in spite of any odds or difficulty. A leader of these kind of men would have to emulate the kind of traits he desired in his men. Hannah, Brown, and Williams provide examples of the caliber of officers needed to lead them.

The peacetime army always seems to go the opposite direction on this issue of discipline. The longer it has gone without a war, the more traits have crept in that Jake ridiculed. The army in the post–Cold War has gone even further to this extreme. One recruiter claimed that all he was allowed to recruit were college kids and altar boys. This just makes the job of leadership easier. An academic education does not make a man smarter nor provide him more common sense. While a fight between one unit and another was considered a sign of good esprit, it has been considered a lack of discipline in the post-Vietnam and post–Cold War army. The excuse is that war has become more technically advanced. A higher caliber of man is needed to operate the weapons. Yet with all the technology in the world, the battle is not won until the infantryman occupies the ground and plants his flag on the hill. It still comes down to a contest between fighting men. In many ways the kind of men who won World War II are not the kind of men the army is searching for today.

Jake did not tell these stories to teach any lessons though. He would always remind his audience that the Filthy 13 were not criminals. If he felt strongly about a contemporary issue such as draft dodgers during the Vietnam War, he would add it. All he wanted with these stories was to make people laugh. The more they laughed the better he told the stories. He had the best time in his life in the army and wanted to share that experience.

If Jake bragged about any personal achievement, it was that he was never promoted to Private First Class during his three and a half years of military service. Anyone could make PFC. Keep in mind that as an acting sergeant, his rank was made automatic upon jumping into combat. However, this distinction of never having been promoted was taken away from him on July 15, 2000. The 95th Regional Support Command made him an honorary colonel of the 95th "Victory" Division with all the privileges that rank would bear. After hearing Jake tell the story of his military service, however, the officers were a little alarmed that members of the unit were bound to carry out any of Jake's appropriate orders. The colonel solved the dilemma by stating that, from what he had heard, Jake had never given an appropriate order in his life.

More recognition followed. In 2002, Jake was inducted into the Oklahoma Military Hall of Fame. His friend, Truman Smith, probably best summarized his postwar contribution to society: "Jake has probably done more to promote patriotism and knowledge of World War II in this part of the country than any other person." To this day, Jake McNiece continues to entertain audiences with tales of his experiences during the greatest war in history. And in such endeavors he continues to be the lifeblood of the unit he founded—one of the best the United States has ever put into the field—the Filthy 13.

A Soldier's Prayer

by John Agnew

Dear Lord, not all the tears we shed today
Are for those we lost along the way
Some tears are for those who dare to say
We must have lingered on the way

Tears for those who fought so brave and gave their lives
And those of us who died inside
We had been in hell and did return

God's mercy will be shown to them
Who served so well and suffered long
They who are the humble in this land
And did proclaim freedom to all in God's domain

Guide us, dear Lord, in Your great way
We who were not trampled on the way.

Notes

Chapter 1: Creating a Legend

1. Tight-shoe night referred to dressing up. One's dress shoes tended to fit rather tight.
2. The Osage tribe retained the mineral rights to their land after vast quantities of oil was discovered on it. If a white man married an Osage woman, he could have access to her share of the fortune.
3. The 506th PIR was organized at Camp Toombs, Georgia, beginning July 20, 1942. The camp was later redesignated Camp Toccoa on August 21, 1942.
4. Pronounced "Zink."
5. Harold Hannah, the company commander, wrote of First Sergeant Albert Miller, "There was something about him that spoke of the country, of understanding men, knowing their foibles, and allowing for such without impairing the discipline he knew was needed. In my book, he was a gem." (Hannah, *A Military Interlude*, p. 173.)
6. Pug was short for pugilist or boxer.
7. Jake refers to anyone who drank heavily as being an alcoholic.
8. "We made Jake an honorary Polack [sic], and tried to teach him some of the Polish language, but he was an Indian from Oklahoma, so we gave it up as a bad job, he was plain hopeless." (Frank Palys to Laura Erikson, Jan. 14, 1995.) Jack Agnew claims that the Warsaw Seven was the first group of men to come up with a name. Jack Agnew enlisted in the 506th from Pennsylvania. He started out in a different demolition section than Jake McNiece. A hell of a soldier in his own right, he admired the antics of Jake so much that he sought to join his section. Jack would serve alongside Jake in every adventure.

9. Most of the regular army men did not fit into the independent nature of the 506th. Jack Agnew admitted that they were instrumental in teaching the recruits their basic demolitions though.
10. Stick refers to a group of men to jump out of an airplane on one pass. Jake uses it in this context as another unit.
11. Colonel Sink had established a live fire obstacle course to climatize his men to combat. They had to crawl under machine-gun fire with explosive charges set off by the demolitions men on the ground and in the top of the trees. He also had pig guts scattered around to add to the feeling of combat.
12. This was the demolitions platoon's first casualty. Jack Agnew said Joe was one of the nicest guys that he ever met and a bitter loss to the platoon.
13. Kitchen Police. Soldiers assigned to work in the mess hall for the day.
14. Private First Class. This was the first promotion. This rank was denoted by a single chevron on the sleeve.
15. The Post Exchange was a store for soldiers.
16. At the time Jake only knew his mother was part Indian. It was not until after the war that he even found out what tribe she belonged to. His mother did not practice nature worship. Jake in his usual quick wit had just made up this answer.
17. Up to that time no one had given Jake a direct order to stand retreat. He knew Captain Hannah had him. Hank Hannah did not remember any of the conversations that Jake described. This is not to say they did not happen but that Hannah had forgotten many of the details. Hannah mentioned that if he did say the things described in this chapter, he was glad. Hank Hannah was very well-respected by his men. Jack Agnew remembered, "He was a real gentleman and one of the finest officers that I ever met anywhere."
18. Military Police. Paratroopers considered MPs airborne rejects. They believed many of them had washed out of the airborne physical training.
19. Paratroopers received $50 additional hazardous duty pay for jumping out of airplanes. Subsequently, it was called "jump pay." This was a big increase to a private's pay of $21 a month.
20. .45 caliber automatic pistols.
21. Jack Agnew remembered that Regiment wanted to court-martial the two but Captain Hannah interceded and said, "No way, these are the kind of men that I want!"

    Gene Brown explained that since Regimental Headquarters Company was so close to Colonel Sink in proximity, it was hard for him not to know what Jake and the Filthy 13 had been up to. Their antics became a joke at the morning breakfast table. Sink was not concerned as long as the leaders did something about it. Hannah and Brown both agreed that Top Kick Miller did the best he could to keep things quiet and deal with them himself. Colonel Sink was not above kicking men out for discipline. The fact that Hannah stood up for Jake and Shorty saved them for a later day.

22. Consequently the 506th PIR adopted Currahee as its motto which means, "We stand alone."
23. In horse races heat is the finish. In this context Jake was trying to encourage Hannah to a race at the finish line.
24. Jack Agnew said Hannah ran like a deer. "The officers went hunting one time and we joked with him if he shot the deer or ran him down."
25. Jack Agnew remembered that the stockade was located at the bottom of the mountain and Jake and Shorty would make fun of the company when they'd run by every morning. "They're in the stockade and we're the ones busting our tails running up and down this mountain."
26. Malcolm Landry recalled that three MPs brought Jake and Shorty back during the morning formation with their blue dungarees with white Ps painted on them. He believed that Top Kick Miller had deliberately scheduled the MPs to bring them back at that time to make an impression on the rest of the company.
27. Each battalion marched a different route. Regimental Headquarters marched with Third Battalion from Atlanta and completed the 136 miles in 83 hours and 50 minutes. Actual marching time was 45 hours and 20 minutes. It rained all three days of the march. Several men fell out at intervals but only 11 enlisted men could not finish the march. (Hannah, *A Military Interlude*, p. 45.)

    Jack Agnew remembered marching across muddy country roads and one of the favorite sayings was, "What's behind that hill?" Then someone would answer, "Another hill!"
28. In the South at that time there were two sets of justice, one for whites and another for blacks. No court in the South would convict a white man for fighting with a black. Jake in his typical fashion was reaching for any excuse he could.
29. This story is Jack Agnew's version since it is more detailed. Jake's account is added as footnote 31.
30. Miguel and Armando Marquez had enlisted out of El Paso, Texas. Mike, who was the oldest of eight, had quit high school during the

Depression to work and help the family. He later enlisted in the Civilian Construction Corps which was run by the military. Mike and Armando had planned to enlist in the air corps but the recruiting sergeant gave them a good line of propaganda and convinced Armando to join the airborne instead. Mike wanted to be a pilot but followed his younger brother. Both ended up in the demolitions platoon. Although Mike was assigned to another section he would end up fighting alongside the Filthy 13 in Normandy and Holland.

31. Jake McNiece remembered saying, "Let's throw all these beds down the stairs." He continued, "Another guy and I grabbed the frame of a bunk and another yanked the door open. Here come this officer, I believe it was Horner, and about ten MPs up the stairs. I just set the bunk down crossways and blocked their entry. They came on in and the officer said, 'You're going to pay for every penny of this!'

    "I said, 'We don't even know what happened. We couldn't be guilty of these charges. Another guy came in here and started all this. I didn't even know him. We were just protecting ourselves.'

    "The lieutenant said sarcastically, 'I can see that much.'

    "Everyone else agreed with me. They just put us under arrest of quarters. That was all they could do."

32. The 506th PIR was assigned to Camp Mackall, North Carolina, from February 26 to June 5, 1943. They left there for Sturgis Army Airfield, Kentucky, June 6, and to Fort Bragg, North Carolina, July 23, 1943, then to New York on August 28.

33. Absent Without Leave. Leaving without permission of the commander.

34. Richard Killblane's interview with Agnew and Pierce.

35. "Well, I'm in the sabotage business," Jake said. "Besides, it sure came in handy one night back in South Carolina when I'd missed the Liberty Run truck back to camp."

    "You mean you stole—'borrowed'—a train locomotive to get back to camp?" I asked.

    "Well, I was already AWOL, but I had to get back to ship out or they would've put me in the brig if I had missed the departure of my unit." (Truman Smith, *The Wrong Stuff*, p. 160.)

36. Jack Agnew was walking guard at that time and remembered it was the adjutant who came tearing up to the barracks in a jeep. Any time there was an explosion in the area, for some reason everyone automatically blamed the demolition platoon.

37. 2nd Lt. Charles W. Mellen from Stanhope, New Jersey, became the leader of Jake's demo section after Leach left.

38. Jack Agnew, who was again walking guard, said they set the charge on top of a cinder block against the floor. The guys in the barracks were playing cards with a GI blanket thrown over a couple foot lockers. When the charge went off, floor boards were blown up and coins were sticking in the tile ceiling. Fortunately, no one was hurt.
39. The 506th staged at Camp Shanks, New York, August 29, 1943, and departed for England, September 5, 1943.
40. Hannah was sent to the Command and General Staff College at Fort Leavenworth, Kansas, in February 1943 and became the regimental operations officer (S-3) upon his return. (Hannah, *A Military Interlude*, p. 49, 55.)
41. The military prison was also at Fort Leavenworth, Kansas. Brown was well respected by the men and he treated them fair, but was very stern with them when one got out of line.
42. Jake takes great pride in this.

Chapter 2: Fuel for the Myth

1. "Colonel Sink came up to me one day and said, 'Hank, I would like to transfer Majewski and Mihlan from Headquarters Company to your S-3 Section. They are giving Captain Daniels a headache, and he would like to get rid of them.' The only answer I could give of course, was 'Yes, sir,' but I really didn't mind because when I'd been Regimental Headquarters company commander, I learned to like both of these jokers." (Hannah, *A Military Interlude*, p. 78.)
2. John F. Hale enlisted from Pulsbo, Washington.
3. Jack Womer was 26 years old from Dundak, Maryland. The 29th Infantry Division had formed its own Ranger Battalion which was unfortunately disbanded in November 1943 before it could hit the beaches of Normandy. Jack Womer had joined the battalion because they ate better. The volunteers went to Scotland for training under British commandos. This was the toughest training Jack had ever experienced but when offered a promotion to take other volunteers through it, he went back a second time. After his return the division disbanded the battalion and returned the men to their original units. While in a YMCA club in Cornwall, Jack ran into a first sergeant from the 101st Airborne Division. He was impressed, especially with the $50 dollars a month pay raise. So Jack asked his outfit to let him volunteer but since he was an expert BAR gunner, they refused his request. He complained to the chaplain who in turn issued him a pass to go down to Newburry, the headquarters of the 101st, to volunteer. There he bumped into the

commander, General Bill Lee. After he explained his situation, General Lee told him what he needed to do to join his division. Jack returned to his unit. After two weeks of waiting without a response, he again secured a pass from the chaplain and visited the 101st. This time his transfer was finally accepted and he made his five parachute jumps in one day. When asked what unit he wanted to join, he asked for the demolitions platoon of the 506th because Myers was there.

4. Jack Agnew from Philadelphia remembered, "I did not play cards and I did not smoke and I did not drink, well at least not as much as those guys anyhow. I volunteered as a dispatch rider. I also went to the division switchboard school. In riding the dispatch, you had two saddle bags and also two little platforms on the back of the bike that carried two jerry cans full of gas or water. Of course, I made a couple of runs to the local pubs for the guys and got the water cans full of beer and they had a couple of parties. Things got a little wild once in a while."
5. Jack Agnew said he had been with Jake's section since Toccoa.
6. Robert S. Cone, a 23-year-old from Roxbury, Massachusetts, joined the 506th in January 1944. He was assigned to the barracks of the Filthy 13. He found them a great bunch of guys and always in trouble. He liked them and fit right in. He spent some of his time away from the company boxing for Special Services so he did not have a lot of demolitions training. Cone remembered that Jake was "so good, he was made for combat." He expected Jake to win the Medal of Honor.
7. Roland R. Baribeau, 29 years old, was from Brighwood, Massachusetts As the father of two children, he did not have to enlist but volunteered for the airborne.
8. Herb Pierce remembered that Baribeau was kind of slow-thinking and spoke real slow. During the big invasion rehearsal for Eisenhower and Churchill, Herb and Frenchy had to blow a hole through barbed wire entanglements so the infantry could cross. After they had the charges set, Herb yelled, "Blow it! Blow it!" Frenchy looked up and said, "I don't have my matches." With everyone watching, Herb ran back to get them. He lit the fuze, then ran about 10 or 15 feet flipping in the air and landed facing the charge when it went off. Luckily he only ruined his watch.
9. Charles R. Plauda, 20 years old, came from Minneapolis, Minnesota.
10. According to Brown, Leach's peers did not think highly of him either while he was still a lieutenant. He was not one of the guys and did not share his liquor ration even though he did not drink. When he moved up to staff, Hannah thought he was a very good officer. There are some

officers who do not do well interacting with people in leadership roles but excel as staff officers. William Leach may have been one of those. Evidently Colonel Sink also thought he was good. Leach rose to major as the officer in charge of the intelligence section.

11. Charles W. Mellen, 26 years old, came from Stanhope, New Jersey, and took over the section before Christmas 1943. Sensationalizing the myth of the Filthy 13, author Arch Whitehouse told how the Dirty Dozen, all of them American Indians, hated officers and would fight anyone who tried to impose authority over them. Their lieutenant bested them in a fight and became their blood brother and so completed the Filthy 13. (Arch Whitehouse, "The Filthy Thirteen," *True Magazine*, date unknown.) Whitehouse picked up the story from Tom Hoge's June 8, 1944 *Stars and Stripes* article, "'Filthy 13' Squad Rivaled by None in Leaping Party."
12. 1st and 2nd Battalions billeted at Alderbourne, 3rd Battalion billeted at Ramsbury, and the regimental staff lived in the Littlecote Manor House with Sir Wills.
13. Jake weighed about 165 pounds but 250 pounds was the average combat load of a paratrooper.
14. Exercise Eagle was a final dress rehearsal for the invasion held on May 12–13. Almost 500 paratroopers were injured. Armando Marquez broke his leg and Jim Eib landed on a wall and injured his back. Brince Stroup and the other two missed the Normandy invasion. (Koskimaki, *A Short History of the 101st Airborne Division in England,* p. 4.)
15. John H. Mohr, *A Paratrooper's Memories of World War II*, pp. 18–19.
16. Jack Agnew said the hollow tree was right at the end of their barracks. They wrapped the deer in a mattress cover and pulled it up inside the tree with a toggle rope that had been issued to each man. A Scotland Yard officer came out to investigate the missing deer. He was asking if anyone knew who was killing the king's deer and everyone was snickering. He did not know he was leaning against the tree with the deer in it.
17. Jack Agnew remembered, "One time we were making close-order drill and were walking out past the Manor and made a lefthand turn and headed up for the woods. Top Kick said, "Okay everybody, grab a stick. We'll go get rabbits." So rabbits go in a hole and can't go in too far. If you can't reach them with your hands, you put the wire in there and keep turning it around until it locks up in their fur and you yank them out on the end of the stick. We would give them a rabbit punch and knock them out then put them in our jump coat pants and take them back to the barracks. I would go get some warm beer and they

would cook them in a deep fry on top of the pot-bellied stove. We were hungry."

18. Whang is a Southern expression for leather as tough as a leather boot lace. It takes tough leather to make boot laces.
19. Jack Agnew recalled that one time "The officers had a party and they had beer barrels delivered out in the back of Littlecote Manor. Some of the guys got the bright idea that we could use some of that beer. So they were rolling the barrel down. Dave Marcus came along. Dave was in communications and was into weight lifting. He was a husky kid. He said, "Where do you want it?" He just picked it up and carried it over his head back to our barracks. They chopped a notch in the bottom bunk and set the barrel in there. They had their barrel of beer right in the bottom bunk at the barracks. The officers never did find out where it went or who had it."
20. Tom Young claimed that his demo section also hunted deer and gigged fish. He said the heavy weapons platoon also participated but that they fished with hand grenades. He thinks that is what got everybody in trouble.
21. Olive Drab wool service uniform.
22. Jack Agnew said they had a sign on the barracks, "The Filthy 13." Everybody who slept in the barracks claimed they belonged to the Filthy 13 but it was only the members of the 1st Battalion Section.

    This was the origin of the myth that the Filthy 13 had sworn not to bathe until D-Day.

    "They boasted that they hadn't washed since Christmas and men here will testify that this was only too true—so true that it earned them a secluded spot on the leeward side of the other barracks. Time enough to wash after D-Day, they said." (Tom Hoge, "Filthy 13 Squad Rivaled By None In Leaping Party," *Stars and Stripes*, June 8, 1944.)

    "Some months ago when men were being carefully selected for airborne infantry work, it was noticed in one training area that whenever a certain group of sluggers got together, they produced a most remarkable odor. At first the patrons of the Red Cross hut put it down to new leather, the scarcity of water or the natural chemical reaction of eating too much Spam and Brussels spouts." (Whitehouse, "The Filthy Thirteen.")
23. 1st Lt. Shrable D. Williams was leader of another section in the demolition platoon.
24. The increased demand for whiskey on account of the tremendous influx of thirsty American soldiers in England did not allow for pro-

duction to keep up with demand. The alcoholic beverage became a scarce commodity. Jake, however, discovered that he could purchase all he wanted directly from the employees at a distillery.

25. Smith, *Wrong Stuff,* pp. 157-161.
26. "As a Lieutenant, and Jake as a Buck Private, I started to pay our check, but he stopped me and pulled out a roll of pound notes as large as two fists, and ordered me to put my money back into my pocket.

    "'You mean you've got that much money left over from what they gave you for the booze?' I asked.

    "'Ohh, this is my money here.' he said.

    "'Even Generals don't have that much money, Jake.'

    "I wasn't about to ask him where he, a Buck Private, had gotten so much money. It was better I didn't know.

    "'Oh, it's legal,' he said, 'It's the treasury of a little club I've founded. It's called the Dirty Dozen. Well, that's the way it started out. It's now called the Filthy Thirteen. I'm the president and treasurer.'

    "The Dirty Dozen? I had to know more.

    "Jake explained that his little band of blood-brothers, who had accepted his ritual of mixing their blood with each other, had vowed not to bathe and to remain dirty and filthy until D-Day when they—demolition saboteurs—would be jumping ahead of the invasion behind enemy lines." (Smith, *Wrong Stuff*, pp. 157–161.)
27. "D-Day was coming up awful soon and we knew it. The Demolition Company [platoon] wanted to have a booze party on a Saturday night. Jake McNiece collected money from the boys who wanted it and went to London to buy the booze. I was on guard at the main gate when Jake got off a vehicle and walked in. He had a barracks bag half full of booze bottles. They had the party at a house out in the big pasture north of the castles. They tried to get me to be their bartender at the booze party. That made me mad because they knew I didn't drink." (Mohr, *Memories*, p. 27.)
28. Audiotape by Mike Marquez, October 15, 1996.
29. "'Those scalp-locks caused a number of incidents. A bare skinhead under a steel helmet can get mighty cold,' recalled [Jack] Agnew, with a pained expression." (Ted Zenender, "We Were Trained for a Suicide Mission," June 7, 1990.)

    It was common belief that the Filthy 13 painted their faces with red and white grease paint. Jake remembered they used black and white paint. Jack Agnew said they wiped the still-wet black and white invasion stripes painted on the planes with their fingers to paint their faces.

Tom Hoge, who wrote the first story, did not mention the color of the face paint. A June 19, 1944 *Time* magazine article, "13 Paratroopers," stated that they painted their faces with red, black, green, and white war paint. Arch Whitehouse's *True Magazine* article said they used red and purple paint.

30. Tom Hoge's June 8, 1944 *Stars and Stripes* article, "'Filthy 13' Squad Rivaled By None In Leaping Party," seemed to have started the ball rolling. This article created the myth that they had sworn since Christmas not to bathe until D-Day. He also claimed that all of the Filthy 13 but one were full-blooded Indians. They had a ceremony to make the single paleface a blood brother before the invasion. All the other writers embellished this basic story.

Chapter 3: A Bridge in Normandy

1. Carentan and Ste. Mere Eglise were the two major transportation networks behind the Utah beachhead. The 82d Airborne had Ste. Mere Eglise as its main objective and the 101st focused on seizing Carentan and the surrounding bridges. Every commander from Eisenhower down saw the importance of Carentan to the success of the Normandy invasion. The Filthy 13, with 3rd Battalion, 506th PIR, essentially had the bridges on the Douve Canal and the 501st PIR had the locks of Barquette upstream from Carentan.

   "Two principal roads led from Normandy into the Cherbourg peninsula. One ran through the bottleneck at Carentan, the other up the far west coast. Between those two roads the Douve River severed two-thirds of the neck. If we were to plug the peninsula, our mission was clear; First, we must seize the bottleneck at Carentan, then hold that east-west river line of the Douve to the west coast road. Finally we would plug the nine-mile gap between that west coast road and the sea. These tasks were to be split between two airborne divisions, the 82d and the 101st." (Omar Bradley, *A Soldier's Story*, pp. 232–33.)
2. All through training the paratroopers were reminded to expect high casualties on a combat jump.
3. "This was the plan for Third Battalion: Supported by one platoon of 326th Engineer Battalion and two demolition sections, it was to land on DROP ZONE D, which was to the south of VIERVILLE and east of ANGOVILLE AU PLAIN. From this ground, the force was to strike southward as soon as possible and seize the two bridges near LE PORT at the mouth of the RIVER DOUVE. The bridges were to be expanded into a bridgehead as rapidly as the tactical situation permitted. By seiz-

ing the high ground in the direction of BREVANDS, the Battalion would be reaching toward the American forces which were moving northward from OMAHA BEACH. It was believed that all of these things could be accomplished on the first day." ("Regimental Unit Study Number 3; 506 Parachute Infantry Regiment In Normandy Drop," p. 3.)

Frank Palys, who worked in the S-2 of the 506th Regimental Headquarters, confirmed that the Filthy 13 received the mission to prepare the bridges for demolition. (Frank Palys to Laura Erickson, Jan. 14, 1994.)

4. Jake received Staff Sergeant Mariano S. Ferra out of C Co. 326th Engineers.
5. Jack Agnew recalled, "The tension was terrific, though some, like Jake McNiece, tried to treat the whole venture like a joke. Some laughed all the way across the Channel. Even though it was the last day of their lives." (Zehender, *Globe.*) Jake's favorite saying was, "Hell, these guys are trying to get us killed."
6. Robert Cone remembered that the pilots panicked when the plane received flak. The plane pitched so much that the guys vomited. They were so angry that they yelled back to the last man to leave a hand grenade in the plane when he jumped.
7. As soon as the aircraft reached the Cotentin Peninsula they ran into a fog bank which obscured vision with the ground. The aircraft became separated and some took evasive maneuvers against the flak. Since the lead aircraft had the radio equipment to home in on the Pathfinders' signal, the others became lost. Lieutenant Mellen and Brown's C-47s were off course flying from north to south and scattered the two demolition sticks from north of Ste. Mere Eglise near Montebourg to St. Come du Mont with the last half of the sticks landing in the flooded fields.
8. "'Piccadilly Willy' never did jump. 'Just as I jumped there was a blinding flash and a roar,' he [Chuck Plauda] said, 'and the plane went up in smoke. There were 600 pounds of dynamite aboard.'" ("Story of 'Filthy Thirteen' Finally Released by Army," *Springfield Daily Republican*, Dec. 4, 1944.)
9. This method of assembly was referred to as "rolling up the stick."
10. The army issued each paratrooper a small switchblade knife for that purpose.
11. Major General William C. Lee suffered a heart attack just prior to the invasion and Maxwell Taylor assumed command of the 101st Airborne Division.

12. The toy metal crickets made a cricket sound when one squeezed them. One crick was to be answered by two. Some tied them around their necks. Jake had taped his to his web suspenders.
13. This response and Jake's fear that the invasion had been called off are clear examples of the paranoia that sets in when isolated on the battlefield.
14. Jack Agnew landed at St. Come du Mont, near a German battalion command post about a mile from his objective. When he landed, the barrel of his bolt-action Springfield jammed in the mud which drove the butt up into his shoulder. He hid near a hedgerow while Germans ran up and down the road. He then moved across to another field and ran into a mortar man who was scared to death and crying. Jack told him, "Hey, you better come with me or stop making all that damn noise or I'll shoot your ass right now!" He refused to go with Jack. He was shocked that a man like that was a paratrooper. Jack then ran into Keith Carpenter and Mike Marquez of his platoon. Carpenter had landed in the swamp. (Koskimaki, *D-Day with the Screaming Eagles*, pp. 300–301.)

    Mike Marquez also landed in the swamp. When he pulled the three disassembled pieces of his M1 Garand out of the weapons bag, the trigger housing fell in the water and he could not find it. He could hear Germans talking nearby but had no intention of being taken prisoner even though he was only armed with a knife. He finally reached some high ground where he saw two figures approaching. He signaled them with his cricket and they turned out to be Jack Agnew and Keith Carpenter. They proceeded to the bridges and picked up Leonard R. Cardwell before they ran into Jake McNiece and the others. Jack Agnew and Clarence Ware then blew up power lines along the way. The first one was on a concrete telephone pole and the other was in a hole underground.
15. Colonel Howard R. Johnson, commander of the 501st PIR, ran into a German command post about the same time he ran into some men from the 506th. (Rapport, *Rendezvous*, p. 111.)
16. Colonel Johnson's 501st PIR had the mission to secure the la Barquette lock and bridges on the Douve up stream from Carentan.
17. "Jake McNiece, Clarence Ware, Keith Carpenter, and others of our company were walking toward a high bank and a sniper shot Clarence Ware about 30 feet to the left of me. The bullet went in just below his left shoulder and down through his back. I don't see how it missed his heart, but it did. He went down like he was dead but it didn't kill him.

At first I thought it was Jake McNiece that got shot. Carpenter took out his first aid powder and sprinkled it on the bullet holes." (Mohr, *Memories,* p. 31.)

Keith Carpenter and two other paratroopers went back after dusk that first night to look for Ware, but he had already been taken back to an aid station. (Koskimaki, *D-Day*, pp. 300–301.)

18. S. L. A. Marshall headed the European History Division that gathered information and wrote the official history of the Normandy campaign. While Marshall's group interviewing process has been applauded he has recently come under criticism for his research. Spot checks of his work in this area have produced inaccuracies. He admitted to Mark Bando that he did not use the group interview method for the action at the Brevands bridges. Consequently, there are discrepancies between the account by the demolitions men and the official report. However, the demolitions men are all in agreement on what occurred. (Mark Bando, *101st Airborne At Normandy*, p. 110.)
19. The wooden bridges led into the towns of Brevands and Le Port just a few miles northeast of Carentan. Jack Agnew remembered the wooden bridge closest to Carentan was a vehicular bridge with concrete girders and the one closest to the Channel was a foot bridge. They wired only the vehicular bridge leading into Brevands. Because of its proximity, most of the demo men referred to this action as taking place at Carentan.
20. The official history states that the 3rd Battalion, 506th suffered extremely high casualties on the jump. The battalion commander, LTC Robert L. Wolverton, along with most of his officers were killed the first day. Captain Charles Shettle led about thirty-two survivors of the battalion to the two bridges at Brevands and established a bridgehead at 4:30. His force grew as others trickled in. He initially sent groups of men over to the other side but they withdrew as the Germans reinforced the other bank. (*Utah Beach To Cherbourg; 6–27 June 1944*, p. 24, and Koskimaki, *D-Day*, pp. 296–314.)

Donald Zahn was the first to cross the bridge. He remembered seeing the demolitions men with scalp locks and war paint wiring the bridge. (Bando, *Normandy*, p. 106.)

Jack Agnew remembered the demolitions men arrived at the bridges first and established the defense. Captain Shettle arrived sometime after that. Jake did not remember seeing Shettle at all. Jack did not remember blowing up the bridges initially but thought they blew the bridges up after the air force damaged them.

1st Lt. Eugene Dance of G Co., 506th PIR, reached the east bridge with about fourteen men from his platoon. The other stick from his platoon straggled in later. He reported to Captain Shettle, then walked across the bridge to his objective, the high ground on the other side. Word came for everyone to return back to the west side of the canal and dig in. Shettle did not feel he had enough men to hold both sides. They were dug in by sunrise.

John H. "Dinty" Mohr remembered that he also came upon Jake McNiece, Keith Carpenter, Mike Marquez, and others at the causeway. Wounded by mortar shrapnel that first day, Dinty Mohr was evacuated to a house behind the causeway that had been converted by medics into a dressing station. (Mohr, *Memories*, pp. 32–33.)

The official report claims seven engineers and two demolitions men wired the bridges the next night. All the demolitions men agree they wired it the first night. ("Regimental Unit Study," pp. 26–27.)

21. Jack was one of two designated marksman for the company. That is why he carried an M1903A1 Springfield. He admitted that the sniper was just on the other side of the dike and not in the building.
22. Richard Killblane's interview with Jack Agnew.
23. The official report claims the Germans tried to make a sortie across the bridge at 2:00 on the second morning. ("Regimental Unit Study," p. 27.)
24. Jack Agnew said he looked over and saw that Mike kept rising up to shoot from the same spot. He then told Jake, "Hey, look at that crazy Indian. They're going to pick him off."
25. Jack Agnew remembered that many men were killed because of this. As many as three paratroopers were killed in the vicinity of one foxhole. Each time a paratrooper was killed another would come in and take his place. They kept rising up to shoot over the dike in the same spot. The Germans knew the hole was there and waited for them each time. Jack would go over and pull the dead paratrooper out of his hole then take his dog tags to Shettle.
26. Eugene Dance remembered that men trickled in at about the same rate that others were killed. The size of the force on the bridges remained about the size of an infantry company—a little over a hundred men. Jack Agnew only remembered seeing about eight men around them. There were about five or six foxholes and the force on their bridge never exceeded sixteen at any one time because of casualties.

    The bridge was constructed on top of the dike with a road leading up to it. That road embankment separated their group from other paratroopers whom they wanted to make contact with. Jack Agnew remembered, "I went over to Captain Shettle and asked if it was all right to get all the explosives to dig through it. We wanted to blow through the hard road. Only Jake and Mike Marquez offered to help. We blew a trench through the road and then Mike and I dug it out." Mike Marquez remembered they blew the trench through the road because men were killed every time they tried to run across it.

27. There was no contact with the 3rd Battalion for three days. Not until Sgt. Cole of E Company, 506th, left the 501st position and went over to the two bridges did Sink discover that Captain Shettle had established a bridgehead. (506th Parachute Infantry, "Operation Neptune; S-1, S-2, S-3 Journals.")

    Mike Marquez said that three other paratroopers had asked if he wanted to go looking for prisoners and souvenirs. He said yes. Jack Agnew said he and Jake gave him a bunch of prisoners to take back. Jack did not know Mike could not see in the dark. Along the way they came across about a dozen Germans with a white flag. Half of them were wounded and they wanted to surrender. The three other paratroopers still wanted to hunt for souvenirs so they sent Mike back with the prisoners. Eventually he became lost and asked the Germans if they knew where the Americans were. He warned them if they led him to the Americans he would treat them nice but if they led him to the Germans he would kill as many as he could. Jack Agnew described Mike as a fierce looking guy. "I don't think they wanted to cross him." They led Mike to the Americans but not back to his original location. There he asked for directions to the bridges and started walking back in time to see the planes bomb the bridges.

28. Official history claims that P-47s bombed on the second day at 2:30 in the afternoon. Every account including newspaper reports differs as to whether the planes were P-47s or P-51s and whether it was the second or third day. Not everyone could tell the difference between one plane or another just as most soldiers could not always tell the difference between German tanks. The two men, Jack Agnew and Eugene Dance, who definitely knew the difference, claimed with certainty that they were P-51 Mustangs.

29. In spite of the orange panels identifying that Americans held the bridges, the fighter-bombers bombed anyway. Each plane carried two bombs. Dance also remembered that the planes dropped all their ordnance on the bridges but not the troops. Debris landed on the men in their shallow foxholes.

30. On the third day, Lt. Charles "Sandy" Santasiero saw the Germans approaching and told his men to hold their fire until the Germans were within 75 yards. After cutting down the Krauts he pursued those who fled into the hedgerows. After killing many more, he brought in the rest as prisoners. They were added to Shettle's growing group of prisoners. Santasiero won the Distinguished Service Cross for his actions. (Bando, Normandy, p. 108.) The official history claimed a battalion of the German 6th Parachute Regiment ran into the force on the Brevands bridges on the second day and as many as 255 Germans surrendered to Captain Shettle's force. (*Utah Beach*, p. 72.) Eugene Dance did not remember any force of Germans reaching his bridge. Germans had surrendered to his force in ones and twos.
31. Jack Agnew remembered, "Jake and I went looking for Ware. On the way we ran across this German. He was all green and rotten but still alive. I said that was a disgrace and someone should put him out of his misery. Jake said, 'You've got the forty-five. You do it.'

    "I turned my head so I would not see it and missed. Jake said, 'You missed that son-of-a-bitch.' He has given me a hard time about that ever since."
32. The official history claims the paratroopers were relieved on the third day. Jack Agnew remembered that they left the bridge one day before the 506th participated in the attack on Carentan. That would have been the fifth day. Eugene Dance said within twenty-four hours after his platoon left the bridge he walked through Carentan and it was secured. Carentan was taken on the seventh day. His force would have left on the sixth day. The official history of the action on the bridges on the lower Douve differs from the testimony of the veterans. While fifty years may have caused many to forget lesser important details they have not forgotten more important events such as when they entered Carentan. Jake is adamant that he was on the bridge for five days. There is no record of who or how many people were interviewed for the official history but the veterans I have interviewed tell essentially the same story. They were not relieved on the third day.
33. Jack Agnew, Keith Carpenter, Mike Marquez, Leonard Cardwell, and Chuck Plauda.
34. The 101st plan was to assault Carentan by double envelopment with the 501st attacking from the northeast from the Brevands bridgehead through the 327th Glider Infantry position and the 506th would first attack Hill 30 then enter Carentan from the south.
35. 12:35. ("Journal")

36. "Colonel Sink (506th Parachute Infantry) moved his command post group over the same route which the battalions had followed, but after leaving the highway he missed the way and swung to the south of Hill 30, where he dug in forward of the two battalions." (*Utah Beach*, p. 89.) The S-3 log stated that at 4:30, "Reg. Hq. Co. and attachments spend night wandering around west and south of RR tracks trying to locate position for new CP. We were under enemy M.G. and small arms fire most of the night." ("Journal") This initiated the attack at around 4:30 in the morning and the other battalions had to fight their way to Regimental Headquarters Company. At 5:00, Sink ordered the 2nd Battalion to attack into the city where it linked up with the 327th at 7:30. Sink set up his CP in Carentan at 10:30. The 501st and the rest of the 506th established a blocking position. Schroeder won the silver star medal for leading this assault on Hill 30.
37. Richard Killblane's interview with Tom Young.
38. Tom Young remembered the story exactly the same way.
39. After the war, Robert Sink became commandant of cadets at West Point. Later he was promoted to brigadier-general as the assistant division commander of the 11th Airborne Division. Then in 1953, Major-General Sink assumed command of the 7th Armored Division.
40. Jake received his first bronze star medal.
41. Jack Agnew described a patrol led by Oscar "Skip" Simpson. Leach instructed "Go out past this First Battalion then come around by Second and Third and come back in." The patrol became pinned down and had to fight its way out. When Simpson returned and reported the enemy contact, Leach said, "I just wanted to know if they were still there." Jack said the men lost all respect for Leach then.

    Later Jack was given a motorcycle to reconnoiter the route to Cherbourg. The next day he led a unit down the road but it did not look the same. He warned them of that. They said they would take it from there and proceeded the wrong way. They had a truck loaded with explosives that Leach wanted to bring back for training. That evening the truck blew up killing several men. Having lost all respect for Leach, the demolitions men easily blamed him for the accident.
42. Richard Killblane's interview with Tom Young.
43. Chuck Plauda in an interview with *Stars and Stripes* claimed to have joined up with a group of men and reached the bridge but neither Jake nor Jack Agnew remembered seeing him. He may have fought on the other bridge. ("'Filthy 13'—Their Number Is Down," *Stars and Stripes,* Nov. 30, 1944.)

44. Jack Womer's account was taken from an interview with him by Richard Killblane.
45. Runners were designated couriers who carried messages.
46. That was the common belief of what happened to Lieutenant Charles Mellen. Frank Palys, however, discovered his body in the middle of a field. Mellen's body was in a crawling position with his right leg pulled up and his carbine cradled in his arms. He was shot twice in the left side. Mellen had evidently died instantly from machine-gun fire. (Frank Palys to Laura Erickson, Jan 14, 1994.) Lt John H. Reeder, who was with Palys when he discovered Mellen's body, reported it to Regimental S-1 on June 9. ("Journals.")
47. George Baran was captured after being wounded then sent to a German hospital near Cherbourg. He was freed when Cherbourg fell to the Americans. (*Springfield Daily Republican.*)
48. Hale and Cone landed almost simultaneously with a German between them. Cone fired first and killed the German. Peepnuts was killed two weeks later on June 20. "'He was right behind me,' Oleskiewicz said. 'We were crawling across a field after getting a machine-gun nest. I heard a single shot, turned around and "Peepnuts" was dead.'" (*Springfield Daily Republican.*)
49. "'None of us saw him,' McNiece explained. 'But we heard from the group he joined that he went with them to clean out three machine-gun nests. He got it at the third.'" (*Springfield Daily Republican.*)
50. Rasmussen was shown the grave and dog tags of Baribeau right after he was captured. Evidently, Frenchy had landed in the same vicinity as Rasmussen near Montebourg.
51. Lt. Alex Bobuck was captured but escaped. He turned Cone's dog tags in to Regimental S-1 on June 7 and reported that Cone had been wounded. ("Journals.") Charles Lonegran claimed to have seen Ragsman Cone at the German hospital in Cherbourg. (*Springfield Daily Republican.*)
52. It was a leg pack of explosives and not a flamethrower.
53. "'I helped him through two fields before we ran into an aid man, he [Trigger Gann] said. 'Then I went back to pick up our knives and some equipment. I got into a fight with some Germans and I had to leave Rasputin rather than reveal his position.' When he came back Rasputin was gone." (*Springfield Daily Republican.*) Rasmussen said he broke his ankle because a leg pack would not release and Gann did not find an aid man.
54. Rasmussen jumped out right behind Lt. Gene Brown as the second man in the other stick. He landed near Montebourg in the same vicinity as

Trigger Gann and Frenchy Baribeau of Jake's stick. The Germans captured him a few days later and took him to a hospital in Volognes then to Cherbourg where they placed him in a pill box with a red cross painted on it. There he ran into George Baran. They were scheduled to move to Brest one evening but the Allies bombed the nearby submarine pens, so they stayed. He remained a prisoner for 30 days until the Americans finally took Cherbourg. Because of the broken ankle Rass could no longer jump so he was transferred to the gliders and fought all the way through to Berchtesgaden.

55. Airborne troops were issued the new M1943 field jacket and field pants on which the riggers sewed a cargo pocket.
56. Both were just having fun with each other. Jake and Top Kick actually thought highly of each other.
57. Pinks and Greens was the term for the officer's service uniform. The coat was an olive drab and the trousers were beige with a pink cast.
58. Richard Killblane's interview with Virgil Smith.
59. Virgil Smith continued, "I was assigned my own jeep. I would catch Jake and we would go hunting on the weekends when we were not doing anything. We went hunting quite a few times. We would put the windshield down on that jeep and take turns driving and shooting. Somebody must have heard our carbines and turned us in. We usually came in on one side but that Sunday we came in on the other side and there were the game wardens on bicycles waiting for us. They chased us but never did catch us."
60. "The name Dinty was given to me way back in Fort Benning because of Dinty Moore stew and that's what this one guy started calling me and it stuck. One guy even named his son after me, Dinty." (Mohr, *Memories,* p. 13.)
61. On June 19, Sink made Hank Hannah commander of the 1st Battalion and put him in for the Legion of Merit. He assumed command three days later. On June 30, General Maxwell Taylor promoted Hannah to lieutenant colonel as the division operations officer (G-3). (Hannah, *Military Interlude*, pp. 119–122.)

    Captain Edward A. Peters had taken over the company after Daniels tranferred to the OSS. On D-Day, Peters led five men against a machine-gun nest. He singlehandedly knocked it out but was killed in the process. ("Journals") The demolition platoon only lost two officers. Charles Mellen was killed in action and Gene Brown was promoted to company commander.

    Lieutenant Shrable Williams moved up to platoon leader.

Lieutenant Sylvester Horner also survived Normandy and was SSG Davidson's section leader. Lieutenant Edward Haley survived Normandy and joined the platoon to replace Mellen as Jake's section leader. Lieutenant Eugene Dance transferred in from G Company and asked for SSG Myers' section since they had known each other from their time in the 29th Ranger Battalion. SFC Charles G. "Chaplain" Williams had been wounded then captured in Normandy. Baran said he saw him in the German hospital at Cherbourg. (*Springfield Daily Republican.*) Earl Boegerhausen replaced him as the platoon sergeant.

Chapter 4: Surviving Holland

1. The Airborne troops were the best trained units the Allies had and Eisenhower knew it would be a waste not to use them. Consequently, a number of airborne drops had been proposed, but Patton's Third Army kept overrunning the drop zones before any jump could take place. Finally the British proposed an airborne operation that made sense: seize a series of bridges along a major transportation artery and then push up the corridor with tanks. This was essentially Germany's 1940 invasion of Holland in reverse. The problem lay in the details, an unknown German SS panzer corps at Arnhem, and the lack of British urgency.
2. Jack Agnew said that they were not allowed to write anything on the planes when they jumped into Normandy but for the Holland jump they wrote their names and "The Filthy 13" on the side of their C-47.
3. Mike Marquez jumped in with an M3 "Grease gun." He threw it away as soon as he could pick up an M1 Garand, because the Grease gun was "ugly and only good for close in fighting."
4. Tom Young remembered, "I was the last man in the stick [of Lt. Dance's plane]. Our plane was being jostled about due to flak. I went into the cabin and saw the navigator and radio operator slumped over dead. The pilot was leaning over to one side with blood spurting out of his head. I yelled at the copilot to turn on the green light. He calmly reached over and flipped the switch. We were in such a rush to get out of the plane that I went out the door with three others."

   Jack Womer remembered that before the jump Jake made him the number three man in the stick. This position was important because he stood next to the door with his hand on the green light. He could see everything that went on inside and out of the aircraft. They did not expect trouble from too many Germans on the ground but expected lots of trouble with the flak. The flak made Jack nervous. Lt. Dance's plane was hit and swerved in front of theirs and the paratroopers were jumping out and hitting the propeller of Jack's C-47. Jack told his stick to go. They went out on the red light.

Steve Kovacs was in the other plane which was hit by flak and caught fire a minute short of their drop zone. The men bailed out and the aircraft crashed. (George E. Koskimaki, *Hell's Highway; Chronicle of the 101st Airborne Division in the Holland Campaign, September–November, 1944*, p. 58.)

5. Lefty McGee was another paratrooper from Jake's hometown of Ponca City, Oklahoma. He survived the war and died in 1998 still living in Ponca City.
6. The 506th took Son, Holland, the first day but the Germans blew the bridge. The 506th reached Eindhoven the next day. 3d Battalion led into the city from the north followed by 2d Battalion with the 1st Battalion behind in reserve. As soon as the lead battalion encountered resistance, Sink deployed the 2d Battalion to the east. Enemy resistance quickly broke, giving way to celebration by the citizens.
7. There is some confusion as to how Davidson and Myers actually died. Eugene Dance did not remember any conversation with Jake. Very few of the men even remembered who Dance was. Dance remembered that the British convoy was backed up bumper-to-bumper. When the Messerschmitts came in, the drivers abandoned their trucks. Dance and Myers ran forward to get the drivers back in their trucks to get them moving again. A bomb landed fifteen feet from Dance. Myers's body absorbed the blast, which saved Dance's life. Steve Kovacs remembered Myers was out in the open yelling at everybody to take cover when he was killed. (Koskimaki, *Hell's Highway*, p. 131.)

Herb Pierce was on outpost duty in Davidson's section. Davidson yelled at him, "Let's get out of here!" They started out of the building for an air raid shelter with Myers in the lead. When Herb saw the bombs falling, he turned back into the building but the blast killed Davidson.

CPL Tom Young said there was a shelter near each bridge. When the Messerschmitts came, he could see what they were going to do. He told his squad—Armando Marquez, Steve Kovacs and Frank Kough—to get into the shelter. He told Bill Myers and Jim Davidson to get in there too but they just stood out in the open. The planes dropped three bombs. A piece of shrapnel about the size of an egg hit Myers in the kidney and another piece hit him on the back of the leg slicing the muscle in two. Myers fell on Tom who carried him into the shelter. The planes returned on a strafing run and set the convoy of trucks ablaze.

Davidson stood there shooting at them with his Thompson submachine gun when he was hit. The rounds had taken his legs off.

When the bombing began, Jack Agnew saw Manny Freedman lying under a plate glass window in an alley way. He called over, "Manny, get out of there!" He came over and with the next bomb "the window just popped out and went right down like a knife blade."

Manny turned to Jack, "Boy, I wouldn't have made it would I?"

Jack answered, "No, you would not."

From there Jack ran around trying to find an air raid shelter. He came upon the bodies of Davidson and Myers. They were not more than three feet apart. He could see from the bullet holes where he believed Davidson had been killed by strafing while standing against a wall. When he picked Jim up, Jack's fingers went right through the back of Davidson's head. A round had blown his brains out. Myers had his legs blown off but was still alive. Jack said he carried Myers down into the air raid shelter where he found Armando Marquez.

Mike Marquez had dug a foxhole over in Jake's sector. His brother, Armando, was on the next bridge. Mike did not want him anywhere near because he would have worried about taking care of him. In Mike's mind, Armando had no business even being in Holland in the first place. He had broken his leg on that last practice jump before the Normandy invasion. Armando, however, wanted to see action and talked Gene Eib into releasing him from the hospital for the Holland jump. After the bombing, Mike ran over to check on his brother. Armando had brains and blood dripping from under his helmet. After a few words with him, Mike realized that Armando was all right. He had evidently put on Davidson's helmet. To Mike's relief, the bombing, however, re-injured Armando's leg so he was later evacuated which caused him to miss the Battle of the Bulge. Myers was evacuated that morning but died on the way to the field hospital.

8. Tom Young said that shrapnel from one bomb hit part of the shelter, then his leg. It did not go in very deep and he was able to pick it out. It did not hurt too much so he marched with the platoon to Son. A medic saw the blood on his leg and checked it out. He then had Tom evacuated.
9. The bombing had inflicted significant casualties on the platoon. When the bridge was turned over to the British there was no longer a need for the demolition platoon. All the demolition officers were sent to other assignments according to need. Eugene Dance was one of the most senior first lieutenants in the regiment. He was promoted to captain with command of Headquarters Company, 1st Battalion.

10. The Germans realized how vulnerable the corridor was. German armor tried to sever the corridor at Veghel on the morning of September 22. In anticipation, Division ordered the 506th, minus 1st Battalion, north to Veghel and Uden. The regiment moved up on the morning of the 22nd both in trucks and on foot. Lead elements of the 2nd Battalion with Lieutenant Colonel Charlie Chase and Regimental Headquarters Company reached Uden around 11:00 and then were immediately cut off. The Germans had severed the road between them and Veghel and tried to take the two towns. Veghel and Opheusden turned out to be the hardest fought battle of the 506th in Holland. The demolitions platoon more likely ran into the Germans at Veghel and fought their way up to their company in Uden. (Koskimaki, *Hell's Highway*, pp. 270-290.)
11. Mike Marquez was pulled to guard Sink's headquarters. Jack Agnew was again detailed as a dispatch rider and sent up to communicate with the British.
12. In spite of his callous humor, the subsequent event would lead to Jake's one recurring nightmare. His wife, Martha, said the cold would always bring on the memory of this event.
13. Herb Pierce remembered they were driving into Uden when a GI stepped out in the road and warned them not to go any further. They could hear artillery up the road. A lieutenant was riding in the front of the truck. As soon as they stopped everyone climbed out of the truck. On the right side of the road was a row of beautiful houses. On the left were hardly any buildings. Suddenly the Germans opened up on them. From this point the stories differ significantly. Evidently everyone scattered in different directions.
14. Herb Pierce said many of the paratroopers stayed in the ditch for a while and then Jake yelled, "We're going into that house over there!" They ran for the building. "Once inside, the walls came apart. The Germans laid those 88s right down our throats. Evidently they had seen us go in there." Jake yelled, "Let's get out of here!" Herb jumped out of the kitchen window and buried himself in a grease pit. The Germans blew that house apart. The paratroopers then started back up the road.

    The field was six feet above the road. The Germans attacked with a captured American tank. An officer charged the tank with a hand grenade only to be killed when he climbed on it. The rest of the paratroopers fought their way up the street.

    Herb remembered that the tanks were firing on them at pointblank range. While he was in one house he saw a little girl wearing a white dress run out of a house into the street. A German tank shot her and she was a mass of blood. Herb ran out to pick her up but a medic got to her first and yelled that he would take care of her. He heard she lived.

Jack Womer jumped into a ditch with a bunch of other paratroopers. He saw a guy with his head blown off. Jack followed the ditch to a house. There were paratroopers all around the house. He figured he would go down into the cellar but could not because it was full of paratroopers "waiting for orders." He remembered only tanks attacking them.

Jack Agnew and Mike Marquez both missed the ambush. Jack did remember experiencing the heaviest mortaring in Veghel. When he crawled out of his foxhole, he could not see how anyone could have survived it.

15. Herb Pierce remembered, "Jake and I were in a foxhole together. I was scared to death. I was shaking so bad I could not shoot or even hold a cigarette. Jake just chewed tobacco and spit, chewed and spit, chewed and spit. It seemed like it did not bother him. I told him I was scared. Jake said to me, 'Kid, you show your fear by shaking. I'm just as scared as you and my guts are tearing me up.' He told us to get out of there and we ran."

    Herb Pierce later told Jake's wife, Martha, how he had once threatened to kill Jake when they got into combat but it was Jake who threatened to kill him and in turn saved his life.
16. Jack Womer remembered a captain coming over to the house hiding the paratroopers. He said, "We've got to go back in town. The tanks have left." Jack came out and a lieutenant asked if anyone could fire a bazooka. Joe Oleskiewicz had a bazooka. The officer told Jack where there were some bazooka rounds. Jack and Joe ran across the road to get the rounds. Then the 88s opened up on Joe. Jack did not see what happened to him. He later saw a pistol Joe had carried next to the body missing its upper torso.
17. Jack Womer remembered, "When the mortars landed in the ditch, Jake and I took off. I went back to finish digging my hole and Graham and the others were gone. They had run out of the ditch and left their equipment. I looked around. The ditch ran under a road and there was Graham. I said, 'This is a good place, so we stayed in there for two days."
18. The mission to reopen the road fell to Sink's 506th PIR. On September 25, a British armored brigade joined the 506th in Veghel from the north. Sink's force then pushed its way up to Uden to clear the road and

rejoin Chase's advance guard. The next day the 506th marched back to Veghel to reopen the road south of the town cut by their old friends, the German 6th Parachute Regiment. Leaving at 1:30 in the morning, the regiment arrived at 5:30. At 8:30 the 3rd Battalion attacked to the south with 1st Battalion on the right and 2nd Battalion in the reserve. Upon reaching resistance, the two battalions were stopped. Then the 2nd Battalion deployed to the left of the 3rd. 1st Battalion swung around to the right and made contact with the 501st while the 502nd came up from the south and linked up with 2nd Battalion. In an enveloping attack on the 26th, the 1st and 3rd Battalions of the 506th held while the 2nd Battalion and the 502nd forced the Germans to abandon the Koevering roadblock. The attack to the south on the 25th is more likely the setting for this story. (Koskimaki, *Hell's Highway*, pp. 291–322.)

19. A bar ditch is a "V" shaped ditch dug alongside a road for drainage.
20. Jake took Jack Womer along to check out the house. Womer checked for booby traps while Jake searched the pantry for food. Womer discovered a mattress in the upstairs bedroom which he pitched out through a hole in the wall. After Jake passed the lieutenant's inspection, Womer then ran around to pick up the mattress so he could sleep on it that night.
21. LTC Hank Hannah had just finished coordinating with the British and on his return trip an 88 struck a tree next to his jeep. Shrapnel ripped through his right shoulder joint, requiring his evacuation to England and the United States. (Hannah, *A Military Interlude*, pp. 138–143.)
22. The British paratroopers had evacuated Arnhem on September 25.
23. American paratroopers were intended for use as shock troops trained to conduct intense fighting for a short period of time and then return to the rear to rest and train up for the next mission. The paratroopers had fully expected to be returned after six days when they had handed their corridor over to the British, but were instead used to drive back the German penetrations of the corridor and reinforce the British on the Rhine. The Americans bitterly resented this, especially since they felt the British had not aggressively pursued their end of the fight, highlighted by the fact that they regularly stopped for tea.
24. On October 2, the 506th moved north by truck to Nijmegen. Herb Pierce remembered leaving Uden in a "six-by." They rode to the "Island," a stretch of land between the Waal and Neder (Lower) Rhine Rivers. Upon reaching Nijmegen, they ran into an MP who instructed them on which route to follow. At the bridge another MP stopped

them. They saw dead bodies and craters. The German artillery had the bridge zeroed in and the MPs only let one truck across at a time. The MP told the driver, "When I tell you to go, you floor that thing." When he gave the order, they took off with shells landing all around them. The paratroopers made it safely to the other side. That was the only time they listened to MPs.

From there the 506th turned west about ten miles to occupy a line of defense near Opheusden. Sink placed the 3rd Battalion on the left while the 2nd Battalion held the right along the Neder Rhine. He held the 1st Battalion in reserve. As German pressure increased around Opheusden, Sink deployed the 1st Battalion on line to hold Opheusden on October 5 as 3rd Battalion shifted its line to the south. After two days of intense fighting, in which the town changed hands, the 327th Glider Infantry relieved the 1st Battalion on the night of the sixth. 1st Battalion then fell back to bivouac in an apple orchard. That same night the Germans broke through the 327th and ran into the 1st Battalion in the orchard and were repulsed. (Koskimaki, *Hell's Highway*, pp. 369-394.)

25. Jerry Higgins had previously been the division's chief of staff but was promoted to brigadier-general as the new assistant division commander after General Pratt was killed in a glider crash in Normandy.
26. Richard Killblane's interview with Virgil Smith.
27. Jake said that Lieutenant Whitehead was originally assigned to G Company, but the name does not appear on any roster. Lieutenant Guthrie Hatfield did transfer from G Company to C Company at this time and may be the officer Jake remembered as Whitehead.
28. When 1st Battalion moved up to support 3rd Battalion at Opheusden it was continually pounded by artillery and mortars. C Company was soon reduced to Lt. Hassenzahl and 26 men. (Mark Bando, *The 101st Airborne; From Holland to Hitler's Eagle's Nest*, p. 69.)

    The bombing and fighting around Veghel had depleted the Filthy 13. Plauda had not jumped and did not return to the unit. Freedman and Graham had both been wounded, Oleskiewicz was still missing and somehow Zemedia was pulled away by Regimental Headquarters Company. Only McNiece, Agnew and Womer remained out of the original Filthy 13 who jumped into Normandy.
29. On the Island, the demolitions men found an old abandoned halftrack, either French or German. Jack Agnew figured out how to get it to work by covering the carburetor with a perforated can. They used it for transportation until they were assigned to OP duty on the Rhine. The noise of the vehicle would give away their position.

30. Jack Agnew remembered, "We ended up in listening posts on top of the dike. Two guys would be in there and you would listen to hear if there was any activity. If there was, then you would try to get back without getting blown out of there because the Germans on the other side of the river in Arnhem were on high ground. The only time you could really move was at night and you did not go back until you were relieved. If someone was not out there for you the next night, you just stayed there until someone did come. So, it was the loneliest spot in the world, a listening post out on that dike."
31. Lieutenant-Colonel D. Dobie of the 1st British Airborne Division had escaped a German hospital and was hidden by the Dutch underground. He then swam across the Rhine and reported to Sink that 125 British paratroopers, 5 American pilots, and 10 Dutch resistance fighters wanted by the Germans were hidden away across the Rhine waiting for rescue.
32. The name Brock does not show up on any map. Randwyck matches Jake's description. At that point the Rhine River made a bend away from the Americans and the stretch of land to the river was covered by trees. It was the only place where the Germans occupied the same side of the river as the Americans. This sector also belonged to E Company which was in charge of the evacuation. (Koskimaki, *Hell's Highway,* p. 364.)

    Jack Agnew remembered that they had established their CP in a thatched-roof farm house in Zetten. He did not remember moving to another location for the rescue. From there they conducted patrols and relieved the OPs. They could not move about during the daylight because of German snipers and artillery. He remembered that this was where the stories of milking the cows, cooking the chickens, and Marquez killing the pig took place. The house later caught fire.
33. Jack Agnew complained, "Jake always made fun of me about not knowing how to milk a cow. I knew how to milk a cow as well as anybody. My parents were dairy farmers. One of the cows had been shot through the utter though. When I tried to milk her, milk squirted out the bullet hole." The three cows later disappeared. Jack thought they had been stolen but it turned out the owner had come and claimed them. He was grateful for Jack having milked them for him.
34. Because the paratroopers were hidden in different Dutch homes, some as far as 15 miles away, it took nearly a week for them to move to the evacuation point.
35. There is no reference to the demolition men's participation nor even the

existence of the minefield, but only that a route had to be laid out with white engineer tape by the engineers. One can only assume the path was through a minefield and not just to keep men from getting lost in the dark. At that time Jake was the only demolition sergeant left and his section was probably the only demolition section still intact in the 506th. His section would more likely have been the only one left to clear the minefield.

36. Jack Womer remembered on another occasion: While up there one night, a "90 day wonder" (lieutenant) from a line company came over and told the demolition men to clear a path through the mines along the bank. The place he wanted cleared was four houses up. The line company had their side covered with a .50 caliber machine gun upstairs in a house but the Germans had theirs covered by an 88 millimeter cannon. As the lieutenant led Jack Womer and two other men along the sidewalk, the 88 opened up on them. Jack Womer figured if they had been out in the open on the bank, they would have been killed. Jack was mad. He told the lieutenant that they did not need the other two men. "You and me go."

    The lieutenant agreed. With only their jump knives they probed for shoe mines. The snow had melted and they had only made it out about ten yards when the Germans sent up a flare. Jack had figured correct. The lieutenant realized clearing the mines was not worth the risk. He said, "We've got to go back." They waited as another flare went up. After it burned out the two got up and walked back to the house. He just wanted to know what was out there.

37. "Our men killed a pig while we were there and they ate that. They sort of had a party with the pig but I didn't eat any pig. It had a bad leg but they ate it anyway. Then there were chickens in the house and a Mexican and I went and got them chickens and cut their heads off. I didn't eat any of the chickens. I don't know why I didn't." (Mohr, *Memories,* p. 45.)

38. "We went to a big farm and our regiment camped there. There was a great big barn and some other buildings, a big-wheel man and 3 daughters." (Mohr, *Memories*, p. 45.)

39. Herb Pierce remembered walking down a road on the wire detail. "I was whispering. It was my way of letting off tension. Jake came back and said, 'Kid, shut up,' then he returned to the front. It was not long until I started whispering again. Jake came back and told me, 'Pierce, I told you to shut up.' He left and I began whispering again. He came back and stuck his gun in my gut and said, 'If you don't shut up, I'm going to shoot you!' I believed he would do it."

40. The 101st Airborne Division withdrew from Holland on November 28, 1944.
41. Frank Kough was also in the demolitions platoon.

Chapter 5: Rescue of a Division

1. Captain Virgil Smith, General Higgins's aide, said that immediately after Holland, General Maxwell Taylor had been ordered to report to General Marshall in Washington, D.C. on account of the crimes by some of the men in his division. Evidently there were reports of the men looting property and blowing safes. The men had accumulated fine furniture in their fighting positions. He had not heard anything of the press release of the Filthy 13. Momentum was building for the airborne divisions to finally get rid of their troublemakers.

   Afterwards the 17th, 82nd, and 101st Airborne Divisions unloaded their worst cases for transfer out of the theater. They were loaded on a train. Stories came out of how they would sell overcoats and shoes for high prices to civilians at the train stops, and then another paratrooper with an MP brassard would come up and confiscate the government property from the unsuspecting civilian. He would then return it to the original owner and they would repeat the process. This scam made them a fortune. The unruly paratroopers eventually took over the train and stopped in a town where they raped a number of the local women.
2. In Normandy, units had initially had limited quotas for the combat infantryman's badge. So it was initially viewed as an award. In time every infantryman who served in combat was issued the badge.
3. Jake is not sure who the acting company commander was when this happened. He did not think Gene Brown would have done something like that.
4. Jack Agnew remembered, "When I heard Jake had volunteered for pathfinders, I said, 'Hell, he's not going without me.'"
5. SSG Jake McNiece, Jack Agnew, and Max Majewski were survivors of the original Filthy 13 from Toccoa. Corporal Jack Womer was the only member from the days in England left in the section after that. Chuck Plauda and George Baran were still alive but did not return to the demolition section. But essentially, the majority of the survivors who created the legend of the Filthy 13 had volunteered for Pathfinder training in England.
6. To this day, first sergeants still supervise formations, police call, and recommend discipline to the company commander. Since these functions are all most soldiers ever see their first sergeant do, it is easy for

an enlisted man to think that is all the top sergeant does. What the Pathfinder company commander needed was what one calls a field first sergeant. The U.S. Marines still reserve those training duties for the company gunnery sergeant.

7. Jake's Pathfinder stick was made up of men from his own regiment: Lieutenant Shrable Williams, Sgt. John Roseman from A Co., Sgt. Cleo Merz from C Co., Sgt. Leroy Shulenberg from B Co., Cpl. John Dewey, T-5 George Blain from Headquarters Co. 1st Battalion, Pfc. Jack Agnew, Pvt. Bill Coad, and Pfc. George Slater from B Co. (*The Pathfinder*, Vol. I, No. 4, October–November–December 1986, p. 6.)
8. Pathfinders were not permanently assigned to the IX TCC but belonged to their parent units. It was coincidence that they happened to be training with the IX TCC when the German counteroffensive began. (Captain Frank L. Brown, "Report of Airborne Pathfinder Operation 'Nuts,'" to Commanding General, XVIII Corps (Airborne), 7 Jan. 1945.) The reason that the Pathfinders were alerted so late to resupply the 101st Airborne Division was that the two regiments of the 106th Infantry Division cut off behind German lines had priority. These regiments ended up surrendering and the priority then shifted to Bastogne.
9. The 106th Infantry Division had just arrived in France on December 6. They replaced the 2nd Infantry Division on December 11. When the Germans attacked on December 16, two of the regiments surrendered and the other fell back in complete disarray. The 99th Infantry Division was just north of them. It had arrived in France on November 3. It had seen a little prior action but also fell back and suffered heavy losses.
10. The 28th Infantry Division had been pulled out of the Huertgen Forest on November 19. It was recruited from Pennsylvania and wore a red keystone patch which earned them the nickname of the "Bloody Bucket."
11. "I passed this order on to General Tony McAuliffe, commanding the 101st in the absence of General Maxwell Taylor, who had gone to the States, at my request, to confer with General Marshall on certain matters pertaining to the airborne." (General Matthew B. Ridgeway, *Soldier: The Memoirs of Matthew B. Ridgeway*, p. 114.)

    According to Captain Virgil Smith, General Marshall refused to let Taylor leave. McAuliffe was the highest ranking officer left in the division.
12. "My decision to hold Bastogne, at all costs, had been anticipated by [MG Troy] Middleton [Commander of the VIII Corps] even as his front was crumbling to pieces. When I called Troy to give him the order to

hold that crucial road junction, he replied that he had already instructed his troops there to dig in and hold. Elements of the 10th Armored Division raced north to Bastogne to reinforce tanks of the 9th Armored in their defense of that key position. That evening the 101st Airborne Division roared into Bastogne after a wild truck ride from Reims while the 82nd Airborne continued north to blunt the pincer that had forced its way between Malmedy and St. Vith." (Bradley, *Soldier's Story*, p. 467.)

13. "Intelligence reports relative to enemy and friendly situations on the ground indicated that the situation in the area was fluid and close map reconnaissance of the DZ was impossible due to lack of large scale (1:25000) maps of the area. . . . The time limit from the receipt of necessary information to take off (thirty minutes) did not allow time for proper briefing, plotting of course and preparation for an emergency operation under the circumstances. Combined Air Corps and Airborne teams took off at 1452 hours." (Brown, "Report.")
14. "Commanding Officer, IX TCC Pathfinder Group returned to this headquarters at 1455 hours and checked prior preparations made in his absense [sic]. After checking weather and sunset time he radioed the Flight Leader to return to the Base. Message was confirmed and flight returned." (Brown, "Report.") Jake claims they turned around only after they failed to find Bastogne. Agnew said they should have kept trying.
15. LTC Joel L. Crouch was the crackerjack pilot. Crouch had originated the pathfinder concept. (*The Pathfinder*, pp. 1, 3.)
16. "In as much as up to the minute intelligence reports were unattainable it was decided to drop one stick and wait for a predetermined signal (orange smoke grenade) prior to dropping second stick in order to definitely establish the fact that the Airborne pathfinders were in friendly territory." (Brown, "Report.")

    The official report states that the Executive Officer of IX TCC Pathfinder Group and the XVIII Corps Pathfinder Officer, CPT Frank Brown, made the decision to commit two identical teams. The decision had to be approved by IX Troop Carrier Command. (Brown, "Report.") Jack Agnew said that Jake McNiece originated most of the plans even though Lieutenant Shrable Williams was the stick leader. The reason that the men thought Williams was such a great officer was that he listened to them.
17. "During the night of 22 December 44, all available information in reference to the operation was obtained. Maps (1:50000) were furnished

to Airborne Pathfinder. Briefing was accomplished and flight took off as scheduled at 0645 hours." (Brown, "Report.")

18. "Take-off time was 0645, 23 December 1944. I was in the lead aircraft (#943) piloted by Lt. Col. Joel Crouch. We were followed by a second aircraft (#681) piloted by Lt. Lionel Wood. The flight from Chalgrove to Bastogne was uneventful but as we approached the 'DZ' and the red light came on for 'Hook-up,' tension mounted and you get a lot of 'funny feelings.' Suddenly there was a burst of ground fire and you could see the tracers go by. It came from a German gun emplacement, directly in front of our flight path. Quickly Col. Crouch, dove the aircraft directly at the Germans (we were looking right down the barrels of their guns) who thinking they had shot us down and we were going to crash on top of them, jumped out of their gun emplacement and ran for safety. The colonel then pulled the aircraft back up to jump altitude. However since we were all standing (loaded with heavy pathfinder equipment) the suddenness of this maneuver caught us by surprise and most of us sank to our knees due to the 'G' force exerted. Luckily we all recovered our balance just as the green light came on, and out the door we went, and George Blain signaled the second aircraft to commence their drop." (Jack Agnew, "Live From Bastogne," *The Pathfinder*, p. 4.)
19. "Troops landed on the exact spot agreed upon by pilot and jumpmaster. Orange smoke and signal from Eureka indicated that troops were safe. Second stick and bundles were dropped at same location by 1st Lt. (now Capt.) Lionel E. Wood flying A/C 681." (Brown, "Report.")

    "While we were still airborne I coded OK. The 2nd plane made a 180 degree turn and dumped #2 stick - Boy!! what a party." (Note by George Blain on the Brown Report to Jake McNiece, Dec 5, 1985.) Blain had the Eureka set.
20. The Pathfinders landed southwest of Bastogne in the 327th Glider Infantry sector. They brought in the supply drops on the same DZ that they jumped in on. The cemetery was in that sector. Each regiment had recovery crews with jeeps waiting at the drop zone to speed the supplies back to their comrades. LTC LaPrade was killed when German artillery hit his CP.

    Jack Agnew did not remember seeing anyone around when they jumped in. He said they landed in the backyard of the Massen house across the street from a huge brick pile that had been stacked for construction. The Massen boy, Loui, came out and helped carry their equipment to the brick pile.

21. "After the shock of my chute opening, I looked around to orientate myself and saw what I thought to be a German tank. I started loosening my "Tommy Gun" in anticipation of a fight. Suddenly I hit the ground in what I think was the hardest landing in my career as a paratrooper. My "Tommy Gun" slammed into my face and I became a bloody mess. A medic quickly patched me up and after assembly we sought shelter in an old metal building, which the Germans quickly blasted us out of. Next we tried the basement of a damaged building, but the Germans zeroed in on us again. We lost some of our equipment this time and some of our people were trapped in the basement for a while, but Dewey and I managed to get them out. Finally we took shelter in Mrs. Massen's house and across from her place, on high ground, was a big brick pile. We set up our equipment (CRN4's) there and waited for the first sound of incoming aircraft. We didn't dare turn on the sets until the last minute, because the Germans would have homed in on us and blasted us to bits. Shortly, the sound of approaching aircraft grew louder and louder so we turned on the CRN4's. Even though the Germans started firing at us, the sight of the aerial armada distracted them and we suffered no casualties. The air drop was a great success and a Christmas present that the beleaguered troops at Bastogne wouldn't forget for a long time." (Agnew, "Live From Bastogne," *The Pathfinder*, p. 4.)
22. The number of drops was taken from Brown, "Report."

    "The road center of Bastogne could not have been held by the 101st Division during the German counteroffensive in December 1944 except for the airplanes that delivered 800,000 pounds of supplies to the division during the critical days between the twenty-third and twenty-seventh of December." (Dwight D. Eisenhower, *Crusade in Europe*, p. 452.)
23. Mohr, *Memories*, p. 57.
24. The two lieutenants reported straight to Division Headquarters to ask where they wanted the drop zone. McNiece and Agnew did not remember them returning but understood that they were tasked somewhere else. This had left Jake McNiece in charge of the Pathfinder operation.
25. This was the Massen house.
26. Max Majewski was on the second stick to jump in.
27. Jack Agnew visited Bastogne after the war. He dropped by the Massen house and the same family still lived in it. They remembered him and invited him to stay with them during his visit. Loui Massen had grown up to become the president of the Bank General.

28. Dr. Kurt Yeary was also from Ponca City, Oklahoma.
29. Gene Brown had been given command of a rifle company. Foy lay on the main road to the north of Bastogne in the 506th sector.
30. While back in England, Gene Brown and the other lieutenants were going to have a party. They needed some whiskey and they knew Leach had several bottles hoarded in his foot locker. Leach did not even drink. The officers did not get along well with Leach so Brown decided to break into his foot locker. Brown was able to place the right amount of explosive to pop the lock in a way that did not destroy it. After they cleaned out the booze, he put the lock back together so the damage was not even noticeable. Of course Leach raised hell when he discovered his loss. Brown was considered the best demolitions man in the platoon.
31. Herb Pierce had wanted to join the fighting in World War II in the worst way. He had tried to enlist in any service that would take him but he was slightly colorblind. After walking out of the Marine recruiter's officer he was so angry he kicked their sign. He then went in and talked to the airborne recruiter. They accepted him. As he was processing in it was again discovered that Herb was colorblind. Herb complained about how being colorblind could keep him from killing Germans. A very practical airborne officer handed him a couple of cards and asked him what color they were. Herb answered correctly. It turned out that he only had trouble distinguishing between the different shades of colors. Herb became a paratrooper. Although he may have shown his fear more than the others, he did not shirk his duty and wanted to carry his own weight.
32. General George Patton's 4th Armored Division broke through to Bastogne at 4:00 on December 26. The 101st had survived seven days of siege.
33. Most units did not make more than two or three combat jumps. Consequently, very few paratroopers can claim to have made four.

Chapter 6: End of the War

1. On January 17, 1945, the 101st withdrew to the corps reserve at Haguenau, France. After February 25, the division returned to Mormelon. By the end of March, it was ordered into the Ruhr Pocket to secure the surrender of German soldiers. After April 20, the 101st moved to southern Germany and then into Bavaria. Major Leach took his patrol out while the division was in the Ruhr Pocket.
2. German for young woman.
3. Up until that time Leach had not led a combat patrol. It was beginning

to become a joke among his peers. As a newly promoted major with the war winding down, he decided to finally take out his only patrol. (Stephen E. Ambrose, *Band of Brothers: E Company, 506th Regiment, 101st Airborne From Normandy to Hitler's Eagle's Nest.*)

4. Browning Automatic Rifle. It is a light machine gun which fires 30.06 ammunition.
5. Actually, E Company shot up Leach's boat. (Ambrose, *Band of Brothers.*)
6. The 45th Infantry Division was the Oklahoma National Guard. The original Oklahomans saw action as early as 1942. By the end of the war, most had been wounded at least once. If they could not return to duty within a few days the men were thrown into the replacement pool and sent out to other divisions.
7. Sink commandeered local boats on the lake and Jack Agnew's job was to operate and maintain them.
8. Upon return from the hospital in England, Gene Brown was reassigned to command of Regimental Headquarters Company.
9. Because of bad weather, the 506th's Fourth of July celebration was postponed to the 6th. The day began with speeches by the officers and then the men participated in athletic events and listened to a local band. At 11:45, a C-47 appeared overhead. At 3,800 feet, Lt. Sterling Horner jumped out following the wind dummy and opened his chute at about 2,400 feet. The plane came around and buzzed the lake and then climbed to 1,000 feet and disgorged its remaining ten parachutists over the water: Lts. Robert Haley, Leo Monoghan, Edgar MacMahan and John Stegeman, Sgts. Jake McNiece and Harold Anderson, and Cpls. John Dewey, Leonard Cardwell, and Stacey Kingsley, and Pvt. Ed Borey. After a lunch of hot dogs, lemonade, and ice cream, the regiment held a baseball tournament against other teams in the division and staged the "Curahee Downs" with German cavalry mounts. ("6 Celebrates Fourth On 6th," *Paradice Press*, July 13, 1945, Vol. 1, No. 5.)
10. Standards for good conduct in war tended to be different than in peace. Jake even received a Good Conduct Medal.
11. Pigalle, an area of Paris that became a red light district and black market center after liberation.
12. The military prison is at Fort Leavenworth, Kansas.

Chapter 7: Get-Together

1. A sap was a short leather whip about eight inches long loaded with buck shot on one end.

2. It was a long trough with a long handle that came clear down to one's waist that carried cement or stucco to the masons. Hod carriers climbed ladders with them.
3. His first wife was killed in an auto accident while he was in the service.
4. City Service Oil Refinery was owned by the city and was adjacent to CONOCO which bought it later.
5. Screaming Eagle was the name given to the 101st Airborne Division patch.

BIBLIOGRAPHY

INTERVIEWS BY AUTHOR

John "Jack" Agnew
Betty Agnew
Elihue Boilla
Gene L. "Browny" Brown
Robert S. "Ragsman" Cone
Eugene A. Dance
Harold W. "Hank" Hannah
George E. Koskimaki
Mike Landauer
James "Jake" McNiece
Martha McNiece
Miguel "Mike" Marquez
Herbert L. "Kid" Pierce
Andrew E. "Rasputin" Rasmussen
Virgil "Smitty" Smith
Jack N. "Hawkeye" Womer
Thomas W. "Tom" Young

OTHER SOURCES

Audio Tape by Miguel B Marquez, Oct. 15, 1996.
Audio Tape by Jack Agnew, ca. Oct. 1999.
Video Interview of Jake McNiece by Truman Smith, May 5, 1994.

Video Interview of Jake McNiece by Joe Todd, March 2, 1988, Oklahoma Historical Society.

Letter, John Reeder to Laura Erickson, May 1, 1994.

Letters, Frank Palys to Laura Erikson, Apr. 29, 1994 and Jan. 14, 1995.

BOOKS

Ambrose, Stephen E. *D-Day; June 6, 1944; The Climactic Battle of World War II*. New York: Simon and Schuster, 1994.

_____. *Band of Brothers: E Company, 506th Regiment, 101st Airborne From Normandy to Hitler's Eagle's Nest*. New York: Simon & Schuster, 1992.

Astor, Gerald. *A Blood-Dimmed Tide: The Battle of the Bulge by the Men Who Fought It*. New York: Donald I. Fine, Inc, 1992.

Bando, Mark. *The 101st Airborne At Normandy*. Osceola, WI: Motorbooks International, 1994.

_____. *The 101st Airborne; From Holland to Hitler's Eagle's Nest*. Osceola, WI: Motorbooks International, 1995.

Bradley, Omar. *A Soldier's Story*. New York: Henry Holt and Company, 1951.

Brown, Frank L. "Report of Airborne Pathfinder Operation 'Nuts.'" Jan. 7, 1945, D769.345 A521, Army War College Library.

Burgett, Donald D. *Currahee! A Paratrooper's Account of the Normandy Invasion*. Boston: Houghton Mifflin Company, 1967.

_____. *The Road to Arnhem: A Screaming Eagle in Holland*. Novato, CA: Presidio Press, 1999.

_____. *Seven Roads to Hell: A Screaming Eagle at Bastogne*. Novato, CA: Presidio Press, 1999.

Center of Military History. *Utah Beach To Cherbourg; 6–27 June 1944*. Washington, D. C., 1994.

Eisenhower, Dwight D. *Crusade in Europe*. New York: Doubleday & Company, Inc., 1948.

506th Parachute Infantry. "Operation Neptune; S-1, S-2, S-3 Journals."

Hannah, Harold W. *A Military Interlude; Cornfield to Academia to Parachutes*, np. 1999.

Harrison, Gordon A. *Cross-Channel Attack*. Washington, DC: Center of Military History, 1989.

History Section, European Theater of Operations. "Regimental Unit Study Number 3; (506 Parachute Infantry Regiment In Normandy Drop)," n.p., 1945.

Howard, James. *Currahee, 506th Parachute Infantry Scrapbook, 20 July 1942–4 July 1945*. n.p. 1945.

Koskimaki, George E. *D-Day With the Screaming Eagles*. Sweetwater, TN: 101st Airborne Division Association, Third Edition 1989.

_____. *Hell's Highway; Chronicle of the 101st Airborne Division in the Holland Campaign, September–November, 1944*. Sweetwater, TN: 101st Airborne Division Association, Second Edition 1989.

_____. *The Battered Bastards of Bastogne: A Chronicle of the Defense of Bastogne: December 19, 1944–January 17, 1945*. Sweetwater, TN: 101st Airborne Division Association, First Edition 1989.

_____. *A Short History Of The 101st Airborne Division In England, Normandy, The Netherlands And Bastogne*, np. nd.

Marshall, S. L. A. *Night Drop; The American Airborne Invasion of Normandy*. Boston: Atlantic Monthly Press, 1962.

Mohr, John H. *A Paratrooper's Memories of World War II*. Ames, IN: Huess Printing, Inc., 1996.

Rapport, Leonard and Arthyr Northwood Jr. *Rendezvous With Destiny.* Washington, D.C: Infantry Journal, 1948.

Ridgeway, Matthew B. *Soldier: The Memoirs of Matthew B. Ridgeway.* New York: Harper & Brothers, 1956.

Ryan, Cornelius. *A Bridge Too Far.* New York: Simon and Schuster, 1974.

Smith, Truman. *The Wrong Stuff; The Adventures and Mis-Adventures of an 8th Air Force Aviator*. St Petersburg, FL: Southern Heritage Press, 1996.

Stanton, Shelby. *World War II Order of Battle*. New York: Galahad Books, 1984.

Webster, David Kenyon. *Parachute Infantry: An American Paratrooper's Memoir of D-Day and the Fall of the Third Reich*. Baton Rouge, LA: LSU Press, 1997.

ARTICLES

"'Filthy 13' Bathed—In Blood." *Stars and Stripes,* Dec. 4, 1944.

"'Filthy 13'—Their Number Is Down." *Stars and Stripes,* Nov. 30, 1944.

Hoge, Tom. "'Filthy 13' Squad Rivaled By None In Leaping Party." *Stars and Stripes*, June 8, 1944.

Hollenbeck, Lynda. "Williams, the 'Silent War Hero,' Dies at 77." *The Benton Courier*, Oct. 21, 1997.

Kondo, Shareese. "Silent Hero Loved U.S., Old Fords, Aiding Others." *Arkansas Democrat Gazette*, Oct. 21, 1997.

Middleton, Troy H. "Report of the VIII Corps After Action Against Enemy Forces on the Cotentin Peninsula, Normandy, France, for the Period 15–30 June 1944." Headquarters VIII Corps, APO 308 US Army, 20 July 1944.

9th TC Command Pathfinder Associaton, *The Pathfinder,* Vol. I, No. 4, October–November–December 1986.

Para-Dice, March 1949, Paradice Press, Vol. 1, No. 5, July 13, 1945.

"Story of 'Filthy Thirteen' Finally Released by Army." *The Springfield Daily Republican*, Dec. 4, 1944.

"13 Paratroopers." *Time*, June 19, 1944.

Whitehouse, Arch. "The Filthy Thirteen." *True Magazine,* date unknown.

Zenender, Ted. "We Were Trained for a Suicide Mission." *The Globe*, Huntingdon Valley, PA, June 7, 1990.

INDEX